Learners, Learning and Educational Activity

The Foundations and Futures of Education series focuses on key emerging issues in education as well as continuing debates within the field. The series is interdisciplinary, and includes historical, philosophical, sociological, psychological and comparative perspectives on three major themes: the purposes and nature of education; increasing interdisciplinarity within the subject; and the theory–practice divide.

Learners, Learning and Educational Activity offers a new and creative approach to the subject of learning by bringing together ideas and research from psychology and socio-cultural theory. The central idea in the book is that learning in schools and other educational settings is best understood by paying attention to both individual learners and the educational contexts in which learning takes place. Taking a broad educational perspective, the author explores a variety of settings – including homes and families as well as classrooms, schools and colleges – to see how they promote learning and encourage different learning outcomes.

The book provides an accessible introduction to new ideas and recent developments in psychology and socio-cultural perspectives. It reviews advances in selected topics that are especially relevant for teachers and other educators, including:

- learners' conceptions of the nature of learning
- the development of advanced levels of learning and thinking
- the role of motivation and self-regulation in learning
- how learning and thinking relate to social and cultural contexts
- the ways in which these contexts influence interactions between teachers and learners.

By illustrating connections between individual and social aspects of learning in educational settings in and out of school, the book will encourage teachers and other educators to think about learners and learning in new ways.

Judith Ireson is Professor of Psychology in Education at the Institute of Education, University of London, UK.

Foundations and Futures of Education
Series Editors:
Peter Aggleton, *University of London, UK*
David Halpin, *University of London, UK*
Sally Power, *Cardiff University, UK*

Education and the Family
Passing success across the generations
Leon Feinstein, Kathryn Duckworth and Ricardo Sabates

Education, Philosophy and the Ethical Environment
Graham Haydon

Learners, Learning and Educational Activity
Judith Ireson

Schooling, Society and Curriculum
Alex Moore

Gender, Schooling and Global Social Justice
Elaine Unterhalter

Learners, Learning and Educational Activity

Judith Ireson

Routledge
Taylor & Francis Group

LONDON AND NEW YORK

First published 2008
by Routledge
2 Park Square, Milton Park, Abingdon, Oxon OX14 4RN

Simultaneously published in the USA and Canada
by Routledge
270 Madison Ave, New York, NY 10016

*Routledge is an imprint of the Taylor & Francis Group, an informa
business*

© 2008 Judith Ireson

Typeset in Galliard by
HWA Text and Data Management, Tunbridge Wells
Printed and bound in Great Britain by
TJ International Ltd, Padstow, Cornwall

British Library Cataloguing in Publication Data
A catalogue record for this book is available from the British Library

Library of Congress Cataloging-in-Publication Data
Ireson, Judith
  Learners, learning and educational activity / Judith Ireson
      p.   cm.
  1. Learning 2. Teaching I. Title
  LB1060.I74 2008
  370.15′23–dc22   2007038790

ISBN10: 0–415–41407–5 (hbk)
ISBN10: 0–415–41406–7 (pbk)
ISBN10: 0–203–92909–8 (ebk)

ISBN13: 978–0–415–41407–4 (hbk)
ISBN13: 978–0–415–41406–7 (pbk)
ISBN13: 978–0–203–92909–4 (ebk)

To my family

Contents

List of figures and tables   viii
Series editors' preface   ix
Acknowledgements   xi

Introduction   1

1 Perspectives on learning   5

2 Acquiring skills and expertise   30

3 Taking control of learning   51

4 Cultural perspectives on learning and thinking   70

5 Interaction and learning   94

6 Exploring connections between individual and culture
   at home and at school   116

7 Connecting spheres of learning   137

References   147
Index   163

Figures and tables

Figures
2.1   Using an analogy to solve a problem   39
4.1   Ecosystemic model   72
4.2   Influences on secondary school learning   76
6.1   Average GCSE grades for students in high, middle and
       low sets, by Key Stage 3 levels   135

Tables
1.1   Central metaphors of major theories of learning   22
2.1   Novice, advanced beginner and expert teachers' interpretations
       of video footage of classroom activity   36
3.1   Self-regulatory processes reported by expert athletes,
       musicians and students   54
3.2   Conceptual framework for studying self-regulation   64

Series editors' preface

One of the most remarkable transformations over the last 200 years has been the universal development of mass education. With each successive decade, provision has expanded to encompass more learners at more stages in their lives. The ambitions for education systems have also expanded to encompass objectives as diverse as personal fulfilment and wellbeing, cultural transmission, active citizenship, social cohesion and, increasingly, international economic competitiveness.

The broad range of ambitions and the sheer pace of change have created a climate in which it is sometimes difficult to stand back and make sense of what education is for and where it should be going. The Foundations and Futures of Education series of books provides an opportunity to engage with these fundamental issues in new and exciting ways. The series adopts a broad and interdisciplinary stance, including historical, philosophical, sociological, psychological and comparative approaches as well as those from within the fields of media and cultural studies. The series also reflects wider conceptions of education embedded in concepts such as 'the knowledge economy', 'the learning society' and 'lifelong learning'.

In each volume, the academic rigour of the arguments is balanced with accessible writing which engages the interest of those working in and for education, as well as a wide range of undergraduate and postgraduate students. Although it will be clear that there are few 'easy answers' to many of the questions currently being asked, we hope you find the debates and dialogues exciting and thought-provoking.

This book examines one of the most fundamental issues in education – learning. Once understood as a highly individual process, learning is now recognised to be a strongly social event, influenced not only by mental processes, but also by the context in which it occurs. Much learning takes place in contexts outside the education system, in homes and families, for example, as well as in classrooms, schools and colleges. Insights from across these different contexts shed light on what learning is, and how opportunities for it can be maximized.

In this lively and accessible book, Judy Ireson maps out a range of views on learning, including psychological and socio-cultural perspectives as well as the perspectives of learners themselves. She examines the acquisition of skills and expertise as well as the development of self-regulated learning. In recent years, teachers and educators have taken more seriously the importance of preferred learning environments in influencing learning outcomes, the use of different cognitive strategies for remembering and understanding, and the importance of monitoring and reflection. Up-to-date research on all of these issues is presented and discussed.

Finally, *Learners, Learning and Educational Activity* examines the social and cultural factors shaping the settings for interaction between adults and children – in school, at home and in the community. It highlights how the beliefs and values of parents and teachers, cultural expectations and customary practices, and pedagogical culture affect the experiences of learning and the outcomes of learning itself. Understanding the links between the individual, interpersonal and cultural dimensions of learning is central to individual and education system success.

Peter Aggleton
David Halpin
Institute of Education, University of London

Sally Power
Cardiff University

Acknowledgements

Many people have contributed to this book, though I take responsibility for the final product and of course for any errors or omissions. Several chapters are developed from my teaching with students taking masters courses in psychology of education and their thoughtful comments over the years have contributed to these pages. I refer to several studies undertaken by masters and doctoral students and to collaborative research undertaken with colleagues, all of which has informed my thinking. Findings from several funded research projects also feature here and this research would not have been undertaken without support from research councils, charitable organizations and government. Virtually all the research referred to in the book involves participants and collaborators and the discoveries made would not have been possible without the help of children and young people, teachers, parents and others. Colleagues, family and friends have given support in various ways and Kate Sym assisted with preparation of the final manuscript. Series editor Peter Aggleton's skilful editing helped to polish the final version and his patience and that of the other series editors and publishers is much appreciated.

Introduction

This book is about learning and how individual learning is shaped by the various contexts in which it takes place, both inside educational institutions and in informal settings such as the home. It takes a creative approach to the subject of learning by bringing together ideas and research from psychology and sociocultural theory. In so doing, it argues that these two fields of study are complementary in certain respects and when used together provide a more complete picture of learning than has so far been achieved by either one independently. Psychology offers strong models of the mental processes involved in learning but tends to be less concerned about aspects of the social world that affect learners' opportunities to learn. Sociocultural theories, on the other hand, have much to say about the cultural contexts in which learning takes place but tend to be less concerned with mental processes involved in different kinds of learning.

The seeds of the book and its focus on relations between individual learning and the educational contexts in which it takes place were sown many years ago when I was researching psychological studies of learning and thinking. These studies were designed to compare the performance of people in different cultural groups on a variety of mental tasks. Psychologists tended to highlight differences between groups in the mental operations tested, such as categorization or logical reasoning. A small number of researchers drew on insights from anthropology to shed light on the cultural practices that might permeate and go some way to explain differences in the performance of participants in these studies. These two perspectives seemed to me to complement each other in productive ways even though they were based on very different theoretical foundations.

More recently my attention has turned to education, which arguably provides some of the most important contexts for learning. Here, learning is frequently seen as an individual process, yet there is ample evidence that schools and classrooms influence teachers and learners and the learning outcomes they achieve. Educational researchers have made considerable progress is identifying and measuring the effects of individual school and classroom variables on students' achievement. For understandable reasons more progress has been made with variables that are relatively easy to measure such as student time on task (or academic learning time). Yet when interpreting the findings of these studies it is not always easy to see why differences in such fundamental aspects of classroom life come into existence.

It is now widely acknowledged that much learning takes place in contexts outside the education system. From a broad educational perspective, therefore, there is an important agenda to understand a variety of settings including homes and families as well as classrooms, schools and colleges that promote learning and how they encourage different learning outcomes. Insights gained from studies of learning in one of these settings can be used to think productively about learning in other settings.

Socio-cultural approaches offer conceptual tools for thinking about learners and their contexts, in and out of school, and have added to our stock of knowledge concerning pedagogic interactions between teachers and learners.

A tendency for there to be limited interaction between the realms of cognitive and socio-cultural psychology, which has been noted by several scholars, makes it difficult to construct a coherent account of learning that encompasses both individual cognition and the social and cultural settings in which children and young people grow and learn. The task is made more challenging due to the complexity of each setting, the content of learning and differences among learners themselves. This book aims to contribute to this agenda by bringing elements of these different perspectives together and identifying key ideas and processes that connect individual learning with the settings in which it takes place. It offers a fresh approach to educational activity and how activities are constituted as sites for learning.

Chapter 1 maps out a range of views on learning, including psychological and socio-cultural perspectives and the perspectives of learners themselves. It starts with an overview of psychological theories of learning, each of which is based on a set of assumptions about the nature of learning and a particular view of learners. Learners are characterized variously as absorbers of information, observers and imitators, thinkers and problem solvers, processors of information, strategists and appropriators of information. Students in school and university provide a similarly broad range of interpretations of learning, although their categories do not map neatly on to those identified in psychological theories. Evidence suggests that very young children have a restricted set of conceptions of learning whereas young people and adults exhibit a wider range. Similarly, teachers have a variety of conceptions of teaching and these relate to the means they use to promote learning. These different views of learning and teaching are important as they have the potential to influence young people's experiences of learning.

Chapter 2 is concerned with the acquisition of skills and expertise. In the past, psychological perspectives on learning were relegated to the performance of basic skills and implicit forms of learning through association. Contemporary approaches now encompass cognitive skills and professional expertise and suggest that similar principles apply to many different domains of learning.

Complex skills build on more basic forms and expertise is achieved through extensive practice that is carefully organized to achieve specific goals.

The organization and regulation of learning that is needed for extensive practice is taken up in Chapter 3. The notion of self-regulated learning encompasses a wide range of thoughts, feelings and actions employed by learners before, during and after completing tasks and activities. These include awareness of preferred learning environments, use of cognitive strategies for remembering and understanding, monitoring and reflection. Connections between self-regulation, motivation and learners' beliefs suggest that self-regulation relates to affective components and to learners' beliefs about the nature of learning and ability.

Chapter 4 moves on to more cultural ground and focuses on several theoretical frameworks that link between individuals and cultural settings, including ecosystemic, post-Vygotskian and participation perspectives. Bronfenbrenner's ecological model and its integration with the idea of a developmental niche highlight the significance of parental beliefs and ideas about children's learning, including beliefs about developmental milestones, the nature of activities children are encouraged to engage in and the people with whom they are allowed to interact. Customary practices also set bounds on children's activities in and out of school. Thus beliefs and customary practices have the potential to affect the learning opportunities provided for children and young people and the knowledge and skills they are encouraged to develop.

Vygotsky (1978) and his followers proposed that interactions between learners and more knowledgeable people were crucial for the development of more advanced types of human learning. This proposal raises a host of questions about the nature of such interactions and how they assist learning. It inspired a generation of observational studies of interactions between adults and children performing a variety of different tasks, which produced ideas and metaphors such as scaffolding and contingency. Chapter 5 reviews a selection of these studies undertaken in a variety of cultural settings and identifies a number of key components of individual pedagogy that affect learning.

Many of the studies referred to in Chapter 5 are experiments in which adults and children complete tasks designed by a researcher. Chapter 6 then turns to the social and cultural factors that shape the settings for interaction between adults and children, in schools, homes and the community. It takes forward some key ideas identified in previous chapters, such as beliefs and values of parents and teachers, customary practices and pedagogical culture, and demonstrates how they may be relevant in school contexts. Linkages are explored between these factors and learners' experiences of learning, demonstrating ways in which cultural beliefs and practices permeate and influence the nature of interactions between teachers and learners in school. Some of these linkages are to be found in classroom dialogues between teachers and learners.

Chapter 7 provides a summary of the first six chapters before moving on to take stock of progress made in understanding how educational activity is shaped by the settings in which it takes place. It also focuses on the indeterminacy that is inherent in the interactions between learners and more knowledgeable others and highlights some sources including participants' goals, their conceptions of learning and teaching, responsibility for regulating task performance and learners' active participation. It concludes that there are strong connections between cultural, interpersonal and individual aspects of learning and that these are evident in schools and colleges and in settings outside school. It is hoped that drawing attention to these connections may illuminate teachers' understanding of learning and assist them in the task of providing productive learning environments for all learners.

1 Perspectives on learning

When we think about learning, the images that come to mind are usually connected with going to school, attending classes, having a coach, or working through a self-help book or computer program. We often tend to think of learning in terms of acquiring skills and knowledge with help from an instructor. For most people, learning is both an individual and a social process. Individual students see themselves as responsible for learning yet they recognize that other people have an influence on what they learn and the quality of the learning experience.

It may come as a surprise, therefore, that much theory and research on learning is concerned with either individual processes or with the broader social dimensions and that until recently there has been relatively little work relating them. Theories concerned with individual processes tend to describe and explain changes in behaviour, memorizing, thinking, reasoning and problem solving and also a range of cognitive and self-regulatory strategies that make the process of learning more productive. Theories concerned with social processes focus on the nature of a learner's participation in learning activities and their interactions with others in the settings in which those activities take place. They consider the role of others in supporting an individual's learning and the social contexts in which this assistance is offered.

Theories of learning offer views of the learner that range from an absorber of information, to a thinker and problem solver, a strategist who regulates learning, and a participant who appropriates information. Traditionally, texts on the psychology of learning tend to work from a single perspective. Learning is considered either from a cognitive, or mental processing, perspective or a socio-cultural perspective. This is understandable as the phenomenon of learning is complex and it makes sense to break off manageable chunks to examine in detail. Yet it leaves us with a rather fragmented view of learning. Now that considerable advances have been achieved from each of these approaches, it is timely to bring them together to give a more complete picture.

The first part of this chapter gives an overview of psychological and socio-cultural theories of learning. The second part documents students' subjective reports of their experiences of learning in schools, colleges and university and explores differences in both students' conceptions of learning and teachers' conceptions of teaching.

Concepts of learning in psychology and education

In everyday usage, learning generally denotes the deliberate acquisition of information or skills. If you ask a group of adults to give examples of something they learned they might suggest learning a foreign language, driving a car, playing a musical instrument, taking a course in history, taking up a new sport or learning to paint. All of these are readily identifiable as forms of deliberate learning, involving skills and knowledge that the individual set out to learn. A more in-depth discussion often reveals awareness of other kinds of learning, such as changes in understanding of a subject, which leads to seeing the world in a different way. Individuals also notice personal changes in themselves as they learn, some of which might be quite fundamental, leading to changes in their identity or seeing themselves in a different way.

Much learning that takes place in life is overlooked in these everyday notions of learning. For example, if someone starts to smoke or develops an irrational fear we do not generally think of these changes as forms of learning. Moreover, some learning is not deliberate, but happens spontaneously as we take part in various activities during our everyday lives. Perhaps because it is so ubiquitous, spontaneous learning is rarely considered in everyday talk about learning.

Within schools, the term learning is often used in a restricted sense, which relates to learning the prescribed curricular content. Teachers and pupils talk about learning specific aspects of curriculum subjects such as mathematics, history or languages. They refer to knowledge and skills that have been learned and reproduced correctly. Learning that does not conform to expectations is not acknowledged, rather it is more likely to be spoken about in terms of failing to learn. In contrast, when speaking about education in general there is a discourse about learning across the lifespan, in the workplace and in a wide range of educational settings, which indicates that learning is interpreted very broadly.

In psychology, notions of learning became wedded to behavioural perspectives early on with learning being defined in terms of changes in behaviour resulting from experience. More complex types of learning, such as changes in conceptual understanding, were considered by Piaget (1964) and Vygotsky (1978) to emerge as part of a developmental process, rather than learning. The reasons for this state of affairs have their roots in the shift from behavioural to cognitive psychology during the middle of the twentieth century. The emergence of cognitive psychology, with its emphasis on mental processes, was a hard fought battle which left learning in the hands of the behaviourists while cognitive psychologists dominated the realms of thinking, reasoning and problem solving. Nowadays some of these divisions have been overcome, and there is a resurgence of interest in the complex types of learning involved in the acquisition of complex mental skills such as reasoning and problem solving.

Some of the fundamental ideas and assumptions underpinning many modern theories of learning date back to the Greeks. Plato proposed that humans are born with knowledge, or innate ideas of other people and objects in the world around. Learning is therefore a matter of uncovering the knowledge we have in our minds and is achieved through rational discourse and logical thinking. Plato's assumption that knowledge is innate is echoed in many modern theories and beliefs, which emphasize the contribution of innate, genetic factors to learning.

Plato's student Aristotle strongly disagreed with his teacher on this point and he claimed instead that experience forms the basis of learning. It is through sensory experience of the world that we recognize features occurring together in consistent patterns and we are able to form abstract concepts. This line of argument gave rise to Associationism, and the Behaviourist school of psychology (Richardson 1988). These two central ideas, that knowledge is inborn and that it is acquired through experience, are still alive today in psychology and in education. Nowadays they surface in discussions about learning, intelligence and personality where there is still debate about the relative contribution of innate, genetic inheritance (nature) and experience (nurture) in learning.

Many years later, the philosopher Immanuel Kant (1781) proposed a resolution of this debate. He argued that experience is important for learning, but there must also be innate rules for producing abstract mental representations, as it would be impossible for us to have coherent experience of the world without some innate concepts, categories or rules. These rules allow us to abstract general conceptions from the ever-changing flux of sensory information around us and to mentally construct the world. He proposed the notion of a 'schema' or mental representation that reflects the real world as experienced and also reflects certain a priori concepts or rules. These constructivist ideas had a profound influence on Piaget who used the idea of a schema in his studies of the development of children's understanding of the world. He proposed that children are born with rudimentary schemas which develop in complexity as children interact with the world around them (Piaget 1963). Vygotsky (1978) also proposed that children learn through interactions and his social constructivist theory emphasizes the importance of the child's interactions with other people. Both Piaget and Vygotsky saw children as active learners, who construct mental representations of the world. Other approaches that follow in the constructivist tradition include phenomenography, which is concerned with individuals' experiences of teaching and learning (Marton and Booth 1997).

The remainder of this chapter is divided into three main parts. The first part provides an overview of major psychological approaches to the psychology of learning. The second part is concerned with students' own experiences of learning and what these reveal about their conceptions of learning and the approaches they take to studying. The final part considers teachers' conceptions of teaching and how these relate to their approaches to teaching and learning.

In the part that follows, major psychological theories of learning will be outlined. Each of these theories has a central metaphor that characterizes a type of learning that is the main focus of research and a set of presuppositions about the nature of learning. Contemporary theorizing and research draws on insights from several of these perspectives. However, it is sometimes helpful to identify the essence of each one and Table 1 displays central metaphors and views of learners.

Behavioural learning

Learning has been a matter of interest to psychologists for over a century. Early research was mainly concerned with animal learning and with basic forms of human learning. At the beginning of the twentieth century, the study of learning was dominated by the associationists who followed Aristotle's view that all knowledge is acquired through experience. A number of psychologists at that time were concerned to establish psychology as a science and they reasoned that the way to do this was to restrict their investigations to those behaviours that could be observed and documented objectively. It followed that behaviour should be observed using rigorous scientific methods, rather than drawing inferences about unobservable mental states. Behaviourists were unwilling to theorize about mental events that could not be directly observed and instead set out to develop principles of learning based on systematic, verifiable documentation of behaviour. These principles were developed through research with animals and later applied to children's learning.

Laboratory investigations of learning led to a number of important discoveries. Ivan Pavlov discovered that animals in his laboratory learned by associating a stimulus to a reflex response (Pavlov 1927). Animals have a number of reflex responses, each of which is triggered by a specific stimulus. These reactions are inborn and occur automatically, for example, the pupils in our eyes dilate when we look at a bright light and a hungry animal salivates when exposed to the smell of food. Pavlov was studying the physiology of salivation in dogs, which involved measuring the amount of saliva produced when the dog was presented with a meal. He noticed that the dog began to salivate before the food was produced and conjectured that the dog was responding to the sound of the door, when it was opened by the animal's keeper delivering food. He went on to design experiments to investigate this phenomenon more carefully, using a bell as a controlled stimulus. These experiments confirmed that if a keeper repeatedly rang a bell before the food was produced, the dog would salivate to the sound of the bell alone. The response of salivation now became associated with the sound of the bell, whereas originally it had been associated with the sight of food.

This basic form of learning is referred to as conditional learning (or classical conditioning).

Watson used a similar procedure in a famous study to bring about a fear reaction in a toddler named Albert (Watson and Rayner 1920). Fear is a natural, reflex reaction of young children exposed to sudden loud noises and Watson exposed the child to a loud sound to induce a fear reaction towards soft toys. He produced the noise every time Albert caught sight of a furry rabbit and he found that after repeated pairings the child reacted with fear when he saw the rabbit. This study demonstrated that humans have basic learning mechanisms similar to those of animals. Conditional learning provides a foundation for certain physiological responses to the environment. Some responses that appear irrational, such as phobias, may be learned in this way. Little Albert's fearful reaction to a soft toy might appear irrational to those who were unaware of Watson's experiment.

Whereas Pavlov started his work by investigating the associations between events preceding a response, Skinner (1953) was interested in events that followed a response. His early work was also undertaken with animals in a laboratory environment, and he discovered relationships between particular behaviours and the events that followed. He established a principle that behaviour is more likely to occur if its appearance is followed by a desirable consequence and is less likely to be repeated if followed by an unpleasant consequence. He designed what became known as a Skinner box with a mechanism for delivering pellets of food and a lever that a rat could operate by pressing with a foot. A hungry rat placed in the box naturally moved around until eventually it pressed the lever, and was immediately rewarded by delivery of food pellets. It did not take the rat much time to learn to press the lever in order to receive food. Several important principles were established that still hold true today, at least for certain kinds of learning. One of these is that we tend to repeat behaviour that is followed by a pleasant consequence and not to repeat behaviour that is followed by an unpleasant consequence. This means that rewards, or 'reinforcers', can be used to encourage desirable behaviour. For example, parents and teachers use tangible rewards or praise to encourage desirable behaviour in young children and dog owners frequently use food to train their dogs to sit, come to heel or fetch objects.

Complex behaviours can be taught with a technique of 'shaping' whereby an animal is first rewarded for performing a basic move and once this has been learned the animal is no longer rewarded for the learned move but is given a reward for the next move and so on until the complete performance has been learned. The success of this technique convinced Skinner (1954) that the key to effective teaching was to analyse the task to be learned into components and order these into a logical sequence for learning. The learner then worked through each component in turn, receiving reinforcement for correct responses. Each step had to be mastered before proceeding to the next, and if the learner failed to complete a step successfully, the material would be repeated or additional material presented. Successful completion of each step was seen as the key to learning, as this meant that the learner then received frequent reinforcement. It followed that each step had to be small.

> The whole process of becoming competent in any field must be divided into a very large number of very small steps, and reinforcement must be contingent upon the accomplishment of each step. ... By making each successive step as small as possible, the frequency of reinforcement can be raised to a maximum, while the possibly aversive consequences of being wrong are reduced to a minimum.
>
> (Skinner 1954: 94)

Behaviourist views of this kind have several important implications for teaching and learning. One of these is that learning is a process of accumulating knowledge in a sequenced and hierarchical fashion. This is based on a view that learning tasks may be analysed to establish the components that must be acquired in order to complete the task. Such an analysis then suggests the most appropriate sequence of learning. Even an apparently simple task of adding two separate sets of objects entails several components. For example, a child who is asked to give the total number of blocks contained in two sets: one containing two blocks and the other containing three blocks must be able to count each set correctly. Counting a set of objects correctly involves knowing how to count orally, being able to count each object in the set once and only once, and knowing that the number in the set is the final number in the count (Resnick *et al.* 1973). A child who is unable to perform these components of the task will not be able to add small numbers of objects accurately and consistently. Analysis of the components enables instruction to be targeted effectively at components that are weak. Similarly, more complex forms of skilled learning are based on subcomponents that may be analysed and sequenced. These form a hierarchy with complex components at the top and simpler ones at the base. For a complex skill, the hierarchy contains numerous components and learners may work through them in different ways, depending on their preferences and the pattern of components they have already learned (Pask 1976). In general, however, learning a task at the bottom of the hierarchy transfers to, or facilitates, the learning of a more complex task (Gagne 1970; Gagne *et al.* 1992).

It is now recognized that although behavioural principles of learning are pervasive, there are limits to their range of application. Reinforcement can be beneficial, especially in the early stages of learning and is particularly useful in managing children's behaviour. A parent or teacher who makes reinforcement contingent on good behaviour encourages the repetition of that behaviour. Nevertheless, reinforcement is not essential and much learning takes place without it. It is now realized that reinforcement has a dual role, it provides a pleasurable outcome and it also provides informative feedback to the learner about the success or otherwise of a response. Feedback helps a learner see where progress is being made and draws attention to improvements that are needed.

Developments of behavioural theory in education also draw attention to the role of antecedents that affect behaviour, rather than focusing exclusively on the influence of consequences. In a classroom, students' behaviour is affected by the behaviour of teachers and other students in the class. For example seating arrangements can influence the extent to which students remain on task and focused on their work, with more on task behaviour when students are seated in rows than around tables (Hastings and Schwieso 1995). Seating arrangements are antecedents that affect student behaviour.

An important assumption made by behaviourists is that all behaviour is learned. In this sense, behavioural theories of learning convey a very positive view of human learning and suggest that every individual can learn, given the right conditions. They also suggest that behaviour can be unlearned, or at least replaced with new learning. Perhaps the most trenchant criticism of behavioural approaches to learning is that they do not concern themselves with some of the most interesting and important aspects of human thinking. This realization led to the development of other psychological approaches to learning, which will be described in the sections that follow.

Observational and imitative learning

As noted above, learning is more than a process of shaping and moulding responses through reinforcement. Children (and adults) also learn by observing others around them and imitating their actions (Bandura 1977). Imitative learning emerges early in development and is found in animals as well as in humans, for example, young chimpanzees copy successful methods of food gathering used by adults, such as using a stick to extract ants from a hole (Tomasello *et al.* 1993). During the first year of life, babies imitate facial expressions and vocal patterns of their caregivers and others around them. Older children are inclined to imitate the behaviour of people they admire such as parents, teachers, pop stars or sporting icons. Children are keen observers and learn a great deal about customs, conventions and skilled activities by watching and listening to others in their families and communities (Rogoff 1990).

Adults frequently demonstrate, or model, actions in ways that enable children to imitate. Their demonstrations are based on a belief that the child does not know how to do the action, wants to perform it and can learn by being shown. Observational learning is facilitated when the actions are clearly modelled so that the child is able to follow each of the component parts (Bandura 1977). When parents and teachers deliberately model behaviour for a child to imitate, they may perform an action more slowly or overemphasize articulation of spoken language to draw the child's attention to important components. This makes the behaviour more amenable to imitation and assists the child in moving on to the next steps, which involve remembering and producing the behaviour independently, when the model is not present.

Observational learning encompasses more than simple imitation and copying of behaviour. When learning through observation and imitation, children also observe the consequences of the behaviour displayed by the model. Following a series of experiments in which children watched an adult behaving aggressively towards a plastic doll, Bandura (1986) concluded that children were more likely to display the modelled behaviour when it was rewarded than when it was punished. A learner's performance of learned behaviour is affected by the consequences experienced and also by vicarious experience of the consequences for others.

Observational learning appears to be a fundamental type of learning that is found in animals and humans. Together with behavioural learning, it entails the formation of associations and the acquisition of behavioural responses, often without awareness. Demonstration is useful in the acquisition of physical skills, and in certain forms of procedural knowledge, such handwriting or methods for solving mathematical problems. It is now acknowledged that demonstration of the cognitive processes involved in tasks such as creative writing and mathematical problem solving can be very beneficial. Teachers who make these steps explicit, for example by talking through the processes involved in writing a story from brainstorming ideas to drafting and final revisions demonstrate processes that are normally invisible to students. This allows students to become aware of the steps involved and that to realize that authors typically go through a process of drafting and re-drafting before the story is printed in its final form. Similarly, if different methods of solving a mathematical problem are demonstrated in class, students see that there is more than one solution method and become involved in a process of 'cognitive apprenticeship' (Collins *et al.* 1989).

The usefulness of behavioural and observational theories of learning, as originally conceptualized, is relatively limited, however, when it comes to the acquisition and understanding of conceptual knowledge. This is mainly due to the focus on observable behaviour, which effectively rules out the study of mental processes. This gap has been filled by the work of cognitive and developmental psychologists who make the study of thinking a central component of their work.

Learning to think and reason

An increasing interest in mental process fuelled the rise of cognitive psychology during the middle of the twentieth century and attention shifted from observable behaviour to thinking, reasoning and problem solving, especially in adults. Developmental psychologists also turned their attention to cognitive development in children and their work has now revealed a great deal about children's thinking and reasoning. Much of this draws on the work of Piaget (1963) whose main interest lay in understanding how children's knowledge develops. He explored the development of human knowledge through research on children's understanding of a wide range of mathematical and scientific phenomena. He was interested in how knowledge of the world changes during childhood and into adolescence and saw himself as a genetic epistemologist charting the changes that take place with age. He did not assume that knowledge exists somewhere in the world ready for us to absorb, but was a constructivist who believed that knowledge is constructed by individuals as they interact with the world around them. He argued that children are born with some rudimentary mental structures, which he termed 'schemes' (or schemata), which develop and change as a result of children's actions on objects in the world.

Piaget proposed two processes through which this change took place, assimilation and accommodation. New information might be assimilated to an existing scheme or an existing scheme might change, or accommodate, if information could not be readily assimilated. Through their actions, children actively construct knowledge and form mental representations. As they grow older, children develop more advanced knowledge structures and become capable of abstract logical thought. Logical thinking was one of his main interests, and he saw the human capacity for logical thought as a pinnacle of human achievement.

Piaget's work and that of his successors has been valuable in focusing attention on children's efforts to make sense of the world around them. We now know a great deal about the cognitive capabilities that children possess from an early age and about the changes that take place in young people's understanding of specific domains such as biology and physics (Wellman and Gelman 1998). For example, young children demonstrate an awareness of significant ontological distinctions that capture basic conceptions of what sort of entities there are in the world. By about four or five years of age they are able to distinguish between living and nonliving things and between plants and animals. They are also equipped with rudimentary notions of number from birth.

Yet this body of research has relatively little to say about the process of learning itself. Piaget proposed that children experience cognitive conflict when they realize that their explanation for a phenomenon is inadequate and that this conflict provide an impetus for conceptual change. For example, if two children performing a task disagree about the answer to a problem, this leads one of them to realize the inadequacy of their understanding and to search for a better explanation. Such a view assumes that children and young people are thinkers and problem solvers striving to make sense of the world around them. In essence they are adaptive organisms equipped with cognitive structures that develop with maturation and through action on the world.

Although cognitive conflict has received some support, it has also been shown that agreement, too can lead to changes in children's understanding (Bryant 1982). The process of learning involves more than the experience and resolution of cognitive conflict, but was not Piaget's main interest. As a result, psychologists are in a position of knowing *what* children think and know about many important aspects of the world. More work remains to be done to understand *how* children and young people come to know and think.

The cognitive revolution and Piaget's work had an impact on the study of learning, which virtually disappeared from the psychological landscape and has taken a long time to re-emerge. The reason for this is in part due to the strong distinction between learning and development, made by Piaget and his followers (Piaget 1963; 1964). He distanced his work from that of the behaviourists who saw learning as a spontaneous, passive process of association, and he proposed that development was concerned with active processes of constructing knowledge. Indeed, he argued that development was necessary before learning could take place, as maturational processes underpin the capacity to think and learn.

This view has been challenged by more recent work which '... has made it clear that learning processes share all of the complexity, organization, structure, and internal dynamics once exclusively attributed to development' (Kuhn 1995: 138). Advances in cognitive neuroscience also indicate that learning and development are inseparable (Blakemore and Frith 2005; Greenhough *et al.* 1987). When animals such as monkeys learn, there is a typical cycle of change in the nerve cells (neurons) that are activated in the brain. At first there is a spurt of activity in the neurons involved and this is accompanied by the formation of new connections between cells. This proliferation of connections between the activated neurons is then followed by pruning as connections that are used frequently become stronger, whereas those that are not used weaken (Blakemore and Frith 2005).

Building on Piaget's ideas, Biggs and Collis (1982; Biggs 1996) describe growth in young people's understandings of school and college curriculum topics in terms of a taxonomy, which they named the Structure of Observed Learning Outcomes, or SOLO taxonomy. They proposed that a learner starts by abstracting a single relationship in ideas that have been presented and gradually builds connections until a complex network is established. Thus the growth of understanding starts with the quantitative accumulation of task components, which then become restructured as follows.

1   *Prestructural.* The learner does not understand the point and does not attack the task appropriately.
2   *Unistructural.* The learner picks up and uses one or a small number of aspects of the task. This indicates nominal understanding.
3   *Multistructural.* Several aspects of the task are learned but are not related, so the learner treats them separately. At this level, understanding is equivalent to knowing about a topic.
4   *Relational.* Components are integrated into a coherent whole and each part contributes to the overall meaning. At this level, understanding is in terms of appreciating relationships.

5   *Extended abstract.* The integrated whole that is formed at the relational level is reconceptualized, or reorganized in some way. This reconceptualization may be at a higher level of abstraction, which enables generalization to a new topic or area, or it may involve reflection on one's own mental processes.

An illustration of how the SOLO taxonomy may be applied to a geography question is provided by Biggs and Moore (1993). A teacher gave a lesson to a year 9 class (aged 13–14 years) on the formation of rain and asked the question: 'Why is the side of a mountain that faces the coast usually wetter than the inland side?' Students' responses could be categorized according to the taxonomy from prestructural to extended abstract. Prestructural responses included 'Because it rains more on the side facing the sea', which is virtually a restatement of the question posed. Other examples of prestructural responses included personal anecdotes about coastal mountain locations students had visited where the weather was wet.

An example of a unistructural response was 'The sea breeze hits the coastal side first.' This indicates that the student has picked up a relevant piece of information but has not linked it to other relevant information. An example of a multistructural level response demonstrated some basic linking 'Well, the sea breezes pick up moisture from the sea and as they hit the coastal side first, they drop their moisture so that when they cross to the other side there's no rain left for the inland side.' This shows that the student has identified a relevant fact ('the sea breeze hits the coastal side first') and thus linked the notion of wind from the sea picking up moisture and dropping moisture, but does not appear to know why this happens.

An example of a response that relates ideas together is 'Because the prevailing winds are from the sea and when they blow across they pick up water vapour and, continuing, hit the coastal ranges. They are then forced upwards and in so doing get colder so that the moisture condenses forming rain. By the time they cross the mountains the winds are dry.' This is a relational response as it shows the student knows that picking up and depositing moisture is related to changes in temperature. Thus the different features of the problem situation are connected, at least for the specific context given in the question as set.

An extended abstract response goes beyond the others in that it recognises the importance of the specific context in which the phenomenon is likely to occur. In this case, the effect occurs if the prevailing winds are from the sea. Extended abstract responses also show a fuller understanding of the physical processes involved, including that as air is carried up the mountain there is a change in pressure which affects saturation. This is a higher order principle, which the student generalises and applies to other, relevant contexts, for example one student saw a similarity with Chinooks, or warm spells that sometimes occur during the winter on the eastern slopes of the Canadian Rockies. An extended abstract response might also point out that there are a number of assumptions about wind and temperature conditions on which the question is based (Biggs and Moore 1993).

The SOLO taxonomy provides a descriptive framework that may be applied to learning in many different subjects. It implies that conceptual learning is a process of accumulating information, which is progressively integrated into a coherent whole that represents an understanding of relationships between the various components. This is consistent with some students' experience of learning a new subject, when at first ideas and information appear discrete and unrelated, sometimes frustratingly so, but gradually become better linked into a coherent whole. At the most advanced level (extended abstract) understanding is transformed through a process of restructuring or re-conceptualisation. The taxonomy provides a useful framework for thinking about levels of understanding, as opposed to a dichotomy between understanding and not understanding. It suggests that we may identify an inadequate level (pre-structural) and four levels of understanding, from basic to advanced.

Thus the process of conceptual learning involves the formation and strengthening of connections between ideas and information, and in some cases a process of transformation and re-conceptualisation. Knowledge structures are built up and used to solve problems such as those set by teachers in the classroom. This may require hard work on the part of a learner, but the process of re-conceptualisation may be experienced as particularly challenging.

Learners' subjective experiences suggest that coming to know and understand a topic involves a sense of integration, as proposed above. University students revising for an examination often reach a point where they experience their knowledge as having object-like qualities, leading Entwistle and Marton (1993) to refer to them as 'knowledge objects'. When this point is reached, students report a sense that information is integrated into a coherent whole, which they can consider from different perspectives. Being able to take a different perspective enables more flexible use of information, as a student can select aspects that are relevant to answer a given question as opposed to reading off chunks of information from memory.

Acquiring strategies and skills

Although the cognitive revolution turned attention away from learning as such, cognitive psychologists have made important discoveries about mental processes that are involved in learning (Anderson 2000). These include how we remember and why we forget and the processes involved in cognitive skills such as reading. Perhaps the most enduring legacy of adult cognitive psychology is the model of information processing, which likens the brain to a computer with a limited capacity for processing information. According to this model, information that impinges on our senses is filtered by sensory systems before being passed on to a central processing system. This system then passes the processed information to long-term storage and to the motor system to produce physical actions.

Limitations on the amount of information that can be held in working memory restrict the brain's capacity to deal with more than a certain quantity of information. Give yourself 20 seconds to look at the string of digits below, then cover it and see how much you remember.

7 2 4 0 9 5 8

Now give yourself 20 seconds to memorize the next string.

6 1 8 0 5 2 7 3 9 4

You should be able to recall the first set, as most people are able to remember a string of about seven unrelated digits. The chances are that you did not recall all digits in the second string in the correct order, as most people struggle if asked to recall more than seven unrelated pieces of information.

To overcome the brain's limited processing capacity, individuals develop strategies for remembering, problem solving and thinking. In the example above, where the information is recalled after a short space of time, digits may be repeated over and over and thus maintained in memory until needed. This is what we do when remembering a phone number just long enough to walk over to a phone and dial it. Other strategies involve the use of mnemonics to remember information, such as anatomical names, historical dates and events, and foreign language vocabulary. They are useful for remembering information in its original form.

Strategies such as organization and elaboration are also widely used. Organization includes categorizing information presented and recalling it by category. For example, when memorizing a list of nouns a student might realize that although at first sight the list appears random, the nouns belong to several categories such as foods, tools and clothing. Memorizing the words by category is an efficient way of remembering the list. Elaboration involves greater transformation of the information presented, such as summarizing a chapter or drawing a concept map, identifying links between ideas presented. Both organization and elaboration are general strategies that may be used with a variety of subject matter (Weinstein and Mayer 1986).

Some strategies are more specific to the content of the subject at hand. For example, we use specific strategies to solve basic arithmetic problems. A child might solve a simple addition problem such as 5 + 2 by counting five objects (or fingers) and then two objects. A more sophisticated strategy would be to count on from the larger number, in this case five, so the count would be '5, 6, 7'. Children who are able to use the faster, more sophisticated strategy sometimes use the slower strategy of counting all the objects (Siegler 2000). This is also true of adults, for example when shopping in a market where there are no computerized tills to work out bills, shoppers may want to add up the cost of their purchases. At a fruit stall suppose that a shopper buys 4 oranges at 16p each, two punnets of strawberries priced £1.20 each, 3 grapefruits at 25p and a pineapple priced £1.60. There are several different ways to add these amounts mentally. One strategy would be to add each individual item in turn and keep a running total. Alternatively a shopper might prefer to calculate the amount for the four oranges first and this could be achieved using different strategies such as repeated addition (16p + 16p - 32p and 32p + 32p – 64p) or multiplication (4 × 16p = 64p). A strategy for the 3 grapefruits might be to draw on memory and 'read off' 75p, as the shopper knows that 3 × 25 is 75 without having to calculate. Individual shoppers have their own preferred strategies, which they rely on when they want to be sure of arriving at the correct total. Nevertheless, they may not use this strategy consistently for different problems and may even switch from one strategy to another during a problem-solving session. It might be instructive to reflect on your own use of strategies when calculating totals or dividing a restaurant bill between a group of friends, without the use of a calculator.

Information processing theories of development treat cognitive growth in terms of changes in children's use of strategies and their conceptual understanding. Researchers investigate how these changes relate to children's age and experience, rather than focusing on stages of development. A central metaphor of information processing theory is that of a computer with limited central processing capacity. Early models proposed a single processor, which limited the capacity to handle information. More recent models incorporate parallel processing so that the system is not limited to one central processor but has the capacity to process information through several channels simultaneously. Parallel processing also allows for greater variability between individual responses as learners may use different mental pathways to process information (Klahr and MacWhinney 1998).

An important feature of information processing theories is that they recognize the complex world in which children live and grow. Children are continually trying to achieve goals with insufficient knowledge and limited processing capacity. By deploying strategies to think and solve problems, they obtain information about the effectiveness of their strategies, which in turn affects the strategies used in future. This is seen as a fundamental process involved in the acquisition of skills and strategies, which is adaptive and self-modified.

Awareness and regulation of learning

Discoveries about the use of strategies soon led on to questions about learners' awareness of strategies. Early studies were concerned with strategies for remembering and the extent to which awareness of these strategies was related to successful memorizing. Flavell and Wellman (1977) proposed a taxonomy of knowledge about memory that included knowing when intentional memorizing is required and when it is not. They proposed that metamemory includes knowledge of strategies for memorizing and when to deploy them.

Since then, interest in the learner's awareness of strategies and their effective use has expanded into other aspects of cognition. The term metacognition is used to refer to awareness and use of a wide range of cognitive strategies involved in thinking, studying and solving problems. Metacognitive knowledge refers to knowledge of one's cognitive processes and encompasses knowledge of self, knowledge of task, strategy knowledge, and knowledge of plans and goals (Alexander *et al.* 1991). Self-knowledge in relation to learning includes individuals' understandings of themselves as learners or thinkers, such as knowledge and beliefs about the nature of learning in general, about a learner's performance relative to others, and about the tasks a learner finds easy or hard. Task knowledge includes recognition of the demands of different types of learning activity. Strategic knowledge includes an understanding of specific strategies that may be used to accomplish tasks with different requirements. Self-regulated learning is an umbrella term that encompasses a wide range of strategies that are deployed before, during and after performing a task (Pintrich 2000). Advances in our understanding of metacognition and self-regulation suggest that learners are thinkers and problem solvers who are able to take control of their own learning.

Socio-cultural learning

The majority of work referred to above is concerned with understanding mental processes involved in learning and thinking. It has advanced our understanding of these processes but has paid relatively little attention to the more social dimensions of learning. In contrast, contemporary socio-cultural theories see learning as an integral part of cultural and historical processes. Children grow up in a social world, first within the family and later within the school and local community. This social world provides an arena in which parents, siblings, peers and teachers influence children's learning. Socio-cultural theories are concerned with relationships between children's learning and the social and cultural environment in which it takes place. Social activities are formed as part of the cultural context in which they are located. These social activities are constitutive of learning, as over time they become part of the individual, who appropriates concepts and ways of thinking and acting.

Whereas in social learning theory (Bandura 1977; 1986), the individual child and the social world were originally seen as two separate entities, socio-cultural theories see a much closer connection between the child and the social system. These theories draw on the work of the Russian psychologist Lev Vygotsky (1896–1934) who saw the child and the social world as part of a single system. Vygotsky was influenced by Marxist philosophy and profoundly affected by the social upheaval in Russia at the beginning of the twentieth century, which fuelled his interest in cultural influences on children's development. Like Piaget, he viewed children as active in their own learning, eager to acquire the skills and knowledge needed to function in the world. He was also impressed by his experience that, historically, cultural environments change and make new demands on the population calling for different skills and knowledge to cope with these changing demands. Children and young people learn the skills needed to function in a particular culture and a major part of Vygotsky's agenda was to understand how social processes are involved in children's learning and development (Vygotsky 1978).

Like his contemporary Piaget, Vygotsky (1978) distanced his own work from learning, by which he meant a passive process of association. He drew a distinction between what he called the 'natural line' of development that took place through direct association between a stimulus and response and the development of 'higher' mental functions through mediation by another person or cultural artefacts (Vygotsky 1978). Higher mental functions included concept formation, memory, voluntary attention and the development of volition. In his theory, these functions form part of the culture into which children grow and they are passed on from one generation to another through children's interactions with parents and others in their social world.

Whereas Piaget argued that development is necessary for learning, Vygotsky argued that learning and development proceed hand-in-hand. He criticized the use of standardized tests of ability to determine children's cognitive level as he reasoned that such tests indicated developmental stages already completed. He argued that to lead the child forward, attention must be focused not only on what the child has already achieved but also on the next stages in learning, or what the child can achieve with help from others who are more capable. As he put it, 'the only "good learning" is that which is in advance of development' (Vygotsky 1978: 89). This means that for Vygotsky, learning is an essentially social process achieved through interaction with more capable members of the culture. He proposed that learning processes are transformed into developmental processes '… properly organized learning results in mental development and sets in motion a variety of developmental processes that would be impossible apart from learning.' (Vygotsky 1978: 90). This transformation takes place through a process of internalization through which children appropriate understanding of concepts, transforming them in the process and making them their own. He established an important research agenda to investigate how this process unfolded during interactions with other people and inspired a generation of research on such interactions (e.g. Rogoff 1990; Wertsch 1985; Wood and Wood 1996a). This research promises to increase our understanding of the processes through which children come to understand the world. Some recent advances in this field of enquiry will be described in Chapter 5.

Implicit learning and tacit knowledge

Much of the theory and research referred to above is concerned with deliberate learning. In contrast, implicit learning takes place 'in the absence of consciously accessible knowledge' (Eysenck and Keane 2005). Early research demonstrated that adults are able to learn rules and patterns in information without being able to verbalize the rules (Berry and Broadbent 1984; Broadbent *et al.* 1986). It is not easy to demonstrate that implicit learning occurs as even when participants are not consciously aware of having learned something, it does not necessarily follow that learning is implicit. Ingenious experiments make use of a complex learning task that involves participants deciding whether strings of letters conform to the rules of an artificial grammar. The majority of people learn to judge grammatical and ungrammatical strings, even though they are unable to state the rules of the grammar (Reber 1993). Implicit learning appears to be common to many species and in humans is affected very little by age or intelligence. It is also relatively unaffected by mental disorders (Reber 1993).

It is now widely acknowledged that from birth, children are predisposed to learn about the world. They are equipped with cognitive structures that help them to make sense of the physical and social world around them. One of the most pervasive characteristics of young children, demonstrated before they start school, is a search for causes. They appear to have a core belief that events do not occur at random and that causes may be found to explain them (Wellman and Gelman 1998). Their achievements in the domain of language acquisition are perhaps the most obvious and dramatic. During the first five years of life, children learn a large vocabulary, syntax and pragmatic use of language. What is striking about this remarkable achievement is that it appears to occur with very little deliberate teaching. Parents and other conversational partners certainly support children as they acquire their native language but they appear to do this naturally and with little awareness (Bruner 1983). Similar achievements have been documented in mathematics, showing that many children learn to count, compare quantities, add and subtract before they start school. Children appear to learn from a wide range of different activities, including transactions in shops, games involving counting, reading numerals on the clock and finding pages in books (Guberman 1999).

The ubiquitous nature of implicit learning means that individuals acquire a large amount of information as tacit knowledge. Every individual has a stock of tacit knowledge built up through their life experiences and although there will be some commonalities between individuals in general forms of representation, each individual's experiences and tacit knowledge differ. This knowledge, or parts of it, may become an 'object of thought', in which case it is brought into consciousness (Prawat 1989). Similarly, information that has been an object of thought can move out of consciousness when it is no longer of interest, or for some other reason. Explicit knowledge, or knowledge brought to mind, represents only a small fraction of an individual's tacit knowledge (Alexander *et al.* 1991). The processes involved in bringing information to mind and making it an object of thought are not well understood or explicated in much research on learning.

It seems that fairly complex information can be learned implicitly, through engaging in tasks and activities in everyday life and in work. The brain is designed to pick out patterns and regularities in the complex arrays of information that are perceived by the senses. This form of learning contributes to young people's understanding of the world, which they acquire as they take part in everyday activities.

Summary of main psychological approaches to learning

By way of summarizing the main theoretical approaches overviewed so far, Table 1.1 displays the central metaphor and view of learning associated with each theory. Its purpose is to highlight the main ideas of each approach and as such it is a simplification, which captures a central idea but does not do justice to the complexity of each theory. It is also worth noting that contemporary theories often draw on a mix of ideas.

Behavioural theories and social learning theory are both concerned with observable behaviour, rather than with the mental processes involved in learning, thinking and problem solving. The central metaphor is one of shaping and moulding learners through the manipulation of the consequences of behaviour and antecedent conditions. Rewards and reinforcers are used to encourage and shape behaviour and antecedent conditions may also be manipulated to increase the frequency of desirable responses. The process of learning entails absorbing knowledge and behaviour or observing and imitating behaviour exhibited by others.

Developmental theories following in the Piagetian tradition view the learner as an adaptive organism. Children are seen as active thinkers and

Table 1.1 Central metaphors of major theories of learning

Theory of learning	Central metaphor	Key view of learners
Behaviourist	Shaping and moulding	Absorber of behaviour and knowledge
Social learning	Modelling	Observer and imitator
Developmental	Adaptive organism	Thinker and problem solver
Information processing	Computer	Information processor
Meta-cognitive	Mental control	Strategist, regulator of learning
Socio-cultural	Participant	Appropriator of information

problem solvers, or little scientists, eager to explore and investigate the world and make sense of it. They are born with rudimentary mental structures, which develop and change with age as a result of their actions in the world around them.

Information processing theories liken the brain to a computer with limited capacity. Children and adults are seen as striving to achieve goals with limited knowledge and processing capacity. To overcome these limitations they develop a range of cognitive strategies and they obtain information about the effectiveness of strategies, which influences the strategies they deploy in future.

Becoming aware of strategies and knowing when to deploy them are functions of metacognitive systems. Theory and research on metacognition and self-regulation see learning in terms of the deployment of effective strategies for the mental control of learning. Learners are seen as executives, managing and regulating their own learning processes.

Socio-cultural theories acknowledge an important role for the child's participation with others in a social and cultural setting. It is through participation in activity that learners interact with more capable people who guide their learning. Learning is seen as a process of appropriation, involving constructive transformation as the learner internalizes knowledge and makes it his or her own.

Learners' conceptions of learning

As noted above, developmental psychologists such as Piaget and Vygotsky attempted to identify general developmental processes and as a result they paid little attention to differences between learners. Similarly, the behavioural and information processing perspectives gave valuable insights into the conditions under which learning took place yet they had little to say about learners' experiences of learning. This gap has now been filled by numerous studies that have explored the experiences of learners in school and university with the aim of finding out how they perceive and approach learning and why some learners are more successful than others (Marton and Booth 1997: 16). These studies use qualitative methods to explore and describe learners' subjective experiences when completing tasks they might encounter at school or university. For example, Säljö (Marton and Säljö 1976) gave university students a text to read and asked them to read it as though they were preparing for a seminar when they would be asked questions. He interviewed them to find out how they had gone about reading the text. His analysis of themes and commonalities in the transcribed interviews revealed that there were some important differences in students' ideas about learning and how they approached the task of reading an academic text. These early findings have been confirmed in later studies and in all, six different conceptions of learning among university students have now been identified, as follows (Marton, and Säljö 1976, Marton *et al.* 1993; Marton and Booth 1997):

A   increasing one's knowledge
B   memorizing and reproducing
C   applying
D   understanding
E   seeing something in a different way
F   changing as a person.

Some university students see learning as a process of increasing knowledge, memorizing and reproducing, they mention learning by rote, cramming and reproducing information in exams. They view learning as essentially a process of accumulating information, and they talk about it as memorizing, acquiring information or knowing more. A related view of learning is concerned with the use and application of knowledge acquired. Other students view learning in a qualitatively different way, for them it is a process of finding meaning, they see things in a new light, and relate new information to their earlier experiences and to the world they live in. Some university students describe learning in terms of changing as a person, thus producing a more fundamental change in themselves, as opposed to their understanding of a subject or field of study.

Secondary school students appear to have similar conceptions about learning as increasing knowledge, memorizing and understanding but do not see it in terms of changing as a person (Marton *et al.* 1997). Students in a Hong Kong secondary school experienced memorizing in two different ways. The first was rote learning of words and information, whereas the second involved a process of understanding meaning, which was then committed to memory. Similarly, understanding was experienced into different ways. The first involved abstracting content and making it the learner's own in some way, whereas the second involved going beyond the content to be learned and relating it to the world at large.

Similar conceptions have been found among 13–14-year-olds in a school in England (Evans 2001). These students expressed conceptions of learning as doing for example 'I learned how to use a drill' and they spoke of learning to know, for example, 'We've learned trigonometry'. They also spoke of learning as understanding, for example, referring to a discussion about a prominent figure one student said, 'We all spoke and we kept changing ideas so we had a whole picture about him'. In this same study, the students were also presented with the idea that learning could be characterized as doing, knowing and understanding and were asked for their comments. Their responses were somewhat similar to those of the Hong Kong students mentioned above, as they thought that understanding was the most important aspect of learning and preceded knowing and doing. As one of the students commented, 'it's understanding when you first learn about it then doing it so you know it then using it' (Evans 2001: 48). Students' views related to the curriculum subject they had in mind, so for example, they were more likely to speak about learning as doing when referring to design and technology and more likely to speak about learning as understanding when referring to history.

Even very young children have more than one conception of learning. Pramling (1988; 1996) asked children aged between three and eight years old to tell her about something they had learned and then asked them how they went about learning. She found that the children held three different conceptions of learning, which she characterized as learning to do, to know and to understand. When children perceived learning as doing, they spoke in terms of learning a skill, performing an activity or behaving in a certain way, for example, 'I have learned to ride my bike'. Learning to know meant that the children perceived learning as knowing facts or receiving information about something, for example, 'I have learned that there is a country called Canada'. Learning as understanding involved a qualitative change in thinking for example 'Although I knew about cars when I was three years old, I did not know anything about traffic' (Pramling 1996: 571). Children's conceptions developed and expanded with age, the youngest children spoke of learning as doing whereas a quarter of the eight-year-olds also spoke of knowing and a very small number spoke of understanding.

Bereiter and Scardamalia (1989) suggest that primary school children see learning as an activity, whereas adults see it as a goal. They asked children in third grade and sixth grade about their long-term goals in life and about what they could do if they had an hour a day to work towards their goals. They also questioned six adults with graduate degrees in the same way. Most of the children indicated topics or activities without an objective, whereas adults specified knowledge and skills they hoped to achieve. The older children were more specific about topics and skills and they also identified components or stages to focus on, whereas more of the younger children only indicated a subject. These ways of thinking about learning were associated with different ideas about how learning took place. The youngest children thought that learning was a matter of doing, whereas some of the older children thought learning was related to age for example 'When I am five I will be able to ride a bike'. At the most advanced level of understanding children realized they needed experience to learn.

Clearly, learners have a variety of conceptions of learning and these expand with age. Children and adults alike realize that we learn by doing, however with age comes an increasing awareness of learning as a process of coming to know and understand. Some university students experience learning as involving more fundamental transformations, such as seeing the world in a different way or affecting their identity. Older learners are also more able to formulate goals for their learning.

These different conceptions of learning are significant, as they relate to students' approaches to their academic work at school and university. Students who see learning as a process of accumulating information tend to take a surface approach to learning. This means that when they read an academic text, they tend to focus on memorizing facts, rather than trying to reach an understanding of the meaning of the text. Students who see learning as a process of understanding tend to look for the deeper meaning of texts and other materials they encounter (van Rossum and Schenk 1984).

It is important to note that in most of these studies, students were talking about their learning in a particular subject. This means that they might have different conceptions about their learning in different domains. It would be possible to have a deeper understanding in a subject that encourages different points of view and a more interpretive perspective, such as history, and a sense of accumulating facts in a subject such as anatomy. A learner's interest in a subject might also affect their conception of learning, as greater interest is likely to be coupled with a desire to understand the material. It is therefore possible for learners to have several conceptions of learning, just as they have several strategies for accomplishing learning tasks. Specific conceptions might come to mind when considering different types of task. Nevertheless, learners who have a restricted view of learning as accumulating facts may experience difficulty in seeing learning in a more transformative sense and thus face difficulty reaching higher levels of understanding needed for success in higher education.

Teaching and learning

The metaphors of learning discussed in the first part of this chapter and displayed in Table 1.1 have important implications for teaching. They imply different, commonly held models of learners' minds, each of which may be identified among teachers and others who work with children and help them to learn. These models range from seeing children as imitative learners to seeing them as thinkers, constructing an understanding of the world around them (Bruner 1996). Different conceptions of children as learners may be associated with different approaches to teaching, which in turn may impact on students' learning.

Evidence suggests that just as learners have a variety of conceptions of learning, teachers have a variety of conceptions of teaching. These have been located on a continuum from a focus on curriculum content and knowledge to be imparted to a focus on student learning (Samuelowicz and Bain 1992), as follows:

1   imparting information
2   transmitting knowledge
3   facilitating understanding
4   changing students' conceptions
5   supporting student learning.

This continuum suggests that university teachers vary in the extent to which they focus on the subject matter to be taught and on their students' learning. School teachers also exhibit a range of conceptions from a content focus in teaching to a student focus (Boulton-Lewis *et al.* 2001; Marton and Booth 1997).

Teachers who see teaching as a process of imparting information and transmitting knowledge tend to have a focus on the subject matter and how it may best be organized and presented to facilitate acquisition by students. The model they work with is based on the notion that the learner's mind is like a receptacle to be filled with facts, principles and rules of action. It reflects an associative view of learning in which the teacher's task is to present information for the learner to learn, remember and apply.

It is hardly surprising to find that teachers view teaching as a matter of imparting information and transmitting knowledge, as a school or university curriculum contains a large body of knowledge to be acquired. Yet such a view focuses on teaching and how it might be most effectively organized, rather than on students' understanding. Teachers who see learning in terms of facilitating understanding and changing conceptions have a greater focus on their students' current conceptions. This suggests that teachers have a view of students as thinkers, constructing a model of the world to help them understand their experience. They see it as useful, therefore, to gain insight into learners' mental strategies for solving problems and for learners to gain access to teachers' knowledge through dialogue (Askew *et al.* 1997; Marton *et al.* 1993). In this way, teaching can help children to gradually develop more advanced understandings of world.

There is evidence of connections between teachers' conceptions of teaching and the means they use to promote the type of learning they had in mind. So for example teachers who see teaching as a matter of imparting information or skills say they would tell, describe, show, repeat or go over work again, or give practice. Those who see teaching as the facilitation of students' understanding speak of using discussion, questioning, stimulating and encouraging students to think about their own thinking (metacognition). This suggests that there is consistency in teachers' views of teaching and their views of learning. Teachers who have a transmission view of teaching tend to view learning as the acquisition and reproduction of content and skills whereas teachers who see teaching as the facilitation of understanding tend to see learning as the development of their students' understanding, and teachers who espouse a more transformative view of teaching see learning as the transformation of learners (Boulton-Lewis *et al.* 2001).

Many of these categorizations of teachers' conceptions rely on information obtained through interviews and therefore give a general view of teachers' awareness and ways of thinking. They do not tell us what actually happens in classrooms, and it is well known that teachers do not always enact their intentions in the classroom context, for a variety of reasons, not least that classrooms are complex environments. Teaching does not take place in isolation, but is a part of a complex system, which embraces the teacher and the teaching context, students and their learning activities and the overall outcome. Classroom constraints and the demands of assessment systems may limit the extent to which a teacher is able to support student learning, and teachers who profess an orientation towards supporting student learning may find it necessary to impart information and facilitate understanding. In a system, the various components interact with each other and work towards a state of equilibrium (Biggs and Moore 1993). If curriculum objectives address higher order thinking and understanding but assessments address lower levels of cognitive activity, the system will settle on the lower level. In this case, there will be 'backwash' from testing, which will have a negative affect on teaching and learning (Frederiksen and Collins 1989).

Summary

Close analysis of the term 'learning' indicates that it is subject to many different interpretations. In its everyday, or vernacular, usage learning is generally taken to mean the deliberate acquisition of information or skills. Within psychology the study of learning has had a chequered history and although it was a major topic of research in the early part of the twentieth century, this was very much associated with behavioural theories. The rise of adult cognitive psychology and Piaget's theory of cognitive development gave prominence to children's conceptions, reasoning and thinking which were seen as fundamentally distinct from learning. Children's learning as a topic in its own right virtually disappeared from the psychological landscape and has taken a long time to re-emerge. The legacy of this situation is that a relatively small number of diverse concepts of learning emerged from various theoretical positions and there is no single unifying framework. The diversity includes associative learning, observational learning, learning to think, acquiring skills and strategies, being aware of and exercising control over cognitive processes and socio-cultural learning. Each of these approaches carries with it a set of assumptions about what is learned and the nature of learning processes involved. An individual is variously seen as acquiring knowledge through association and shaping, observation and imitation, a constructive process of understanding, and a social process of interaction with a knowledgeable other.

Teachers and students alike carry a diverse set of notions about learning. These range from memorizing, to seeing something in a different way and changes in students as learners. Whereas young children appear to hold a limited number of conceptions of learning, older students and adults exhibit a wider range. It is likely that fundamental conceptions of learning as doing and knowing persist and that other conceptions are added as students progress to more advanced levels in the education system.

It is now acknowledged that some learning is ubiquitous and occurs spontaneously as a natural part of everyday life. Nevertheless, deliberate learning is a major concern in education where it is necessary for children to follow a prescribed curriculum. Children and young people are not always interested in the subject matter presented to them and in these circumstances assumptions made by some of the theories discussed above are questionable. Specifically, the tendency to assume that children have a natural inclination to find out about the world around them has meant that theories of cognitive development pay little attention to the issue of motivation. While there is certainly some truth in the view that children are curious to learn and to hone their strategies for solving problems, this view downplays the effort and hard work that children and young people must invest if they are to master the school curriculum.

2 Acquiring skills and expertise

Introduction

During their lives most young people and adults acquire a remarkable range of skills and knowledge. These include oral language, reading, mathematics, sports, musical and artistic activities, geography, navigation skills and game playing, to mention just a few. Recent advances in understanding the development of skills and expertise suggest that there is some commonality in the way that we learn and become expert in a wide variety of different skills, including physical skills such as football and cognitive skills such as reading. This chapter is mainly concerned with cognitive skills and expertise, as these are especially important in education. It provides a review of what is known about the learning of skills and development of expertise and synthesizes findings from theory and research.

Numerous studies have made comparisons between experts' and novices' mental representations and processing. They indicate that as a result of acquiring large amounts of information in a domain, experts' representations become more efficiently organized and more strongly based on principles. Practice plays an important part in this process and the acquisition of complex skills typically takes around 10 years, or 10,000 hours of practice. To achieve an exceptional level of performance requires dedication and those who go on to achieve expertise commit themselves to their chosen domain for many years. Families play an important role in stimulating children's interest and supporting them in their learning, indicating the value they place on their child's education and achievement. The chapter ends with a discussion of educational implications of this body of research.

Skills and expertise

What do we mean when we say someone is highly skilled, an expert or exceptional? In everyday language, these terms are generally used in a comparative way, to identify people who perform at high levels relative to others. The child or adult who achieves the highest academic grades or wins international competitions in sports or music is said to be exceptional. In popular thought, the notion of expertise is entangled with stereotypes such as talent, experience and specialization (Bereiter and Scardamalia 1993). There is a tendency to think that experts are people with particular talents. Similarly, children who show remarkable achievements at an early age are thought to be prodigies with innate talents and abilities. This way of thinking leads us to a view that certain individuals are endowed with special abilities, whereas extensive research in cognitive psychology indicates that many abilities are acquired. Common processes are involved in learning of a wide range of skills and expertise (Speelman and Kirsner 2005).

A comparative view of skills and expertise encourages a focus on exceptional individuals and can blind us to the achievements of typical people. Many everyday activities are highly skilled, for example reading, writing, calculating, navigating round cities, driving and playing sports. All these activities take years to acquire, yet they tend to be taken for granted, and their complexity can be underestimated. Watching a young child learning to read, write or calculate brings home the difficulty involved in these skills, which to most adults appear simple.

A distinction is frequently made between physical skills and cognitive skills. Physical skills that involve perception and a physical response are sometimes called 'psycho-motor skills' or simply 'motor skills' (Fitts and Posner 1967). Examples include many sports, typing, and physical work on factory production lines. Cognitive skills include those involved in playing chess, problem solving, reading and other complex mental activities. In the past, the terms 'skill' and 'expertise' were used to refer to motor and cognitive skills respectively, and it was thought that these types of skill were dissimilar. Nowadays this distinction is not always made as it is thought that there is a common set of principles underpinning both psycho-motor and cognitive skills (Speelman and Kirsner 2005). This position is reflected in a recent definition of expertise as 'highly skilled competent performance in one or more task domains' (Sternberg and Ben Zeev 2001: 365).

So what are the characteristics of highly skilled performance? Three key components are speed, accuracy and fluency (Sloboda 1986). Top dancers, sports players and musicians are able to perform complex moves with great accuracy at high speed. They also integrate one part of an activity seamlessly with another, which makes their performance appear almost effortless. This integration constitutes the 'fluency' of performance, where one move leads into another without a break. Speed, accuracy and fluency are evident in skills and expertise in many different domains.

Learning curves

It is widely accepted that practice is necessary to develop skills and expertise and that practice speeds up performance in a variety of tasks and activities. Over a hundred years ago, Bryan and Harter (1899) plotted learning curves showing the rate at which people learned to send and receive Morse code.

They found that typically there was rapid early learning followed by a period of slower improvement. They also found plateaux where performance levelled off for a while before increasing again with more practice. Similar plateaux were later found in studies of people learning to type.

Since then the characteristic shape of learning curves has been confirmed, showing that during the first sessions of practice, performance improves quickly and this is followed by continued but smaller improvement over a long period of time. This pattern is evident in a very wide range of tasks from solving simple arithmetic problems to writing books and manufacturing ships (Speelman and Kirsner 2005). It is worth noting, however, that these graphs are typically the result of averaging data produced from groups of people and that individual learning curves are not always so smooth.

Performance in a wide range of skills and expertise continues to improve over long periods of time. Crossman (1959) found that workers rolling cigars on a factory production line gained in speed over a period of 10 years, after which gains continued but were very small. Others have replicated this finding and propose a '10-year rule', or 10,000 hours of practice required to become an expert. For example, chess masters studied by Simon and Chase (1973) had spent 10,000 to 20,000 hours looking at chess positions and expert radiologists studied by Lesgold, Glaser, Rubinson *et al.* (1988) had examined between 10,000 and 200,000 x-rays. Children and adults who achieve international levels of performance require about 10 years of preparation (Bloom 1985). Even prodigies such as Bobby Fisher took a preparation time of about nine years (Ericsson *et al.* 1993) and it has been suggested that other child prodigies started at an early age and were thus able to build up 10,000 hours of practice while still young. As in other domains, expertise in teaching develops through extensive practice and typically this takes many years of classroom experience (Berliner 1986). Even skills that are mastered by most people, such as reading and arithmetic, take many years to learn.

Expert knowledge and performance

Our understanding of expertise has been transformed by the realization that it relies on a well-structured knowledge base, rather than straightforward increases in processing speed. Intelligent behaviour relies on the efficient organization of information in the brain as well as on efficient access to that information (Glaser and Chi 1988). These insights have been gained through studies of the way in which experts perceive and process information.

Two main research strategies have been used to uncover the mental processes of experts. One is to ask experts to 'think-aloud' while solving problems and to use qualitative methods to analyse protocols. A second method is to compare the perceptions and representations of experts and novices, sometimes combining this with protocol analysis. This latter method has been used extensively and shows that one of the key differences between experts and novices lies in the way they perceive and store information. Experts' perceptions are far more meaningful than those of novices and this relates to the organization of information in memory.

When experts and novices are given the same information they see and interpret it in very different ways. In a landmark experiment, de Groot (1965) compared world-class chess masters and less experienced players who were nevertheless very good. He was interested in finding out how the world-class players were able to out-think their opponents, so he showed them a board with pieces arranged as they might be during a game and asked them to think aloud while they worked out their next move. He found that all the players thought through their next move in great depth and none of them considered all the possibilities. The only difference was that the chess masters considered possibilities for moves that were of higher quality. He concluded that the masters acquired greater knowledge of chess from the many hours they spent playing the game, which meant that they were more likely to recognize configurations in a meaningful way. Moreover, their representations were also linked to knowledge about strategies, which helped them to think about their next moves. This meant that when masters looked at the configurations, they immediately perceived meaningful patterns, whereas less experienced players had to spend time working out the meaning from individual pieces of information.

Experts' ability to see meaningful patterns of information also helps them to remember large amounts of information. De Groot (1966) went on to compare expert and novice chess players' memory for configurations of chess pieces on a board. He showed them a board with a configuration of pieces as they might be during a game and after five seconds he took the board away and asked participants to reconstruct the configuration of chess pieces on an empty board. Chess masters were able to position 20 pieces correctly whereas novices managed only four or five. This demonstrated that expert players were better than novices at remembering the configurations of pieces.

When experts and novices were compared on a similar task in which the pieces were arranged on the board at random, there was very little difference in the amount they remembered (Chase and Simon 1973; Gobet and Waters 2003). This suggests that good chess players do not necessarily have better memories than other people. Instead their memory for chess improves because they play a great deal of chess. With repeated experience of typical configurations during games and how these affected a player's next moves, experts associate configurations, moves and consequences. In other words, they see configurations in a meaningful way, and are aware of the consequences for their next moves. Novices, on the other hand, see only individual pieces, and fail to realize the consequences. It therefore appears that as an increasing amount of domain knowledge is stored in memory it gradually transforms mental representations. These findings lead Chase and Simon (1973) to conclude that expert performance in chess and other activities arises from the acquisition of large amounts of knowledge and pattern-based retrieval of information from memory. This was a significant realization as it challenged a prevalent view that expert chess players had a greater intellectual capacity that enabled them to search for chess moves.

This ability of experts to perceive patterns and meaning in information that appears random to the novice is not confined to chess. For example, when expert radiologists and novices are shown the same x-rays, experts can identify anatomical structures whereas novices find this very difficult (Lesgold *et al.* 1988). Similarly, photographs or video recordings of a classroom activity reveal a great deal to an experienced teacher, whereas a beginning teacher sees only superficial features (Berliner 1986; Sabers *et al.* 1991).

Compared with novices, experts' knowledge appears to be better organized and this allows them to represent problems in terms of deeper theoretical principles and to abstract features which help them solve problems more efficiently (Chi *et al.* 1982). Many good examples of the different representations of experts and novices come from the domain of physics. Chi, Feltovitch and Glaser (1981) compared the classification of physics problems by experts and beginner physicists, who were college students. The problems were displayed on a set of cards, which participants were asked to sort into categories and then give reasons for their categorization. College students sorted the problems on the basis of surface features, for example they grouped all the inclined plane problems together and all the problems involving springs together. Experts sorted the problems in a very different way, based on underlying principles such as conservation of energy or Newton's second Law. For them, problems that were very different on the surface were seen as similar, as they related to these deep underlying principles. Furthermore, when asked to solve a set of physics problems, novices tended to focus on surface features of the problems, whereas experts represent problems in terms of theoretical principles. Knowledge structures, or 'schemas', are thought to guide how problems are represented and understood, and to link with knowledge about actions and their consequences (Chi *et al.* 1982). It is proposed that these representations are stored in long-term working memory and can be rapidly retrieved thus enabling faster and more efficient problem solving.

In addition to more efficient accessing of information, experts also have a deep understanding of how knowledge is constructed and utilized in their chosen field. Weinberg (1991) compared history experts and a group of high schools students who were high achievers in history. The historians were experts in different fields such as Asian history, mediaeval history, and American history. He gave both groups a factual test about the American Revolution and found that some of the students did better than the experts. He then gave them a set of historical documents relating to the Battle of Lexington, and three pictures of the Lexington battlefield. The task was to select the picture that best represented the battlefield. Whereas students tended to select a picture very quickly, the expert historians took a great deal of time and care reading the documents and looking at the pictures for corroborating evidence. They realized that historical knowledge is a matter of interpretation, and they were able to come up with alternative explanations on the basis of the evidence. This study shows that although the students knew many facts about American history, they did not have a deep understanding of the subject, and how it is constructed through empirical inquiry.

Similarly, expert teachers' knowledge allows them to make inferences and solve problems more effectively than novices. In one study, small groups of expert and novice teachers were shown a slide of a classroom for a brief moment and were asked to say what they saw (Berliner 1986). Novices gave literal descriptions, for example one said, 'a room of students sitting at tables' and another said, 'a classroom. Student with back to camera working at a table.' (Berliner 1986: 10). Experts recognized that the students were taking part in small group work. They did this by drawing inferences from the layout of the classroom and their knowledge of classroom teaching. This knowledge was not available to the novices, who were unable to draw similar inferences. Berliner argues that these differences between expert and novice teachers are very similar to those shown between experts and novices in other domains such as physics.

Sabers, Cushing and Berliner (1991) asked expert, beginner, and novice teachers to view television monitors displaying the work of a high school science class. Expert teachers were carefully selected and all had over five years' experience and taught a wide range of courses within the secondary science curriculum. Advanced beginners were secondary science student teachers or teachers in their first year of teaching who volunteered to participate. Novices were employed in business or industry and had expertise in science but had not been trained as teachers.

Participants were given a complex task designed to simulate classroom teaching. They watched three television monitors showing different views of a science classroom and reported what they saw. As they did this, they also pressed keys to indicate which monitor they were looking at. The findings revealed differences between the scanning patterns of experts, beginners and novices. All participants watched the middle screen more than the other two, however experts monitored the left and right screens more frequently. It appears that the advanced beginners and novices watched the teacher, who appeared more often in the middle monitor. The findings also indicated that the expert teachers were able to process information more rapidly than novices. It seems that in teaching, as in other domains, experts perceive patterns and meaning in classroom activity, which enables them to encode in 'chunks' and therefore process information more rapidly than novices.

Participants also reported what they saw as they watched the three television monitors showing different views of the science classroom. This revealed that the three groups differed in their interpretations of events, as illustrated in Table 2.1. Novices and advanced beginners both focused on surface features, whereas the experts were able to interpret events and behaviour as well as to draw conclusions about their meaning. They refer to the behaviour of

Table 2.1 Novice, advanced beginner and expert teachers' interpretations of video footage of classroom activity

Novices	Advanced beginners	Experts
(1) From the left ... I can't tell what they are doing. They're getting ready for class, but I can't tell what they are doing.	(1) The kids walk in. She doesn't say hello to any of them. They're sort of wandering in.	(2) I haven't heard a bell, but the students are already at their desks and seem to be doing purposeful activity, and this is about the time that I decided they must be an accelerated group because they came into the room and started something rather than just sitting down and socializing.
(2) They seemed to be more studious on the left here ... I'm not close enough to tell if they are doing the actual work, but they are not participating in the lecture.	(3) In the right monitor, we have the teacher lecturing, students taking notes.	(4) Again, viewing the middle monitor, I think there is an indication here of the type of structure of this classroom. It's pretty loose. The kids come in and go out without checking with the teacher.
(3) she's trying to communicate with them there about something, but I sure couldn't tell what it was.		

Source: Sabers *et al.* 1991.

Note
Numbers in brackets refer to participants in each category.

the students and make inferences about their ability (accelerated group) and about the teacher's level of regulation.

Several important conclusions can be drawn from this research. First, the development of expertise involves changes in perception and representation of information. Experts are able to scan information more efficiently and to perceive patterns and meaningful wholes in a stimulus array, such as a chessboard, x-ray, words on a page or set of arithmetic problems. In contrast, novices see only random information, which has little meaning for them. The perception of meaningful wholes triggers responses such as actions or decisions, thus leading to more efficient processing. Expert knowledge is more efficiently organized around principles and this means that experts also have faster access to relevant information. A well-structured knowledge base also allows them to draw relevant inferences from information received. It is important to note that experts' ability to perceive patterns does not imply that they started with superior perceptual abilities. Instead, abilities develop with practice and relate to the development and organization of the knowledge base.

Acquisition of skills and expertise

Although comparisons between groups of experts and novices have successfully highlighted the significance of experts' knowledge base, they do not tell us a great deal about the processes involved in acquiring expertise. An understanding of how skills and expertise develop calls for studies of individuals over a period of time. Such investigations suggest that the process of learning new strategies, skills and knowledge proceeds through at least three modes. The first is the accretion of new strategies or ways of thinking that are more advanced (Anderson 2000; Norman 1988; Siegler 2000; Speelman and Kirsner 2005). Accretion is the most common form of learning and involves the gradual accumulation of information (Norman 1978). It is most successful when new information fits into a framework of prior knowledge, or schema, as this assists retention. If no such framework exists, the new knowledge may be stored in an inaccessible area of memory.

Second, after the initial learning and use of strategies there is a process of refinement so that more advanced alternatives are used increasingly often. Additionally, a learner's choice of strategy becomes better fitted to the demands of particular problems. So in the example of simple addition, given in Chapter 1, a child learns that counting on is a more efficient strategy than counting all the objects, and uses it more often for this type of problem. Conceptual learning, on the other hand, may involve the reorganization of knowledge structures or schemas, a process that Norman refers to as 'structuring' (Norman 1978). Structuring takes place when knowledge structures are inadequate and a new structure is needed to take account of discrepant information.

In either case, once a new strategy has been acquired or a schema has been structured, there follows a process of tuning or refinement, during which more advanced alternatives are used increasingly often. Tuning takes place when knowledge structures exist but are not organized efficiently. This may arise when mental representations are too general or when they are not well matched for the task. Tuning occurs through extensive practice, which leads to a task being completed more quickly and automatically (Norman 1978). There is improved execution of strategies as learners become increasingly skilful in their use (Siegler 2000). These associations are progressively refined until the third stage is reached, when the components become autonomous and less subject to conscious control. During this third 'autonomous stage', skills continue to become faster and more fluent and are less subject to external influence.

These stages correspond with many adults' own experiences of learning a new skill. Take, for example, learning to drive a car, which is an experience that most people remember very clearly and sometimes with strong feelings. If you were one of the millions of people who went through this, it is worth casting your mind back to the time when you first sat behind the wheel, switched on the engine, put the car in gear and set off on the road. A common experience is that the whole operation seems very complicated with too much to think about and do. This is not surprising as driving involves multiple components, several of which are in themselves complex operations. For example, the steps involved in setting off in first gear are as follows:

1 Press down on the clutch pedal to disengage it
2 Move the gear stick into first gear
3 Lift foot up on the clutch pedal to engage it
4 Press down on the accelerator.

On top of this, the driver must check in the rear view and wing mirrors to make sure it is safe to move off and also signal to warn other drivers of the intention to move. At first, each of these steps requires the driver's full attention. However, with practice the driver no longer has to think about when to press the clutch and when to move the gear stick, but simply changes from one gear to another. When this happens, it frees up mental capacity to think about other aspects of driving. Eventually, driving a car takes very little conscious thought, as fewer mental resources are needed to perform each component skill. This allows the driver to pay more attention to traffic and anticipating other drivers' behaviour, or even holding a conversation.

Theories differ on the details, but there is general agreement that during the first phase, individuals draw on their existing skills and knowledge to make sense of the task and attempt to perform it. Skills that have been developed in another context are recruited into the performance of new tasks (Speelman and Kirsner 2005). In other words, when we are faced with a new task we use whatever skills we have available to perform it. Steering a car is easier if we have had experience of steering another vehicle such as a bike. Driving a different car or a larger vehicle uses many similar skills and is relatively easy compared to learning to drive without any previous driving experience.

Anderson (1983) proposes that knowledge relevant to the performance of cognitive skills begins in declarative form. Declarative knowledge is the representation of facts such as 'In England, always drive on the left hand side of the road'. It contrasts with procedural knowledge, which represents what to do in a given situation. Anderson's Adaptive Character of Thought (ACT) theory claims that procedural knowledge is embodied in a set of production rules or condition–action pairs. If the condition of a production rule is true (e.g. we are in England), then the action will follow (drive on the left). Initially, a learner who is faced with a problem uses general problem-solving methods, which can be used to solve problems in many different domains. These include searching for an analogy or analysing the problem and breaking it down into manageable sub-goals (means-ends analysis). Searching for an analogy is a useful general strategy as it is often possible to apply a method used for one type of problem to another problem of a similar type. Students often use this strategy when given a page of similar problems to solve, as in the example displayed in Figure 2.1.

If the teacher then set another problem to solve, such as 85 = 4*x* + 5, the student would be likely to use a weak problem solving method, and in this case analogy would be the most likely method to apply. Analogy would enable the student to mimic the previous solution, providing that the student noticed the usefulness of the previous solution and was able to remember the steps followed by the teacher.

Imagine that a teacher is describing an algebra solution method to a student. The teacher may start with a problem like 79 – 3*x* + 4 and tells the student is that the goal is to solve for '*x*'. To achieve this goal requires achieving a number of sub goals. For example, the teacher may tell the student that the first step in realizing the overall goal is to isolate the '*x*' term on the right-hand side of the equation. This will mean eliminating the '4' from this side of the equation. The teacher will then demonstrate how this is done, by adding '–4' to both sides of the equation:

$$79 + (-4) = 3x + 4 + (-4)$$

so

$$75 = 3x.$$

Having achieved this sub goal of isolating the x term on the right-hand side of the equation, the teacher may then describe the second sub goal, which is to eliminate the coefficient of the x term, which is 3. This is achieved by dividing both sides of the equation by 3:

$$75/3 = 3x/3$$

so

$$25 = x$$

This is then the solution to the problem.

Figure 2.1 Using an analogy to solve a problem (Source: Speelman and Kirsner 2005: 44–5, by permission of Oxford University Press)

During the second phase of skill acquisition, methods that are specific to particular tasks are developed through 'compilation', which involves two processes. The first of these is 'procedularization' whereby new domain-specific productions are created as by-products of the application of general methods and then become independent of declarative knowledge. In the example in Figure 2.1, procedularization would mean that the student developed a set of productions to solve the problems directly and no longer needed to refer to memory of the teacher's instructions to solve further problems. The development of productions reduces the load on the student's working memory, as there is now no need to remember the teacher's instructions (declarative information) and to use analogy at each step of the problem. These productions are domain specific, so will only work when solving algebra problems of a similar kind.

The second process is 'composition', during which sequences of productions are collapsed into single productions that have the same effects. This process leads to more efficient performance. An expert who has had a great deal of practice solving problems of this kind is able to look at the example above and immediately give the answer, without going through the solution steps. Similarly, the expert driver changes gear without thinking about each step. According to this theory, productions gain strength if they are successful and productions with greater strength are more likely to be used. So those that are practised more often gain strength and are executed faster. In the latest version of the theory, practice does not automatically lead to composition, instead improvements in performance result from the strengthening of productions.

Component process theory proposes that skills are made up of 'a number of component processes that perform the various subtasks involved in the skill' (Speelman and Kirsner 2005: 121). This theory highlights the significance of the learner's old (existing) skills and, as noted above, asserts that performance on a new task depends on the extent to which old skills can be used in the new context and the amount of practice an individual has had with these old skills. For example, a student who has mastered basic arithmetic will be able to solve the equation above more easily than a student who has not. Speelman and Kirsner (2005) also claim that the rate at which performance of the new task improves depends on several factors including individual differences in learning rate, the proportion of old and new skills needed to perform the task, and the nature of training.

In a complex task like reading comprehension, many sub-skills are involved, including speech comprehension, letter recognition and combining words to form the meaning of a phrase or sentence. Performance of complex tasks starts with the lower level components that are practised until they become automatic, thus freeing up processing capacity for the learner to develop other components. It is not necessary for speech comprehension and letter recognition to be perfected before reading comprehension can be achieved. Instead, a certain level of each of these components is required before a child can be expected to read and understand a simple text.

Skills and the brain

It has been claimed that all learning follows a set of principles embodied in component process theory (Speelman and Kirsner 2005). This theory remains to be fully tested, especially with children and young people. Nevertheless, it offers one of the most parsimonious explanations of human learning, with implications for acquiring diverse forms of skills, knowledge and habits of mind, including the formation of social stereotypes. As such, it provides a unifying framework for all learning. The principles have been discussed above and may be summarized as follows:

1 Practice leads to faster performance
2 Practice leads to efficiencies in accessing knowledge
3 These efficiencies lead to less demand on working memory
4 As expertise increases and fewer mental resources are required to perform a particular task, this enables the development of the hierarchy of skills
5 Many skills involve a vast array of component processes.

Underlying these principles is an assumption that the brain is a complex system and like other such systems it contains resources and agents. Agents in the human brain perceive, process and transmit information. The brain is composed of a large number of individual neurons and networks of neurons that receive and pass on information to other neurons and networks. Each neuron is separated from the next by a small gap called a synapse and messages pass across the synapse by chemical transmission. When particular neurons are used, they become more likely to be used in future and more successful processing attracts further use. An important assumption of the theory is that 'the likelihood of an agent being used in the future depends on the success of its processing' (Speelman and Kirsner 2005: 219). Agents compete for resources in complex systems and the competition between agents in the brain is simply to be used in future. The result of these competitions is that successful agents grow and may combine to form larger agents or split into smaller more specific agents, depending on the task presented. Tasks therefore guide the process, as specific agents are recruited to perform different cognitive operations and achieve task goals.

This view of learning receives some support from studies in neuroscience, which indicate that connections in the brain are constantly changing, even in adulthood. It used to be thought that this plasticity in the brain was limited to childhood but it is now known that it extends into adulthood. Certain brain regions continue to develop throughout adolescence and into adulthood, especially the frontal lobes, which are concerned with planning and executive functions (Blakemore and Frith 2005). Moreover, new brain cells continue to grow in crucial areas for learning and memory, and changes in the neurons themselves, which speed up the transmission of information from one neuron to another, also continue into adulthood. All these changes depend on environmental experience, so environmental experience changes our brains and as education is one of the most sustained environmental factors influencing us, it is true to say that education changes our brains.

Adapting and extending expertise

Even though there is more to learn about the processes involved in the acquisition of skills and expertise, it is clear that extensive practice in a domain is essential for anyone to become an expert. Yet as Ericsson (1996) points out, recreational golfers, tennis players and skiers may take part in their sport for many years without achieving high levels of performance. Likewise, doctors may be incompetent even after extensive experience (Bereiter and Scardamalia 1993) and teachers may not become experts even after many years in the classroom (Desforges 1995).

One of the reasons for this is that as skills become automatic, there is a loss of explicit awareness and control over the processes involved the skilled performance. For example, adults read without being aware of the processes involved in decoding and text. Similarly, experts may be unable to explain how they perform complex operations, such as medical diagnosis, teaching or even driving a car.

In some cases individuals may be content to allow skills to become automatic as this achieves an adequate level of performance. If they have no aspirations to achieve higher levels of expertise they may see no point in making the effort to improve. They may also be unaware that they could further improve their performance. There is a commonly held view that experts reach a point when they know everything they need to know in their domain. Without a realization that there is more to learn and they have the capability to do so, individuals are unlikely to search for ways of improving their performance.

Another factor stands in the way of extending conceptual understanding that might form part of expert performance. Whereas accumulating and assimilating information to an existing schema is relatively straightforward, restructuring and re-conceptualizing is more challenging. Numerous studies with children and adults show that existing conceptual knowledge and attitudes may be very difficult to change. This is especially evident in science, where children's and adults' understanding of a range of scientific concepts may be strongly resistant to change (Carey and Spelke 1998; Driver 1994; Driver *et al.* 1985). For example when asked to draw a picture of the Earth, young children often depict it as a round, flat object like a plate. They have difficulty understanding that the earth is a spherical object like a ball. When asked to explain the trajectory of the sun during the day and night young children suggest that the sun disappears underneath the plate at night or that it goes to sleep at night (Nussbaum 1985). These concepts may be altered by demonstrations that reveal their inadequacy and by discussions of more powerful ideas, but tend to take time. Resistance to conceptual change is also found among adults, as will be illustrated below.

An important difference between élite and average performers seems to lie in the way they practise. The notion of practice tends to conjure up an image of someone mindlessly repeating an activity, whether it is a golf swing, playing a piece of music, reciting multiplication tables or foreign vocabulary. This type of mindless practice may increase speed and accuracy, but is unlikely to improve performance to a high level. Instead, research with expert musicians, athletes, chess players and doctors reveals that they practise in a very different way. Their practice is deliberate and involves concentration on specific aspects of the activity they wish to improve (Ericsson and Lehmann 1996). 'Individuals concentrate on actively trying to go beyond their current abilities' (Ericsson 2002: 13). Their practice involves thinking carefully about how to achieve the desired improvements during practice, maintaining intense concentration while practising and evaluating the effectiveness of practice. The need for intense concentration limits the amount of time that can be spent on practice and many expert musicians report practising for only a few hours and choosing times when they feel refreshed.

Young people usually start deliberate practice in their early to mid teens, after making a clear commitment towards reaching a high level in their chosen domain (Bloom 1985). With young children, teachers generally set simple tasks and objectives, and guide children's attention to the goal of the activity. Younger children practise but they do not generally focus intensely and deliberately. With older children, teachers tend to increase the demands for practice and later on they provide general instructions and feedback, which helps learners to monitor their own performance.

Ericsson argues that experts must resist the tendency for performance to become automatic and those who become experts achieve this by acquiring and refining cognitive mechanisms to support continued learning and development. In his opinion, automaticity can prevent progression to higher levels of expertise. For this reason, experts select particular aspects of their performance to improve and work on them deliberately in their practice. 'One of the most crucial challenges for aspiring expert performers is to avoid the arrested development associated with generalized automaticity of performance and to acquire cognitive skills to support continued learning and improvement' (Ericsson 2002: 18). Ericsson and Lehman (1996) asked experts to think aloud as they solved problems in a variety of domains such as medicine, computer programming, sports and games. This revealed that deliberate preparation, planning, reasoning and evaluation were associated with experts' superior performance.

Mental representations form an important part of this process. For example a musician forms representations of what a piece of music will sound like and these then provide a desired performance goal. Musicians also have representations of how to execute the performance and how the audience will experience listening to the music. Similarly, a writer thinks about the structure of a text and how it will sound to a reader and a teacher planning a lesson thinks about the content and design of learning activities and how students will respond to them.

Ericsson and Kintsch (1995) also argue that highly expert performance is adapted to the particular demands of a given situation. For example, expert musicians, athletes and teachers continually adjust their performance according to the conditions in which they perform. Top players in racquet sports are much better at anticipating their opponents' actions, and this enables them to adapt to different types of shot (Abernethy 1991).

Other factors may act as barriers to further progression. Speelman and Kirsner (2005) suggest that '... in most cases where implicit expertise has been observed, the nature of the tasks that experts are expert at do not require verbalization of the underlying knowledge and processing' (p. 236). In other words, experts may not have been asked or encouraged to articulate their knowledge or their processing. So it is not surprising that they have not become expert at talking about their expertise. This point is particularly relevant in teaching as after their initial training, teachers rarely have opportunities to discuss details of their classroom practice with others. There is also very little agreed technical vocabulary for teaching and this inhibits productive discussion of practice. Indeed, Desforges (1995) argues that many teachers fail to develop a knowledge base to inform their practice and therefore do not become experts in spite of many years in the classroom. It is important therefore, to distinguish between expertise and experience (Berliner 1986) as experience may serve only to make existing methods more efficient (a process known as 'grooving'), rather than involve the more fundamental changes required for enhancing and extending performance. Deliberate practice, as noted above, calls for attention to specific aspects of the activity to improve, which involves conscious awareness and a well-organized knowledge base.

Desforges (1995) also suggests that teachers are not generally inclined to critically evaluate their classroom practice in ways that are likely to produce change. They often appear to have in mind a notion of acceptable states in the classroom and to behave in ways that maintain these states (Brown and McIntyre 1992). Their main concern is to maintain discipline, order and predictability (Doyle 1986). A focus on classroom management and student behaviour is accompanied by limited knowledge and understanding of children's learning and a consequent mismatch of work (Bennett *et al.* 1984). It is also associated with a tendency to ignore information that is inconsistent with beliefs, for example teachers who espouse child-centred philosophies of teaching are found to exert a high degree of control over lesson content and to be directive in the way they conducted classroom interactions (Desforges and Cockburn 1987).

In essence, many teachers do not spend time on deliberate practice of the sort found among top musicians and athletes. This is hardly surprising, as they rarely have the opportunity to stand back and evaluate their practice or discuss lessons with an expert mentor or tutor. When thinking about children's learning, it can be easier to explain unexpected events, such as rapid learning by a child who has hitherto made slow progress, in terms of existing theories rather than to challenge and restructure these theories. It is also easier to ignore, reject or exclude anomalous information as irrelevant than to revise our existing beliefs or theories (Chinn and Brewer 1993). Cognitive restructuring is only one of many possible responses to anomalous information and is unlikely to take place unless the information is perceived to be significant and occurs frequently.

These studies indicate that there are many obstacles to be overcome in the pursuit of expert performance. A considerable amount of practice is required and this calls for an investment of time and effort. Additionally, practice needs to be specifically targeted to achieve goals that take learning forward. This calls for learners to reflect on and evaluate their performance and continually seek ways to make further improvements. In spite of this, theories and research outlined in previous sections tend to suggest that the development of skills is a natural process that occurs without any major difficulties.

Typical trajectories to excellence

Interviews with élite performers and their parents and teachers suggest that there is a typical pattern in their early exposure to the domain and their progression to a high level of performance. Bloom (1985) found that most individuals are initially exposed to the domain in a playful way when they are young. If, after a period of time, the child becomes interested and shows some promise, parents arrange instruction with a teacher who has experience working with children. Parental support is also involved at this stage, as parents help children to practice on a regular basis and they also offer general encouragement. As performance improves, more highly qualified teachers and coaches are employed and the amount of practice gradually increases. For most élite performers there is a period during their early to mid teens when they make a major commitment to reaching a high standard in their chosen field. At this point, they look for a master teacher and organize training conditions to maximize the chances of improvement. For some families, this means moving to a different area or providing transport and spending time to give necessary support to their child, watching performances and sometimes travelling with them to distant locations. In both music and sport, nearly all performers who reach an international level have worked with teachers or coaches who have experience of performing at a high-level or have worked with other students at this level.

Parental support plays a major part in élite performers' development. Children and young people depend on their parents for financial resources, organizational backing and emotional support (Bloom 1985; Howe 1990). Apart from the cost of equipment and fees for tuition and coaching, parents provide transport to venues for practice and competitions. The resources involved are so great that families do not usually support more than one élite performer (Bloom 1985).

These findings indicate that an individual's expertise is a culmination of individual and social factors. Individual capability, interest and dedication require support from parents, teachers and others if they are to flourish. Family support is crucial, both in terms of financial resources and demonstrating that they see the value in pursuing the child's interests and activities. When resources are limited it may not be possible for a child to have coaching or music lessons. A career in music or the arts may be considered undesirable or too risky and so children are not encouraged to pursue these paths. Sports that are valued in a society and taught in school provide greater opportunities for all and require less commitment from the family to support an aspiring international performer. Nevertheless, certain children are excluded from these activities through a lack of family or other resources.

Talent and practice

Theories and research considered so far in this chapter have given a general account of the development of expertise but have not addressed the issue of differences between individuals. It is evident that there are large differences in attainments and the speed and ease with which individuals achieve them. This raises the question as to whether special inborn talents or abilities are required for individuals to become expert in particular activities such as music, sport, mathematics, science or foreign languages.

It is widely assumed that exceptionally competent individuals have inborn attributes which are variously labelled 'talents', 'gifts' or 'natural aptitudes' (Howe *et al.* 1998: 399). Such talents are thought to explain why some people excel, while others fail. It is also thought that these talents emerge in early childhood and can be readily identified, so that predictions can be made about who is likely to excel. Furthermore, it is generally believed that only a minority of people are talented and talents are relatively domain specific. Howe, Davidson and Sloboda (1998) argue that there is little evidence for this view and that practice is the most important element in the development of expertise.

There are several methodological issues that make it extremely difficult to assess the relative contribution of inborn characteristics and practice in the development of expertise. First, one way of attempting to establish whether there is an inborn, or genetic, component is to study the precocious development of children in the early years. Many such accounts exist but for practical reasons the majority of these are based on retrospective accounts given by adults looking back on their childhood, or by their parents. Typically, accounts of precocious development are reported several years after the events occurred. Unfortunately retrospective memory is known to be unreliable and so the evidence supplied in this way is suggestive rather than definitive. Individuals' own memory for events in the first few years of their lives is known to be especially unreliable. Second, to establish an innate basis for a talent, it should be possible to find the talent emerging in the absence of opportunities to practice. This is very difficult to do as parents may claim that their child learned unaided when they unwittingly provided opportunities and support for learning. Moreover individuals sometimes practise unobtrusively, so their parents and teachers are unaware of the amount of practice undertaken. For example, individuals who develop exceptional skills in calculation can practise these in their heads without anyone knowing. A third approach is to look for correlations between intelligence and occupation. This evidence, which is reviewed by Eysenck and Keane (2005), gives a mixed picture. Correlations between occupational success and IQ tend to be rather small and diminish with experience in a job. Success in occupations of high complexity such as the legal profession, medicine and accountancy is more closely related to IQ. There have been very few studies that have taken account of deliberate practice, motivation, parental support and IQ, however, there is ample evidence that these factors play an important role in the development of skills and expertise.

The identification of gifted and talented children also presents a number of difficulties. Tests of general intelligence have been used to identify high ability in relation to school achievement. Such tests are good predictors of school achievement and are therefore useful as a general indicator of performance in academic subjects. They have a number of shortcomings, which render them unsuitable as the sole measure of high ability and talent. Perhaps most fundamentally, the construct of intelligence as a general factor pervading all types of academic ability has been contested for much of the twentieth century. Sternberg's triarchic theory (Sternberg 1985) proposes that there are a number of component intelligences and that individuals may demonstrate particular abilities in a group of related academic subjects or in a particular subjects such as mathematics. Some pupils demonstrate high ability in sports, arts or music, while others display exceptional leadership or social skills. Some have an exceptional tendency to become absorbed in a particular topic and sustain this interest over a period of time.

As these observations show, it is extremely difficult to disentangle the effects of genetic and environmental factors in the development of expertise. There is insufficient space here to go into the detail of all the evidence and arguments here, but some main points may be useful. First, there is a strong case to be made that practice is an essential component in the acquisition of knowledge and skills in different domains. Biographies of individuals who reach high levels in their chosen field indicate that they are sustained by interest and enjoyment in the domain together with a capacity for hard work and the ability to regulate their practice. Eisenberger (1998) suggests that this capacity for hard work, or industriousness, is under-rated in Western civilization and he points to the influence of the Romantic tradition that claims 'unique potentialities for each individual' (p. 412). Such a view encouraged the notion that these potentialities would emerge in a gentle, nurturing environment. This stands in contrast to evidence from many biographies of outstanding mathematicians and scientists such as Einstein, which show that remarkable persistence is required to become proficient in a chosen field.

Second, biographies and other accounts also indicate that the family environments of individuals who go on to exceptional achievements tend to be extreme in the extent to which they promote and encourage achievements from an early age (Bloom 1985; Howe 1990). Parents place considerable value on success and achieving the best one can in life. They often structure the child's life around an activity they themselves enjoy and assume the role of teacher when the child is very young, supervising homework and practice and spending time with the child, giving support and encouragement. This strong sense of the value and importance of achievement stems in part from the individual parents' own valuing of an activity and in part from the cultural value placed on specific accomplishments in a domain such as arts, science, mathematics or sports.

The tendency to focus on outstanding achievers can draw attention away from the majority achievements in a society. In a universal education system, children and young people spend many years acquiring the skills and knowledge embodied in the curriculum. Their developing expertise is also founded on industriousness and persistence, and reflects the support of parents and others in the community. The Romantic tradition with its emphasis on the gentle nurturing of children may have more profound effects on the majority of children, as they may not enjoy a high degree of fascination with all the subjects they are required to study at school. A cultural environment that encourages and values intellectual pursuits would help to sustain these young people.

Despite the large literature generated by research on expertise, there is still only limited understanding of how expertise develops, especially in complex, knowledge-rich domains such as medicine. Much of the research involves comparisons between groups of people with different amounts of experience. There are relatively few longitudinal studies that follow individuals over an extended period of time.

Educational implications

For educators, there are a number of issues deriving from research on the development of expertise. First, practice plays an important role not only in the short term but also over extended periods of time. Practice that is designed to achieve specific learning goals continues to improve performance over many months and years, and this is true for young children learning letters of the alphabet as much as for radiologists interpreting x-rays. Mindless, or routine, practice has its place and provides a means of improving some skills but runs the risk of grooving habits of mind, which can sometimes present barriers to further improvement. Deliberate practice appears to be particularly effective in the acquisition of high levels of expertise.

Each individual needs to practice all the components skills involved in a complex task such as learning to read. At any one time, different components will be at various levels of proficiency and a young reader recruits whatever skills they have available to assist in the job of decoding text. As children have diverse amounts of exposure to experiences that are beneficial for reading, component skills will be at different levels of proficiency. Also, during any reading experience children attend selectively, so whereas one child might look carefully at letters and words on the page as an adult reads aloud, another child might be looking at the pictures or gazing round the room. The child who looks carefully at letters and words is more likely to link these with the adult's reading of the text and to learn letter sound correspondences. This component skill is then available to be recruited in the task of decoding text. As most tasks in school involve a complex mix of knowledge and skills, individual trajectories vary so that children need to be offered learning activities that give them the opportunity to develop all the component skills, including oral language, and syntactic, semantic and pragmatic knowledge as well as skills in decoding text.

A related educational issue concerns provision for individuals whose performance is exceptional. Given that resources are inevitably limited in national education systems, students identified as gifted or talented may be provided with special programmes and resources. One of the main difficulties with such an approach is that there are few reliable methods of assessment available, which means that some talented individuals will be missed and others will be incorrectly identified as talented. A clear assessment and grading structure makes the selection process more reliable, but at higher levels of achievement these assessments may not be applicable. Another difficulty is that children who perform well on the various tests available are likely to be those whose families have been able to support them in the early stages of learning and to employ teachers and coaches. It is a challenge to give support to these children while also providing opportunities for those who are less fortunate.

Within schools, common forms of provision for able pupils include acceleration, enrichment and differentiation. Acceleration refers to administrative practices designed to allow students to progress through schools at a faster rate than average. This includes starting school early, grade skipping, accelerated sets that enable students to take examinations early or various forms of additional provision such as summer schools specifically designed for able pupils. Enrichment activities may also be provided either within the classroom or in special groups. These activities are generally designed to encourage the use of higher order cognitive abilities. Placing able children in groups together can foster high levels of attainment, yet some negative, unintended consequences have also been found, such as lowered academic self-concept and isolation from peers (Kulik and Kulik 1992; Whitty *et al.* 1998). Provision for children who show signs of talent or high ability calls for careful consideration to be given to the most appropriate ways of offering enrichment and other opportunities, without making children feel too different from their peers.

Summary

During our lives we become skilled in an amazing range of different activities. This chapter has focused mainly on cognitive or mental skills, as these are especially important in education. Advances have been made in understanding cognitive skills and reveal the importance of domain knowledge in the development of expertise. Experts develop an extensive knowledge base, which affects the way they perceive and process information presented to them. Instead of seeing disconnected arrays of information, experts see meaningful patterns that relate to principles and understanding of the way in which knowledge is constructed. Their knowledge base develops over many hours and years of practice and is associated with more efficient processing. It is now realized that similar processes underpin the acquisition of many different skills that we develop during our lives.

Practice is an important element in the development of any skill. It speeds up performance and leads to skills becoming automated. An individual's enthusiasm and commitment to learn is clearly an important ingredient of success, as it typically takes 10 years or 10,000 hours of practice to achieve a high level of expertise in any domain. Practice that involves deliberate attention to specific aspects of performance is thought to be especially beneficial. This raises questions about the factors that motivate individuals to persevere for this length of time and how they regulate their learning to achieve the results they aspire to. These questions will be considered in next chapter.

3   Taking control of learning

Introduction

As indicated in the previous chapter, practice is an important component in the development of skills and expertise. Deliberate practice appears to be especially beneficial and Ericsson (2002) has argued that this form of practice is essential for the development of advanced forms of expertise. Effective learning involves the deployment of a range of strategies before beginning a task, during task completion and after the task is completed. Good learners monitor and regulate their cognitive processes during learning and they select strategies that are appropriate to meet task demands. Strategies deployed during the completion of learning tasks emerge gradually and are closely connected with an individual's growing knowledge base.

In addition to the various strategies deployed while completing a task, learners also regulate themselves before starting work and when the work has been completed. Self-regulated learning thus encompasses a wide range of strategies that effective learners use to take control of their learning. It includes strategies to maintain motivation and self-belief as well as cognitive strategies such as goal setting, monitoring and self-evaluation.

Learners' conceptions of ability and effort, their orientations towards learning and their motivational beliefs are also associated with self-regulation. During adolescence, beliefs about ability as a fixed or malleable entity become linked with beliefs about learning and with the use of learning strategies. Learners who see learning as a constructive process and who are oriented towards mastery tend to employ a wider range of strategies for self-regulation as compared with those who see learning as an accumulation of knowledge.

Historically, attempts to teach learning strategies using methods of direct instruction met with very limited success. Recent interventions based on more complex models have shown that it is possible to improve students' awareness and regulation of learning. These models incorporate the teaching of key concepts in a curriculum subject so that students are helped to build up a relevant knowledge base. Teachers provide practical tasks to support learners as they develop awareness of the processes involved and encourage reflection and discussion about strategies used when solving problems.

Self-regulated learning

Becoming aware and taking control of cognitive processes, or 'metacognition', has attracted the interest of educational and developmental psychologists for many years and its significance for the development of thinking is widely recognized (Nisbet and Shucksmith 1986; Perkins *et al.* 1993). Metacognition refers to monitoring and regulating one's cognitive processes during learning and includes activities such as selecting learning strategies, matching strategies to task demands, and comprehension monitoring (Brown *et al.* 1983). Contemporary definitions of self-regulated learning generally include metacognitive strategies alongside a wider set of regulatory strategies.

The term 'self-regulation' has been widely interpreted and used by researchers in the fields of health and education, with a resulting proliferation of definitions. Nevertheless, there is some agreement that self-regulation is 'a systematic process of human behaviour that involves setting personal goals and steering behaviour toward the achievement of established goals' (Zeidner *et al.* 2000: 751). There are a number of closely related concepts, some of which overlap with the concept of self-regulation such as self-management, which implies that goals are set by others whereas self-regulation often implies that people follow self-set goals.

When considered in relation to academic learning, self-regulation has been defined as '… self generated thoughts, feelings, and actions for attaining academic goals' (Zimmerman 1998: 73). It is clear from this definition that goal setting is an important component of self-regulated learning, and it implies that learners follow self-set goals. Yet, within a compulsory education system, goals are frequently determined by the curriculum and set by teachers in the classroom.

Actions for attaining academic goals include a wide range of strategies that learners might use such as personal strategies for arranging a productive working environment, and cognitive strategies for completing the task at hand (Weinstein and Mayer 1986). Reflection on the use of these cognitive strategies and self-generated thoughts and feelings are also significant aspects of self-regulation and may be used to maintain motivation.

Cognitive strategies are widely used for memorizing and understanding information. These strategies have been classified into three types, namely rehearsal (rote learning), elaboration and organization (Weinstein and Mayer 1986). Rote learning strategies involve the repetition of items to be learned such as repeating a telephone number, using mnemonics, reciting a verse of poetry, copying and re-reading. These strategies can help a learner attend to information and to remember it in the same form in which it was presented. They can be very useful for memorizing significant historical dates, foreign language vocabulary, a religious text or a part in a play.

Meaningful learning requires more active strategies that involve deeper processing, such as elaboration and organization. Elaboration includes para-phrasing, summarizing, creating analogies, asking questions, explaining the information to another person and applying in new situations. Organization includes comparing and contrasting, drawing diagrams or concept maps and identifying relationships. These strategies involve selecting and organizing the ideas in a text or other sources of information, rather than remembering them in the same form, and require a deeper level of processing, which leads to a deeper understanding of the material.

In addition to the use of cognitive, task specific strategies, learners employ a wide range of strategies for self-regulation before, during and after a task. Zimmerman (1998) identified ten methods for self-regulation that are used for academic learning and also for learning in many other domains. He gives examples of these techniques taken from biographies, autobiographies and instructional texts written by successful writers, athletes and musicians, and from self-reports of successful students. A summary is provided in Table 3.1.

It is clear that there are some commonalities across many domains of learning. Successful learners in many walks of life use similar, deliberate strategies to plan, execute, monitor and evaluate their performance. In addition to task specific strategies, successful learners schedule time for practice, training and studying and arrange an environment that is conducive for work. They also set themselves goals to achieve, monitor progress, motivate themselves, evaluate progress and make positive consequences contingent on performance.

Individuals also adopt strategies that suit them personally and that are appropriate for the task at hand. They know how to motivate themselves and how to create environments in which they can work well. For example, some writers know that they work best in a quiet, secluded room whereas others work productively in other places. Self-regulatory strategies may be used for learning throughout life and once mastered may be applied to a wide range of activities from mundane tasks in everyday life to highly accomplished performance in a specialist field.

Self-regulated learning and achievement

Evidence indicates that high achieving students in school and college employ more self-regulatory strategies than students with lower grades. Zimmermann and Martínez-Pons (1986) developed interviews similar to those conducted with the expert musicians, athletes and writers (outlined above) to compare high- and low-achieving students' self-reports of strategy use on a set of given problems. They developed eight scenarios of commonly encountered learning situations, which they used in structured interviews with the secondary students. Students reported using 14 processes of self-regulation and the higher achievers reported significantly greater use of 13 of these. High achievers not only used more strategies than low achievers, they used them more often. The authors went on to compare students aged 8–9, 11–12 and 15–16 years, from a regular school and a school for gifted pupils

Table 3.1 Self-regulatory processes reported by expert athletes, musicians and students

Self-regulatory processes	Area of expertise		
	Athletes	*Musicians*	*Students*
Goal setting	Setting specific and quantifiable daily goals for training	Setting goals for daily practice	Making lists of goals to accomplish during studying
Task strategies	Knowing how and what to practise	Playing a piece slowly and softly	Creating mnemonics to remember facts
Imagery	Visualize successfully making a shot	Imagining the presence of an audience	Imagining the consequences of failing to study
Self-instruction	Verbalizing confidence statements, for example, 'let's go!'	Verbally praising or prompting oneself	Rehearsing steps in solving a maths problem
Time management	Setting up regular practice times, eating times, relaxation and preparation periods	Scheduling daily practice to avoid extremes	Scheduling daily studying and homework time
Self-monitoring	Keeping a daily record of goal accomplishment or filming matches for replay	Keeping daily records of performance	Keeping records of completed assignments
Self-evaluation	Breaking game into components and evaluating after each performance	Listening to self-recording, setting realistic standards	Checking work before handing it in to teacher
Self-consequences	Self-grading after every match	Refusing to end practice until passages is played flawlessly	Making the viewing of television or telephoning contingent on homework completion
Environmental structuring	Building practice facility designed to develop weak parts of game	Performing with specific tools, e.g. a metronome	Studying in a secluded place
Help seeking	Returning to coach when flaws develop in game	Returning to teachers when techniques slip	Using a study partner

Source: Zimmerman 1998: 76, with permission of Taylor & Francis.

(Zimmermann and Martínez-Pons 1990). All students reported on their use of self-regulatory strategies (self-evaluating, organizing and transforming; goal-setting and planning; seeking information; keeping records and monitoring; environmental structuring; memorizing; help seeking; reviewing). The findings supported earlier research in showing that high achievers used more strategies and use them more often.

Similarly, readers who are more successful in understanding texts make greater use of strategies than readers who are less successful. Successful readers tend to monitor as they read and therefore notice when they do not understand a word or a passage of text, whereas poor comprehenders tend not to notice errors and inconsistencies in text (Garner 1986; Yuill and Oakhill 1991). Good readers employ active strategies of questioning, summarizing, predicting and identifying main ideas to assist in constructing meaning from text (Brown *et al.* 1986).

This differential use of strategies may relate to students' judgements about the relative difficulty of tasks. Owings, Petersen, Bransford *et al.* (1981) constructed two versions of several stories, making one version harder by altering the syntax. Students aged 9–10 years were asked to read and learn the easy version of one story and the harder version of another. They were then asked to say which story was harder to learn and why. Students who were in the top third of the class were able to say which version of each story was harder and they also spent more time studying the harder version. Students in the bottom third were less accurate in judging the difficulty of the stories and they spent similar amounts of time studying the easy and hard versions.

Many studies on self-regulation obtain information on learners' use of self-regulation at a single point in time and so do not provide evidence about the causal direction of influences. For this reason, it is unclear whether students' greater use of strategies leads to higher achievement or that higher achievement leads to a greater use of strategies. It may also be that another factor underlies both the use of strategies and higher achievement. Or, it may be that effects are reciprocal, so that the use of strategies improves learning and this in turn leads to greater use of strategies in the future.

Knowledge and the use of strategies

In general, the deliberate use of strategies for learning and remembering develops with age (Kail 1990). As compared with learners aged 13–14 years, older learners (aged 15–16 years) in the study referred to above by Zimmerman and Martínez-Pons (1986) reported using more self-regulatory strategies and they used them more often. This may reflect maturational changes in the brain but could also be a result of learners' increasing knowledge. As age is so closely related to increases in knowledge it can be difficult to separate the two, but there is evidence to indicate that knowledge acquisition relates to the more effective use of strategies.

The development of cognitive strategies does not take place in isolation but is closely linked with the development of a knowledge base. Indeed, in a review of research Glaser (1984) came to the conclusion that strategies develop as a by-product of learning. Some examples of the important role of knowledge were given in Chapter 2, where it was shown that knowledge representation changes in adults who acquire expertise in a domain and this affects their approach to learning. Similar effects were found in four- to five-year-old children by Chi (1978), who designed an ingenious and well-known experiment comparing children who were very knowledgeable about a topic, such as chess or dinosaurs, with adults who were less knowledgeable about these subjects. In one study she used the task developed by de Groot in which chess pieces were arranged on a board as they might be during a game (described in Chapter 2). The board was then taken away and replaced with empty board and the child was asked to reconstruct the configuration of pieces. A child who was a chess player was able to reconstruct the configuration more accurately than an adult who did not play chess. Both participants were then given a test to assess how well they could remember strings of digits. This test, which is called a digit span test, is frequently used to test working memory and in this case the adult performed better than the child. Similarly, a child who was very knowledgeable about dinosaurs was shown to have a more sophisticated classification system than an adult who knew very little about dinosaurs. These findings suggest that as their knowledge base develops, children are able to use more sophisticated classifications and memory strategies.

Different demands are made during earlier and later stages of learning a new cognitive skill, as discussed in the previous chapter. In the early stages of learning, cognitive resources are used to develop representations of conditions and associated actions, which become linked procedures (Anderson 2000; Speelman and Kirsner 2005). Through repeated use, these procedures become automated thus freeing up mental resources for other activities. Until this point is reached, an individual's processing capacity is occupied with establishing procedures, and there is little capacity for task specific self-regulatory processes (Winne 1995). Similarly, with practice, cognitive strategies may be executed automatically thus freeing up resources that had been needed to monitor execution of the strategies.

Self-regulation is, at least in part, a cognitive process that takes up mental capacity which means that mental resources have to be shared between self-regulatory processes and the cognitive processes directly involved in completing the task. For a learner, the processes involved in studying an academic text might include extracting main ideas and relating new information to their existing knowledge of the subject. These are demanding tasks requiring considerable cognitive resources, especially if the person concerned is unfamiliar with many of the ideas and terminology presented. In this case, a learner may be trying to master new vocabulary, understand new ideas, and build a mental representation of the text. All of these processes require mental resources, so the individual may have no unused capacity for simultaneously working on self-regulation. Therefore, it may be counterproductive to engage in self-regulatory strategies at an early stage in learning (Winne 1995). Learners with limited knowledge and those who lack conditional knowledge about when to deploy specific strategies effectively may not be able to find the mental resources for simultaneously thinking about self-regulation. It may be preferable to practice new strategies on a familiar text or set of problems, which is readily understood and where few demands are made on cognitive resources. This is consistent with findings that children discover new strategies when they are successful in completing problems (Siegler 2000).

It is now clear that learners typically use a variety of strategies and ways of thinking to solve problems (Siegler 2000). Children who are faced with a problem may be able to use a sophisticated strategy yet select a simpler one on some occasions. This variability in use of strategies has been found in a many studies and illustrates that children may use different strategies on two occasions close in time, and even during one problem-solving session (Siegler 2000).

In a review of main findings from studies that describe children's use of strategies over a period of time, Siegler (2000) demonstrates that changes typically take place very gradually with older strategies being used even when new ways of working become available. Children who demonstrate the use of more sophisticated and efficient strategies, such as retrieving an answer directly from memory, often fall back on slower, less efficient strategies when they are confronted with more difficult problems. This is highly adaptive, as it helps children to balance concerns about speed and accuracy in problem solving. Strategies such as retrieval are fast but may lead to errors in more difficult problems. Making use of an earlier strategy such as decomposing difficult problems into two simpler ones is more likely to give the right answer but to take longer. It is not only children who fall back on reliable, slower strategies for solving difficult problems and adults also do this on many occasions (Siegler and Alibali 2005).

Although there may be no capacity for task-specific self-regulatory processes during the early stages of learning, other strategies may be useful before and after task completion. For example, before a task is undertaken, time management may be needed to allow sufficient time for practice and environmental structuring (e.g. finding a quiet place to work) can be used to facilitate concentration during the time available. Likewise, self-evaluation is a useful strategy to employ when study time is completed. The early stages of learning can also be frustrating and anxiety provoking, so techniques for regulating emotional responses may be needed.

These examples illustrate that cognitive strategies emerge alongside the acquisition of knowledge. Learners have a repertoire of strategies, which they draw on in light of the demands of different tasks and situations. Students are more likely to acquire self-regulatory strategies on familiar tasks rather than during the early stages of learning something new.

Awareness and self-regulated learning

Evidence presented above indicates that adults and children deploy a range of strategies to solve problems and remember information. Considerable efforts have been made by researchers to understand how learners develop and use these self-regulatory strategies. Learning activities are generally complex and learners attend to specific cues and information according to their perceptions, continually balancing costs and gains.

The deliberate use of strategies involves becoming aware of them and their usefulness in a given situation. Realizing that we are likely to forget, and thinking of ways to remember, is helpful in everyday life, leading many people to write shopping lists before going to the supermarket. Similarly a sprinter might realize that visualization can improve performance and use this strategy while on the starting blocks.

Marton and Booth (1997) argue that to describe something we must become aware of it and be aware that we are aware. In other words to describe learning we must not only be aware of our learning but also realize that we are aware. Moreover, without awareness we cannot have a will and, therefore, if we are to self-regulate we must first become aware of our own learning. While there is an element of truth in this argument, the situation is not clear-cut as, from an information-processing perspective, cognitive strategies are like other forms of cognition and may become automatized and used without awareness. Indeed, Winne (1995) argues that cognitive and self-regulatory strategies may be used without awareness and therefore 'SRL inherently blends deliberate and non-deliberate forms of cognitive engagement' (Winne 1995: 176). This view receives support from Siegler (2000), who asserts that both conscious and unconscious processes are involved in the acquisition of new strategies. New strategies may emerge without the learner being aware that they are doing something different. Similarly, learners may come to rely on a more efficient strategy without making a conscious choice.

The issue of awareness presents theoretical challenges, as the notion of conscious control is fundamental to the many definitions of self-regulated learning given above. It also presents methodological challenges for researchers, many of whom rely on self- report methods such as interviews and questionnaires to obtain information on self-regulatory processes.

Motivation and self-regulated learning

As noted above, cognitive strategies and self-regulation take time and effort to acquire so we might ask why students are motivated to invest in them and why some people continue to strive to improve their performance (Perkins *et al.* 1993; Pintrich 2000). Cognitive psychologists tend to assume that our brains are designed to develop more efficient ways of working and that self-regulation is just like any other cognitive process, so no further explanation is needed. Motivation researchers suggest that students' subjective experiences and their beliefs about learning play an important role in the take up and development of self-regulation (Pintrich 2000).

In the past, psychologists treated achievement motivation as an aspect of an individual's personality, which was thought to be relatively stable. Contemporary theories pay more attention to the social and cognitive processes involved in students' motivation to learn. There is a strong focus on the role of students' motivational beliefs concerning their ability to perform particular tasks, and about the value of tasks.

In relation to achievement a useful framework for motivation is provided by expectancy-value theory, which proposes that motivation to learn is a function of an individual's expectations regarding the likely outcome of a learning activity and the extent to which the person values learning or achievement (Eccles *et al.* 1998). Within this framework, learner expectations and values are conceptualized in terms of a constellation of beliefs, including students' appraisal of their ability to complete academic tasks, their perceptions of the difficulty of different tasks and individuals' perceptions of themselves and their learning goals (Eccles and Wigfield 2001). The following sections will elaborate on key issues concerning expectations and values and their relations with self-regulated learning.

Students approach their learning with expectations about the likely outcomes of their efforts. Individuals have different levels of confidence in their ability to succeed and the extent to which they are responsible for their own actions. Bandura (1997) emphasized the role of efficacy and human agency in achievement motivation. He proposed that learners base their expectations on previous performance in similar tasks, so individuals who have succeeded in the past tend to be more optimistic about the future. Other factors that might influence a individual's sense of efficacy include physiological reactions to a task or situation, such as anxiety, and encouragement by others.

There is evidence of positive relations between self-efficacy and the use of cognitive learning strategies among middle-school and college students (Pintrich 1999; Pintrich and de Groot 1990). Similarly, Zimmerman and Martínez-Pons (1990) found that students' expectations of achievement (self-efficacy) correlated with the actual grades achieved. This study used two measures of self-efficacy in several academic subjects, one for students' self-efficacy for their achievement in that subject and the second for self-efficacy for self-regulated learning in the same subjects. They found a correlation between students' expectations of achievement and their self-efficacy for regulating their own learning. Findings also indicated that students' beliefs about their ability to self-regulate (self-efficacy for self-regulated learning) predicted their beliefs about their academic achievement (self-efficacy for academic achievement). This in turn related to actual grades achieved. Further evidence of an association between achievement and students' confidence in their ability to self-regulate is provided by research showing that self-efficacy for self-regulated learning is a better predictor of attainment than prior achievement (Pintrich and de Groot 1990). As both these studies were cross-sectional and used statistical methods to establish the ordering of relationships between variables, they provide useful indicators of likely causal links but longitudinal studies are needed to confirm these relationships and to establish causal connections. Taken together they indicate that secondary-age students who have greater confidence in their ability to control their learning tend to have higher expectations about their academic achievement.

Students may be confident and have high expectations about their ability to complete a task successfully and yet have low motivation for learning if they do not value a task. It has been proposed that subjective task value has four components, namely attainment value, intrinsic value, utility value, and cost (Eccles *et al.* 1983). Students may enjoy school learning and gain satisfaction from classroom tasks and activities, in which case there is intrinsic value in school learning (Deci and Ryan 1987). Attainment value is the personal importance of doing well on a task, in other words students gain satisfaction from good performance or doing better than others. Tasks also have utility value if they relate to students' current and future goals and aspirations. The notion of costs includes negative aspects of engaging in a task such as anxiety, fear of failure and the amount of effort needed to succeed, and also lost opportunities such as time for other interests.

Intrinsic value denotes that individuals take part in certain activities out of interest and enjoyment (Ryan and Deci 2000). Given a free choice, we may read, take part in sports, play music, or even work. If these activities are enjoyable, there is no need for external pressure to encourage us to take part. Tasks may also be valued for extrinsic reasons, such as when children are offered rewards such as smiley faces, stickers, sweets or money to encourage them to learn and achieve. These are clearly separate from, or extrinsic to, the learning activity itself as the reward is given only after the task has been completed successfully.

Social approval provides another source of extrinsic motivation and many children work hard in school to please their parents or teachers and live up to their expectations rather than for the inherent satisfaction involved in completing schoolwork (Biggs and Moore 1993; Ryan and Deci 2000). Some students internalize these aspirations and identify with them, making them their own, whereas other students conform to their parents' wishes and feel less personally committed (Ryan and Deci 2000).

Students who value tasks for intrinsic reasons tend to employ more self-regulatory strategies (Pintrich 1989; Pintrich and García 1991). In these studies, task value included students' interest in the task and its relevance, importance and usefulness. Although findings indicated that students who value a task tend to employ more strategies when completing it, the strength of this relationship varied considerably thus suggesting that other factors may be more important in some cases.

Motivation does appear to play a part in self-regulation and evidence is accumulating to show that expectancy-value theory provides a useful way of conceptualizing motivation in this context. Learners who have positive expectations about their ability to control their learning and to achieve are more likely to employ self-regulatory strategies and to do well in school. As yet there is insufficient evidence to confirm the causal directions of these influences.

Learners conceptions of ability and their learning goals

Other factors that have been linked with motivation and self-regulation include students' orientations towards task goals and their conceptions of learning. Many students treat the learning activities presented to them by their teachers as a form of work, a job to be done (Bereiter and Scardamalia 1993; Woods, 1990). Their main goal is to accomplish the tasks assigned to them, just as a worker completes tasks set by a manager. Some of these students may be characterized as work avoidant, and their main goal is to do as little work as possible (Nicholls 1989). When classroom tasks and activities are seen as a 'job to be done', students may be unaware that teachers set these tasks to achieve instructional goals. As a result, these students' learning occurs as a by-product of performing the activity.

Even students who are attempting to work towards instructional goals set by their teachers may differ in terms of their orientation towards the tasks set. Motivation researchers have identified two main orientations, namely a 'performance orientation' whereby students are mainly concerned with showing that they have greater ability than other students, and a 'learning orientation' whereby students are more concerned with understanding the content (Dweck 1999; 2001; Nicholls 1992). Students with a performance orientation are mainly concerned to gain high marks in tests and examinations, as this is a demonstration of their ability. They work to maintain their position relative to others in the class and strive to gain favourable judgements of their competence and to avoid negative judgements (Dweck 2001). Students who pursue learning or mastery goals strive to increase their competence, understand or master something new. They are concerned with improvements in their own learning and are prepared to undertake challenging tasks and make mistakes in the service of learning. Students may have high mastery and performance goals, or they may be relatively high on one and low on the other. This means that in any classroom there will be students with different orientations towards the task of learning. Some will be more concerned about teachers' judgements of their competence, whereas others will be more concerned about their own mastery of the subject matter.

Students' orientations towards learning appear to be linked to their beliefs about intelligence. Before turning to these relationships, some background is needed on children's concepts of ability, or intelligence, and how they change with age. In a research programme undertaken in the US spanning almost 20 years, Carol Dweck and her colleagues have shown that individuals differ in the extent to which they think of ability as a fixed or malleable entity (Dweck 2001). Young children do not appear to have well-formed notions of ability but by the age of 7–8 years, they become concerned with relative ability, or how well they are doing compared to others. They also show signs of developing an understanding of ability as something that is relatively stable. By the age of about 10–12 years, children begin to view ability as a capacity rather than a set of skills and knowledge (Cain and Dweck 1989; Nicholls and Miller 1983). Also around this age there is evidence that competence perceptions start forming links with interest and other ways in which children value particular kinds of learning. Dweck (2001) points out that, although many children come to view intelligence as a relatively stable entity which they cannot change, some children maintain a more optimistic and malleable view of ability. They continue to think that effort can be used to improve their ability.

The orientations to learning identified among students in secondary education bear some similarities with surface and deep approaches to learning identified among older students at university (Biggs *et al.* 2001; Entwistle and Waterston 1988; Marton and Säljö 1984). A surface approach is characterized by a tendency to focus on superficial features of material presented such as facts and procedures to be remembered, whereas a deep approach is characterized by a search for meaning. University students with deep approaches and school students with mastery orientations have a desire to understand material and to relate ideas and arguments to their own knowledge, understanding and experience.

Students who have a deep approach or are mastery oriented are more likely to use meaningful learning strategies and deep processing, whereas students who have an achieving approach or are performance oriented are more likely to employ rehearsal and other shallow processing strategies. Meece (1994) examined relationships between elementary students' orientations and self-regulation in 5th-grade (age 9–10 years) and 6th-grade (age 10–11 years) science classes. Students with task mastery goals used self-regulated learning strategies, whereas students with ego-social orientations, similar to performance orientation (desire to demonstrate ability, please teachers, outperform others) and work-avoidant orientations (desire to do as little work as possible) used effort-minimizing strategies such as guessing or copying.

There are also links between older students' learning strategies, their conceptions of learning and their orientations towards learning (Vermunt 1998; Vermunt and Vermetten 2004). University students who see learning as a constructive process tend to employ more self-regulatory strategies, as compared to students who see learning as an intake of knowledge (Vermunt 1998). Self-regulated students report the use of a wide range of strategies, which include relating and structuring information, critical analysis and processing. These strategies involve reorganizing information and thinking about how it relates to other knowledge. Some students who were less self-regulated were more regulated by external factors such as directions and deadlines. They tended to use a narrower range of strategies, predominantly memorizing and analysing, which involve more superficial processing. These findings indicate that for university students, there is an internal coherence among conceptions of learning, cognitive processing and self-regulation. According to Vermunt and Vermetten (2004), this internal coherence is not found among younger students in secondary education. Younger students do not discriminate as clearly between their learning strategies, conceptions and orientations.

Taken together, the evidence suggests that during adolescence, young people's conceptions of learning, ability and effort become increasingly differentiated and linked with motivational beliefs, interest and the use of cognitive and self-regulatory strategies. Students' beliefs about learning relate to their orientations towards learning and to the self-regulation of learning. Although there is a great deal more to be discovered about the links between these beliefs, orientations and learning processes, it is clear that learners' use of self-regulatory strategies do not exist in isolation from them. At present we have relatively limited information about the source of learners' beliefs and conceptions but they are likely to originate in their exposure to prevalent beliefs and conceptions in the family, school and college.

Forms of self-regulation

Up to this point the various forms of self-regulation have been treated as though they comprise a single entity, whereas there appear to be qualitative differences between the types of regulation required before, during and after a learning task (Pintrich 2000; Puustinen and Pulikinen 2001). Before starting a task, general, self-organizational strategies are involved, such as arranging a place to work and setting task goals. When undertaking a task, cognitive processes and strategies specific to the task are called into service and monitored. After a task is completed, a learner may evaluate his or her performance, the usefulness of strategies and the task itself.

A framework proposed by Pintrich (2000) delineates four phases of self-regulation, namely forethought, monitoring, control and reflection. During each of these phases there are four possible areas of self-regulation involving cognition, motivation, behaviour and context (see Table 3.2). The model provides a mapping of the possible range of activities that might be performed in the four phases but does not imply that the phases occur in a specific order or that full range of areas is necessarily involved in each phase. Phases may occur at any time during a task and in some tasks may be omitted altogether. Some activities within a phase may not be amenable to self-regulation.

In the phase of forethought, planning, and activation, the learner's cognitions include goal setting, whereby desired outcomes are clarified. Learners also summon up their current knowledge relating to the task at hand and their metacognitive knowledge about strategies that may be useful. Goals include task specific goals that may be used to evaluate progress, as noted by athletes, musicians and students in Table 3.1 (Zimmerman 1998). Knowledge of a subject is usually activated automatically as part of the

Table 3.2. Conceptual framework for studying self-regulation

Phases of self-regulation	Areas for self-regulation			
	Cognition	*Motivation*	*Behaviour*	*Context*
Forethought, planning	Goal setting, activate prior content and metacognitive knowledge	Self-efficacy, goal orientations	Time and effort planning	Awareness of task and contexts, that might help or hinder learning
Monitoring	Metacognitive awareness of and monitoring of cognition	Awareness of self-efficacy, values, attributions, interests, anxieties	Time and effort management	Monitor context
Control	Select and adapt cognitive and metacognitive strategies	Maintain motivation	Expend effort	Influence context
Reflection	Cognitive judgements, attributions	Assess motivation	Evaluate behaviour	Reflect on context

Source: abbreviated from Pintrich 2000, with permission of Elsevier

cognitive processes involved in understanding, but highly self-regulated learners may also use deliberate strategies of knowledge activation. Similarly, metacognitive knowledge may be activated automatically or deliberately and includes knowledge of learning strategies that might be useful for the task at hand. Motivational processes in this phase include the learner's self-efficacy, or beliefs about their capacity to complete the task, the value of the task, interest and their goal orientations or reasons for engaging in the task. Behavioural regulation includes time management and self-observation, which provides information on progress during the task. Regulation of the context involves students' perceptions of the task and the context, such as features of classrooms that may help or hinder learning. Away from the classroom a learner may have greater freedom to regulate and organize their own learning environments as in the examples of athletes and musicians studied by Zimmerman (1998) and referred to above.

Monitoring involves awareness of actions and their outcomes, which provides information to enable the learner to control cognitive, motivational, behavioural and contextual factors. Learners monitor their cognitive processes and motivational states and also the changing demands of the task and context. Motivational regulation takes many forms such as giving a reward after work is completed or boosting self-efficacy through positive self-talk.

This might include Zimmerman's (1998) category of self-instruction, as noted in Table 3.2, whereby musicians reported verbally praising themselves and athletes encouraged themselves with statements such as 'you can do it'. Behavioural regulation includes seeking help when needed.

Learner's reactions and reflections include self-evaluations of performance, motivation, behaviour and context (Pintrich 2000). These appraisals may provide useful information about the effectiveness of strategies used. They also involve emotional reactions that may affect learners' perceptions of tasks and their motivation for future learning.

This framework is helpful in mapping out the various strategies that might be used in different phases of a task. It accords motivation a central place in the self-regulation of learning, alongside cognitive and behavioural components. It also draws attention to the context in which learning activities takes place as having potential impact on the deployment of self-regulatory strategies.

Measuring self-regulated learning

It is worth noting at this stage that many of the studies referred to above rely on the use of self-report questionnaires. Several different questionnaires have been developed and each is designed to collect information on particular self-regulatory processes. Each questionnaire reflects the theoretical orientation of the designer and contains a number of sub-scales measuring theoretical constructs of interest. The Learning and Study Strategies Inventory (LASSI), is mainly concerned with cognitive strategies of rehearsal, organization and elaboration (Weinstein *et al.* 1987; Weinstein and Palmer 2002) and was designed as a diagnostic tool for students and their tutors. The Approaches to Studying Inventory (Entwistle and Ramsden 1983), the Approaches and Study Skills Inventory for Students (Tait, Entwistle and McCune, 1998) and the Study Process Questionnaire (Biggs 1987) were designed for use with university students and both include measures of students' approaches to learning. The Inventory of Learning Styles developed by Vermunt (1998) and the Motivated Strategies for Learning Questionnaire developed by Pintrich, Smith, Garcia and McKeachie (1991; Duncan and McKeachie 2005) were initially developed for students in college or university, but have been adapted for use with secondary school students. The Inventory of Learning Styles includes measures of cognitive strategies, metacognitive strategies, conceptions of learning and learning orientations (Vermunt 1998). Vermunt and Vermetten (2004) report that it has been used with students aged 12–14 years.

These questionnaires and inventories obtain information on students' usual ways of working and self-regulating. They generally invite respondents to remember an event or set of events that is representative of their learning experience. Other methods, such as interviews and protocols, obtain information about specific instances (Winne and Perry 2000). Information provided over a period of time may be obtained using think aloud measures, traces or observations. Traces refer to marks students leave when studying, such as margin comments, underlining or highlighting. Think aloud methods require learners to give a running commentary as they study and although these records provide useful information, they run the risk of disturbing the student's learning.

Interventions to enhance self-regulation

When cognitive strategies were first investigated, there were many attempts to teach them in experimental settings and in school. Early training studies involved direct teaching of cognitive strategies under laboratory conditions and met with only limited success. During the 1980s, strategy research moved into the classroom and incorporated a focus on metacognition so students were told how strategies operated and why they were useful. Researchers found that although students were able to learn and use the strategies taught during an intervention, there was limited generalization and application of strategies to new learning (Howe 1991; Paris and Paris 2001). A common finding was that students would use strategies when taught during a lesson yet failed to apply them to other similar tasks. There was also a tendency for lower achieving students to have more difficulty in learning and applying strategies. As these students were often the target of programmes to teach cognitive strategies, researchers looked for other theoretical frameworks to guide their efforts.

One example of this progression from direct teaching of strategies to a more metacognitive approach is to be found in the teaching of reading comprehension. Brown and her colleagues (Brown *et al.* 1983; Brown *et al.* 1986) identified four comprehension strategies that were used by good readers and attempted to teach them to children who had difficulty understanding text. Direct teaching methods were found to be relatively ineffective and this led to a reappraisal of the theoretical basis of the pedagogical approach and to the subsequent development of reciprocal teaching (Palincsar and Brown 1984). This method of teaching draws on the theory of Vygotsky and incorporates a social mechanism for the handover of responsibility for the use of strategies to the learner.

In reciprocal teaching, the teacher works with children in small groups and demonstrates the use of the four comprehension strategies of clarifying, predicting, asking questions and summarizing. First, the teacher and students read a text together and the teacher demonstrates the use of the four strategies. Over time, each student takes turns in leading the group as they use a particular strategy. The results of this study were promising, as student's performance improved significantly on strategy tests and was maintained when students were retested six months after the programme ended.

Other, more recent interventions also suggest that, rather than using direct teaching methods, it may be beneficial to encourage learners to become aware of the strategies they use. For example Borkowski and Muthukrishna

(1995) compared a method of guided discovery and direct strategy teaching for mathematics in students aged 7–8 years. In guided discovery, students are encouraged to be actively involved in the learning process, which in this case meant that they were encouraged to invent their own strategies with help and guidance from their teacher. In direct strategy teaching, the teacher identifies effective strategies, demonstrates them and gives the students practice in using them. Findings indicated that guided discovery teaching was more effective than direct strategy instruction.

Some classroom interventions such as the cognitive acceleration in science education programme (CASE) encourage students to think about their own thinking as one element in the design of classroom activities (Adey and Shayer 1993; Shayer and Adey 2002). As a whole, the programme aims to develop children's thinking in science and the encouragement of students' metacognition is premised on a view '… that students are more likely to develop wide-ranging thinking skills if they are encouraged to think about their own thinking' (Adey and Shayer 1993: 9). The programme therefore encourages reflection on thinking, rather than using a direct approach to teach the use of metacognitive strategies. During science lessons, pupils are encouraged to talk with the teacher and with other pupils about the relative difficulty of problems. They are asked to explain what was difficult about a problem and how they overcame the difficulty. For example, students working on the notion of classification might be given a set of simple exercises such as putting animals into groups, sorting a variety of groceries, or grouping chemicals by colour and by solubility. Having done this, they are asked to reflect on their classifications and identify those that are the most and least difficult for them and to explain why. Reasons why some classifications are harder than others are then shared with other pupils and the teacher. In this way, students become more aware of their own thinking and thus more able to use it as a tool in a new context.

Two further aspects of the CASE programme may support students' development of awareness and their control over strategies (Adey and Shayer 1993). First, lessons start with 'concrete preparation' during which students are familiarized with important ideas and vocabulary for the topic. Second, students are encouraged to develop technical language to describe problems and reasoning patterns. Technical language can provide important tools for thinking, for example students who are able to identify mathematics problems as belonging to particular categories, such as a proportionality problem, are then in a position to use strategies for solving this class of problems (Adey and Shayer 1993).

Reflection also forms a component of Zimmerman's cyclical model of self-regulated learning (Zimmerman 1998). This model has four components, starting with goal setting and strategic planning, followed by strategy implementation and monitoring, then strategic outcome monitoring and finally self-evaluation and monitoring. The cycle is recursive. A recursive approach is also evident in the Strategic Content Learning approach (Butler 1998), which incorporates similar elements of self-regulation into a programme of personalized support for learners. These programmes acknowledge that interventions to encourage the use of self-regulatory strategies need to be long-term and multifaceted, addressing motivational beliefs alongside self-regulated learning strategies, and recognizing the importance of social interaction as a means of developing self-regulation.

Most of the programmes mentioned above have been designed for teenagers or adults. It is worth noting, however, that even young children can be encouraged to reflect on their learning (Adey *et al.* 2002). As noted in Chapter 1, young children have conceptions of learning as doing or knowing and Pramling (1988; 1996) hypothesized that these conceptions might be affected by metacognitive teaching. She went on to compare children in two experimental classes and two control classes (Pramling 1996). The teachers of the experimental classes incorporated certain principles designed to promote the children's metacognitive reflection. They created situations and activities that encouraged the children to reflect on content, structure and their own learning and thinking.

For example, when working on the topic of the weather the teacher wanted to children to learn that there are different symbols and they mean different things that are agreed on as conventions. She asked the children to make symbols to denote different kinds of weather, such as thunder and lightning, storms, sunshine and cold and warm air. Children were then encouraged to talk about different ways of depicting the weather. The class also reflected on structures and cycles, for example they discussed how drinking water gets into their homes. Children's reflection on learning itself was encouraged by activities such as finding out how weather forecasting is done. The children were told to find out after school and the next day the teacher used the information to start a discussion about the various ways in which we can learn and find out. Children's conceptions of learning were tested in two interviews one at the beginning of the study, and the second a year later. At the beginning, the majority of children held a conception of learning as doing. One year later, the conceptions of children in the control classes had not changed, whereas half the children in the experimental classes now thought of learning as knowing and a small number thought about learning as understanding.

Summary

The notion of self-regulated learning encompasses a wide range of thoughts, feelings and actions employed by learners before, during and after completing tasks and activities. It involves cognitive and metacognitive components required for specific learning tasks together with the orchestration of motivational, emotional and behavioural aspects of learning. In the preparatory phase, goal setting is considered to be an important component of self-regulation and one that is adopted by many outstanding performers. Self-regulated learners are aware of their own learning preferences and organize an environment that is conducive to learning. During task completion, the use of cognitive strategies for remembering and understanding is closely connected with the learner's acquisition of a knowledge base. These cognitive strategies appear to develop spontaneously in some instances and, in common with other skills, may become automatic with practice. Monitoring provides the learner with feedback about the various components involved in performing a task and alerts the learner to ineffective strategies, lack of understanding, flagging effort or changes in the environment. Being aware of various factors that might disrupt learning is a first step towards controlling them. All the awareness in the world may be ineffective, however, if the learner has no desire to complete the task. In this respect, intrinsic interest or extrinsic value such as rewards and social approval may be harnessed to increase effort.

Links are now emerging between students' self-regulation and their beliefs about learning and ability. Young children's conceptions of learning, ability and effort are not well differentiated, but by the beginning of secondary education, children become concerned with relative ability and tend to view ability as something relatively stable. Young people's conceptions of learning become increasingly differentiated and linked with motivational beliefs and the use of cognitive and self-regulatory strategies.

Given this complex picture, it is hardly surprising that early attempts to teach cognitive strategies through direct instruction were somewhat unsuccessful. Recent interventions based on more complex models of human learning hold greater promise. They show that improvements in self-regulated learning may be achieved when embedded in a teaching approach that combines an effective approach to developing students' conceptual understanding with metacognitive strategies in a teaching environment that facilitates open discussion of learning and learning strategies.

4 Cultural perspectives on learning and thinking

Introduction

Young people grow and develop in a social world that contributes to the development of their learning and thinking. From the time of birth, children are surrounded by and interact with other people including parents, siblings and other family members. As they grow older and their social world expands, children and young people encounter other adults and children in a variety of different contexts in homes, schools and in the community.

Several theoretical approaches have been developed to link between individuals and their social and cultural context. All these approaches are concerned with children's development, and how it relates to, and is affected by, the social environment in which they learn and grow. Structural models of individuals and their contexts, such as ecological systems theory, map out relationships between the developing child and groups within society, seeking to identify specific groups in which the child is situated and connections between these groups. Socio-cultural models, on the other hand, point to the important part played by purposes and goals in human activity and the mediation of learning through tools and artefacts. Notions of 'activity' and 'participation' have also been used to theorize means through which individuals come together and to explore the interactions that occur between participants as they take part in activities together. This chapter outlines several different perspectives and their contribution to our understanding of learning, both in and out of school.

Ecological systems theory

Bronfenbrenner (1989; 1993) was one of the first psychologists to develop an ecological theory of learning as a way of linking individuals and their social and cultural contexts. His model recognizes that a young child develops within a family, but that this is located within wider social and cultural systems. According to this model, the child lies at the centre of a set of nested systems, rather like a set of Russian dolls one inside the other, and the model is represented as a set of concentric circles (sometimes referred to as 'onion rings'). The child is 'nested' in the family, which in turn is located in a neighbourhood and served by health and education services. The various levels of these systems structure the child's environment, with the immediate surroundings having a direct influence and distal surroundings having indirect effects.

According to Bronfenbrenner, the child's immediate physical and social surroundings include the family, school, neighbourhood and peers. The child comes into direct contact with family members, children in their school and neighbourhood, and other adults in these settings. Bronfenbrenner refers to these immediate surroundings as the microsystem. The model acknowledges that there is communication between elements of the microsystem, such as between the child's family and school, which might affect the child's development. The mesosytem represents these linkages between elements of the microsystem. An analysis of the mesosystem includes asking questions about communication between home and school and how this might affect a child starting school. There are two more systems lying outside the mesosystem, the first being the exosystem, which represents settings that have an indirect influence on the microsystem, such as local and national government, educational organizations and policies, social welfare services, family friends, and the mass media. The outermost ring is called the macrosystem, which represents ideologies and dominant beliefs in a culture. A simplified model, representing the family and school contexts in which a child grows and develops, is shown in Figure 4.1.

In the school context, the child's immediate surrounding, or microsystem, is the class and the class teacher. The child interacts with the teacher as an individual but such interactions take place within the context of the class and the classroom, which affect the interactions that take place. Likewise teachers and learners are part of the wider school community, with its own ethos, policies and procedures. Schools in turn are affected by external factors such as government educational policies, resources and the catchment area in which the school is located. External factors such as the national curriculum have a clear and direct influence on the content of classroom teaching, whereas the effects of other factors may be more subtle.

Bronfenbrenner's model has been very effective in encouraging a simultaneous focus on individual development and the context in which that development takes place. It has encouraged researchers to identify and measure factors in the wider context and to explore their relationships with individual development.

Developmental niche

Several different versions of the concentric rings model suggested by Bronfenbrenner have appeared (e.g. Cole 1996; Dasen 2003), as it is readily adapted for a wide variety of interests. The microsystem is of particular interest as it is here that there are linkages between the various components of the child's immediate surroundings. It represents the culture in which the child

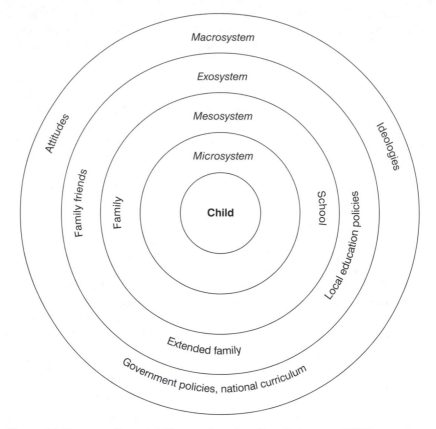

Figure 4.1 Ecosystemic model (Source: based on Bronfenbrenner 1989)

develops and encompasses general aspects of society, such as values and belief systems (Cole 1996). Further analysis of the microsystem is offered by Dasen (2003), who draws on the notion of a developmental niche, as proposed by Super and Harkness (1986). The notion of a niche is borrowed from ecology where it is used to denote the tendency for plants to adapt and thrive in locations where certain soil and climatic conditions prevail. A developmental niche denotes significant features of the contexts in which children are located in any culture. It comprises three components, first the physical and social contexts in which the child lives, which include living space, family structure and language. Second, customs or culturally determined child-rearing and educational practices; and third, the psychological characteristics of caregivers, including parental beliefs about developmental milestones and the types of competencies expected of children. The developmental niche is seen as a system in which the child and the three components interact in a coherent fashion. The child adapts to his or her surroundings and the niche also adapts to the child.

Dasen (2003) proposes that the child's developmental niche is located in the microsystem, as defined by Bronfenbrenner (1989; 1993), and outlined above. By bringing these two notions into an integrated framework, Dasen (2003) redefines significant proximal features of the child's environment in terms of the three components of the niche. Significantly for this discussion, the child's learning is a central aspect of the model and there is an explicit connection between the child's learning processes, competence and performance.

Beyond the developmental niche lie the ecological and socio-political contexts in which the child's family is located. This includes cultural values, especially those that are evident in belief and value systems such as religion. The macrosystem represents the wider cultural, socio-political and ecological contexts while the mesosystem is seen as a set of processes through which these wider contexts influence the child's developmental niche. An important aspect of this model is that there is interaction within each system, and across the levels of the different systems, making a fluid interchange possible between various levels.

In relation to children's learning, Dasen (2003) asserts that parents have a set of beliefs and ideas about the competencies they expect children to acquire. He uses the term 'ethnotheories' to denote parental beliefs about and perspectives on children's development that are shared by groups of people in different cultures. Each society has shared knowledge and conceptions about children and their development and even though everyone in a society may not share these ideas, there are commonalities to be found among members of particular groups (Dasen 2003). These shared beliefs contain tacit understandings about appropriate goals for development (Goodnow 1996). Groups of parents, caregivers and teachers also share beliefs about the influence of genetic and environmental influences on children's development, such as developmental timetables, the types of competencies expected of children at different ages, definitions of intelligence, how learning occurs and whether teaching is necessary.

Furthermore, the patterning of learning activities in the home and in school also impinges on children's learning. In the home, patterns frequently arise from customary childrearing practices such as the way that children are carried when young, the kinds of activities they are encouraged to take part in and the people they are expected to interact with as they grow older. These different practices are well documented in cross-cultural psychology, where there is a long tradition of comparative studies of childrearing dating back to Whiting's six cultures study (Whiting and Whiting 1975). Customary practices are also evident in education, where comparative studies of teaching and learning in classrooms illustrate the diversity of customary practices in different education systems (Alexander 2000; Stigler and Hiebert, 1999) and also in different classrooms within a single system. Such studies help to uncover the customs and beliefs that impact on teachers' classroom organization and the kinds of learning activity they arrange for students.

Ecological systems theory, and its integration with developmental niche theory, provides some useful tools for analysis of the contexts in which children grow and learn. Nevertheless, ecological systems theory is open to criticism on a number of grounds. First, although it tends to encourage a structural analysis of the people and organizations in the child's environment, it has little to say about processes that bring individuals and organizations together and influence the way they interact. Second, although links are drawn between the various levels of the system, indicating that each may influence the other, the model tends to encourage a view suggesting that greater influence flows from the outer levels to those at the centre. This tendency is countered to some extent in models that explicitly show influences flowing in both directions, and linkages between components within levels. When it comes to understanding links between specific social contexts and individual children's learning, a finer-grained analysis is required. The notion of a niche also suggests a somewhat stable entity and has no theory for change over time. Children's niches tend to be well defined in the early years but become more fluid, as they grow up and develop their own social networks. Young people become more independent and have a greater say in their activities and they have multiple sources of information in their environment.

Mapping the school as a context for learning

Ecosystemic models provide a useful starting point for thinking about schools as contexts for learning. They have encouraged many educational psychologists to view the school as a nested system and to attempt a mapping of the factors that influence students' school learning (Biggs and Moore 1993; Brophy and Good 1986; Dunkin and Biddle 1974). A recent review and synthesis of the literature on school teaching and learning used a systemic approach to map contexts for learning in secondary schools (Hallam and Ireson 1999). This identified, from existing research, factors in the wider school environment that influence classroom teaching and learning. As noted above, learners spend much time in classrooms, which are located with the wider school context. In the classroom, an individual learner interacts with the teacher both as an individual and as a member of the class. Interactions between teachers and pupils are influenced by individual characteristics, such as teachers' knowledge of the curriculum, their beliefs about learning and their pedagogic practices. Similarly, a learner's knowledge, beliefs about learning and orientation towards learning also influence the way she or he interacts with teachers.

The composition and characteristics of a class also affect interactions, including the age of students, the range of ability within the class, group dynamics and the behaviour and motivation of the class as a whole. Interactions within the class are influenced by school policies and practices, such as those concerning ability grouping, inclusion, timetabling, and the allocation of teachers to classes. Similarly, the school is affected by external factors, such as the national curriculum and assessment, policies on selection and school intake. Some external factors such as the national curriculum have a clear and direct influence on classroom teaching as it affects the subject matter covered during lessons. In secondary schools, subject areas or departments also affect teachers' ways of working. School characteristics such as school ethos, catchment area and resources impinge on classrooms and the wider school environment (see Figure 4.2).

This mapping exercise give us a useful framework for understanding learning in school as it identifies specific features of schools and classrooms that appear to impact on students' learning, directly or indirectly. Each of these features, and the relationships between them, have been studied in detail (see Hallam and Ireson 1999 for a summary), yet perhaps because of their complexity there is still a need for further investigation. Reviews of the literature on the effects of different factors indicate that proximal factors, or those that directly affect learners, have stronger effects on children's learning and achievement, whereas the effects of distal factors that affect learners indirectly through their influence on schools and teachers, for example, are smaller (Wang *et al.* 1993). Thus, interactions between parents and children at home and between teachers and children at school generally have a greater impact on children's learning and achievement than the organization of schools.

Socio-cultural theories

Socio-cultural theories also set out to describe and explain links between the developing child and his or her social context. A major aim of these theories is to provide explanations of children's development that take account of the social and cultural contexts in which children grow and learn. Many draw on the work of Vygotsky, the Russian psychologist, whose work was mentioned earlier (pp. 19–20) (Vygotsky 1962; 1978). At the time when Vygotsky's work was translated into English the field of child development was dominated by the work of his contemporary, Piaget, who emphasized the role of maturation in development and paid relatively little attention to the influence of others in helping children to learn. Vygotsky's work struck a chord among many educational and developmental psychologists who recognized that a much richer understanding of children's learning could be achieved by theories that addressed the social nature of learning.

Vygotsky's theory was wide-ranging, and this section will sketch aspects of his work that have influenced current thinking about teaching and learning. These include his claim that a child's mental functioning originates in social and cultural processes, and his views on psychological tools and mediation. Before embarking on this agenda, it is worth noting that Vygotsky drew a distinction between two types of learning. He identified learning that occurs spontaneously as part of everyday life and contrasted this 'natural' form of learning with the development of what he called 'higher mental functions' that are subject to voluntary control.

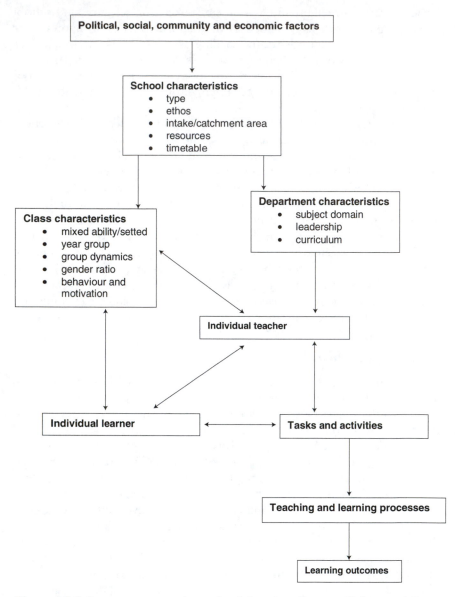

Figure 4.2 Influences on secondary school learning (Source: Hallam and Ireson 1999: 70)

Spontaneous learning occurs as a natural part of our interactions with objects and events that we encounter on a daily basis. For example we rapidly discover that touching very hot objects is painful and so learn to avoid them. Babies also learn about the shapes and textures of objects when they grasp and manipulate them. These examples illustrate that spontaneous learning takes place when we interact directly with objects to achieve certain goals or outcomes. Vygotsky viewed this spontaneous or 'natural line' of development to be a basic form of learning, which was subject to behavioural contingencies.

In contrast with basic forms of learning the 'higher' mental functions include voluntary attention, memory, cognition and the ability to exert control over these mental processes. Vygotsky (1978) drew a line between conscious mental activity and spontaneous learning that takes place without conscious awareness. He reasoned that the higher mental functions are mediated by cultural artefacts, by which he meant that individuals interact indirectly with objects through cultural artefacts.

Thus for Vygotsky the development of higher mental functions was essentially a social process. Individual mental functioning could only be fully understood through an analysis of social and cultural processes as the child's understanding of the world originates in the use of concepts by others in the culture. This claim is made in his 'general genetic law of development' in the following translation by Cole, John-Steiner, Scribner and Souberman (Vygotsky 1978).

> Every function in the child's cultural development occurs twice: first, on the social level, and later on the individual level; first *between* people (*interpsychological*) and then *inside* the child (*intrapsychological*). This applies equally to voluntary attention, to logical memory and to the formation of concepts. All the higher functions originate as actual relations between human individuals.
>
> (Vygotsky 1978: 57 [Emphasis in the original])

This is a strong statement about the origins of important mental functions and consciousness, which places social interaction at the heart of human development. Vygotsky claims that the child is reliant on knowledge and forms of thinking that exist in a culture, or between people (interpsychological). Children acquire ideas and forms of thinking through their interactions with more knowledgeable people in the culture around them.

Although the quotation above gives social interaction a prominent role and downplays the process of maturation, in other writing Vygotsky's position appears to be less extreme. For example, he acknowledged that maturation plays a role in development and saw it as intertwined with cultural development (Vygotsky 1978). In his short lifetime, Vygotsky did not succeed in fully explicating the relationship between these two aspects of development, yet his work drew attention to the interactions between children and others in their cultural world and inspired many of his followers to examine these in great detail.

Subsequently, Tomasello (1999) has argued that humans possess a biologically inherited capacity to understand that other people are intentional agents like themselves. This capacity distinguishes humans from other animals and enables cultural transmission to take place to an extent that is not found among other primates. Advances in developmental psychology show that early recognition of others as intentional agents appears in infancy, at around nine months of age, and develops gradually as children start to employ cultural tools especially language (Tomasello 1999; Trevarthen 1979). Thus there is evidence that maturation and cultural development are intertwined, as Vygotsky suggested.

The zone of proximal development

One of the ways in which Vygotsky developed thinking about the role of social interactions in learning was through the notion of the 'zone of proximal development' (ZPD) (Vygotsky 1978; 1981). This is defined in terms of two levels of performance, the first being that which the child can achieve alone and the second being the level that a child can achieve with guidance from a more capable adult or peer. The first of these levels is one that is frequently accessed by educational and psychological tests and examinations, when individual performance is tested and no help is allowed. Vygotsky argued that such tests gave only a partial picture of an individual's capabilities and did not provide sufficient information about the child's potential to learn. For this, a second assessment was required of the child's achievement when supplied with adult guidance. He defined the distance between these two levels as the 'zone of proximal development', as follows:

> ... the distance between the actual developmental level as determined by independent problem solving and the level of potential development as determined through problem solving under adult guidance or in collaboration with more capable peers.

> (Vygotsky 1978: 86)

The notion of a zone of proximal development generated a great deal of interest in the developmental and educational literature. Much of this work has been concerned with the nature of interactions between adults and children in the zone and the extent to which this affects learning. Some of this research will be considered in Chapter 5. In thinking about the zone of proximal development, Vygotsky came to the view that it was brought into being when the child interacted with other people in his environment. It is through the process of interaction that children internalize ideas and forms of thinking that then become part of the child's independent psychological functioning. He came to the conclusion, therefore, that learning leads to development, as it 'sets in motion a variety of developmental processes that would be impossible apart from learning' (Vygotsky, 1978: 90).

Tharp and Gallimore (1988) expanded on the notion of the zone of proximal development, suggesting that learning in the zone takes place in what they refer to as two 'stages' or phases. The first is where the learner's performance is assisted by more capable others, including parents, teachers, coaches, peers and experts. The amount of help required depends on the child's age and the nature of the task. When a learner attempts the first steps within a new task, they may 'have a very limited understanding of the situation, the task, or the goal to be achieved' (Gallimore and Tharp 1990: 184). As Wertsch (1984; 1985) pointed out, the adult or more expert person has this understanding and takes responsibility for arranging the task in such a way as to enable the child to take part. Gradually, as the child participates and comes to understand the task and how to complete it, the adult hands over responsibility for task completion to the child. Once this has been achieved the process of internalization has taken place and the child moves into a second stage of learning within the zone.

When learning has been internalized, the learner is able to carry out a task without assistance from others and is also able to regulate performance. Additional practice in this stage leads to improved performance but as the learner is able to regulate his or her own learning there is now no need for expert guidance to achieve this. Self-directed speech is frequently used to achieve this regulation and is an important indicator of progress in the handover of control from the adult to the child. A child (or adult learner) uses self-directed speech, or self-talk, as a way of monitoring and guiding progress (Tharp and Gallimore 1991).

Two additional stages beyond the zone of proximal development are also outlined by Tharp and Gallimore (1991). In the first additional stage (stage III) there is no longer any need for self-regulation, as task execution is integrated and automatic. This stage is similar to the stage of automatization identified in research on the acquisition of skills (see pp. 37–40) and assistance from others or the self may even be disruptive. The first three stages (including two within the zone) are repeated for new learning throughout life so that all human learning, for children and adults alike, involves a mix of assistance from others, self-regulation and automatized performance.

Also, every individual experiences situations when something that was well learned in the past is forgotten and has to be recovered. There may be occasions where task demands are great, or the individual is under stress and assistance is needed again. This may lead to overt self-direction or seeking assistance from others in which case the learner re-enters the zone of proximal development. Key questions that arise from this analysis concern the nature of interactions and forms of assistance in stage 1 of the ZPD, and these will be considered in more detail in Chapter 5.

Mediation

As noted above, Vygotsky (1978) and his followers view development as a product of the social and cultural environment. In his or her environment the child encounters a variety of cultural tools and artefacts, such as physical tools, computers, maps, language and mathematics. Vygotsky (1978) distinguished between psychological tools, which can be used to direct the mind and behaviour, and physical tools that can be used to bring about changes in other objects. He gave the example of a person tying a knot in a handkerchief to help them remember something and proposed that this simple action represents an attempt by the individual to take conscious control of remembering. It transforms tying a knot into a psychological tool that mediates the process of remembering.

A more complex version of knot tying is to be found in the 'Quipu' used by the Inca people in Peru. The Inca civilization covered a large area but had no writing system and Quipu were used to help convey information accurately from one area to another. These devices comprised a set of strings tied to a stick that could be carried easily by a runner. Each string had several knots tied on it, representing quantitative and other information to help the runner convey the information accurately. Psychological tools are thus devices that may be used to exert conscious control over mental processes such as remembering. As noted in Chapter 3, a large number of self-regulatory strategies have now been uncovered some of which invoke external representations such as diagrams, while others are more covert.

Cultural tools and artefacts are the products of socially based activity and are handed down from one generation to the next, shaping the activities of those who use them. For example, before the invention of the printing press, books were scarce as they had to be written out by hand. Printing presses allowed for the publication and wide distribution of books and their use in universal systems of education. Nowadays, the internet makes an enormous amount of information available to anyone with access to a computer and a good search engine. Cultural developments such as these affect individuals' thinking through the knowledge they acquire, the kinds of skills they develop and the way they interact with others in their social world.

Some of the best examples of how material tools relate to cognitive representations and mental processes are to be found in research on mathematics. Many different material tools have been used through history to support mathematical activity, such as abacuses, calculators, number tables, computers and slide rules. A comparison of the errors made by students who used an abacus and students who used Arabic numerals indicates that patterns are consistent with the method used (Stigler *et al.* 1986). Also, students who are good at using the abacus appear to use a mental abacus when they calculate solutions in their heads (Stigler 1984). Use of an abacus thus influences representations of information and the steps followed in mental calculations. Likewise, individuals who have learned paper and pencil methods for calculation may visualize a problem, as it would be set out on paper. For example, an addition of two numbers might be visualized with the numbers positioned one above the other so that the hundreds, tens and units columns are aligned. Operations such as carrying numbers forward can also be visualized.

Vygotsky (1978) saw physical tools as less transformative than psychological tools. According to him, a material tool, such as an axe, has a direct effect on an object but does not have a powerful effect on the mind. For example, when we use an axe we make physical adjustments rather than thinking in a fundamentally different way about chopping wood. More recently there has been considerable debate about distinctions between physical and psychological tools, but there is insufficient space here to elaborate on this (Wertsch 1985). Moreover, with the advent of more complex tools such as computers, robotics and electronic control systems the distinction between physical and psychological tools becomes less clear-cut, as a great deal of 'know how' or intelligence is built into advanced, computer-based systems (Pea 1993). Similarly, considerable amounts of teaching expertise may be designed in to materials and other resources used to support classroom learning, as will be illustrated in Chapter 6.

Vygotsky (1978) also considered a third category of mediation by human beings. One of his important insights was that an adult's interpretation of a child's meaning could lead to a transformation of the child's activity. He gives a well-known example of a baby making a grasping movement towards an object that is out of reach. In his view, the grasping movement is a natural reaction to the sight of an object and as such has no inherent meaning. If an adult interprets this movement as a gesture indicating the child's desire to hold the object, the act of pointing becomes transformed. The child uses pointing to influence the adult's activity and pointing may be accompanied by vocalization to add emphasis to a demand for an object to be delivered within reach. Over time, the child internalizes the gesture and uses it as a means of self-regulation. In this way, meaning is constructed through mediation with others.

The notion of meaningful activity is a central premise in many contemporary socio-cultural theories. Human behaviour is considered in terms of purposive, culturally meaningful actions, as opposed to adaptive reactions. Therefore it is seen as goal directed and goals are socially and culturally meaningful.

Cognitive activity in a niche

The notion of a developmental niche was introduced above, where it was considered in relation to children's learning (Dasen 2003). As previously noted, the idea of niche provides a useful, general framework for analysing the influence of family and community contexts on children's social development, but does not go far enough in terms of analysing processes that might connect the various elements of these contexts. Gauvain (1998) draws on socio-cultural theory and argues that three aspects of this theory are useful in delineating subsystems of the developmental niche. The first subsystem comprises activity goals and values that are culturally defined. In the socio-cultural tradition, as outlined above, human activities are considered to occur in meaningful contexts and to be purposeful. These activities and their structures thus provide opportunities and constraints for children's cognitive growth. Consistent with post-Vygotskian theory, activity structures include the goal of a task and the means for reaching this goal. The second subsystem comprises historical means provided by the culture, such as material and symbolic tools, while the third involves routines and rituals that instantiate cultural goals and values. These socially organized activities are seen as the means whereby 'culture penetrates cognitive activity and development' (Gauvain 1998: 70). Everyday practices provide connections between individuals and cultural goals and values.

As compared with Dasen's proposal that parental ethnotheories and ideas influence children's learning (Dasen 2003), Gauvain (1998) suggests more specifically cognitive components. In line with socio-cultural theory, priority is given to activity goals and there is an assumption that most activity is organized in a purposeful manner. The purpose of an activity influences the way it is organized. Cultural values encompass tacit understandings about appropriate goals and about what is considered to constitute good performance. There is evidence to indicate that important tasks are organized differently to those that are less important, economically or for other reasons. If efficient, error-free performance is required, competent adults tend to be directive and learners are allowed to take part in a limited way, observing and joining in only at certain points when they have the required skills (e.g. Greenfield 1984; Lave and Wenger 1991). When error-free performance is less important, learners are allowed to be more actively involved and errors are accepted as part of learning. An explicit recognition of activity goals and values is useful, but other factors may also affect the way that activities are organized. For example, parents' and teachers' beliefs have an impact on their enactment of activities with young learners, as noted by Dasen (2003).

Both models of the developmental niche include the notion of customary practice, formulated as childrearing customs (Dasen 2003) and in more cognitive terms as scripts, routines and rituals (Gauvain 1998). Customary practice, routine and rituals instantiate cultural goals and values, thus forming a direct connection between individual and cultural practice. In cognitive terms, routines are represented mentally as scripts that provide a framework for sequences of commonly occurring events. Scripts are cognitive structures in long-term memory that provide frameworks for predictable and routine events, such as eating in a restaurant (being seated, selecting and ordering food from a menu, being served, eating, paying the bill and leaving). Although scripts provide consistent structures, they may be modified for variations such as different types of eating establishment.

Customary practices in any culture or niche follow specific sequences and one of the child's achievements is to learn scripts for behaviour in many different circumstances. Children also learn conventional ways of organizing knowledge and communicating information in ways that make it comprehensible to other people.

Participation perspective

The notion of activity also features in Rogoff's (2003) participation perspective, which proposes that participation in cultural activity is key to human development. Within any culture, people take part in various activities and groups that affect their development 'Humans develop through their changing participation in the socio-cultural activities of their communities' (Rogoff 2003: 11). She resists the tendency to reduce culture to a number of variables, whose influence is then compared individually or in combination. Instead she argues that culture should not be thought of as an entity that exerts an effect on an individual. Rather, 'people contribute to the creation of cultural processes and cultural processes contribute to the creation of people' (Rogoff 2003: 51). Her agenda is to develop an understanding of how individuals and cultural practices are connected and how each contributes to the formation of the other.

Relations between individual development and the social context are conceptualized in terms of three mutually constituting planes of analysis (Rogoff 1990; 2003). The first plane is familiar in developmental psychology as it concerns the solitary individual. The individual is viewed as an active learner, or meaning maker, and learning is not simply a process of copying information but of 'appropriating' or transforming it to make it one's own. Here, Rogoff is putting forward a constructivist view of learning, similar to those of Piaget and Vygotsky. During the process of appropriation, individuals simultaneously contribute to the transformation of cultural tools, practices and institutions. This view aligns with that of Cole (1985) who argued that the zone of proximal development creates a space for creative invention and changes in thinking from one generation to another.

The second plane is interpersonal, where learning takes place through a process of guided participation and involves interactions with others in the zone of proximal development. There are two basic processes of guided participation, mutual bridging of meaning and mutual structuring of participation (Rogoff 2003). Mutual bridging refers to the interactive process involved when partners actively attempt to find a common perspective or language through which to communicate ideas and coordinate their efforts. This process appears to be peculiar to humans and may be intimately connected with the use of language (Tomasello 1999). Mutual structuring of participation refers to the selection of activities that children may observe or take part in. It also includes the part children are able to play in activities such as conversations, narratives, routines or play. Caregivers and children both contribute to this process of structuring, for example children are adept at placing themselves in a good position to eavesdrop or observe activities that interest them and they have a tendency to stay close to their elders thus gaining a ringside view of many cultural activities.

There are similarities in the process of guided participation in different communities and also differences in the nature of activities that children engage in. For example, Rogoff *et al.* (1993) compared mothers' interactions with their toddlers in four different settings, a Mayan town, an Indian village and two middle-class urban neighbourhoods in Turkey and the USA. In the first two of these communities, mothers encouraged children to observe ongoing activities but did not see themselves as responsible for children's learning. The Turkish and US middle-class mothers were more inclined to organize and direct their child's learning, using verbal instructions and providing home lessons. They scheduled time specifically for children's activities, separate from adult activities, whereas Mayan and Indian mothers shared their attention between adult and children's activities. It seemed as though the US mothers were preparing their children for kinds of activities they would encounter at school. Exposure to school-like forms of speaking helps children to adjust to the demands of classroom dialogue when they start school (Tizard and Hughes 1984).

The social plane is embedded within the third plane, which is cultural–institutional and focuses on the settings in which activities and practices develop. In any institution, ways of organizing and working are established and we may be interested in how these cultural practices develop and change. Rogoff (2003) argues that it does not make sense to investigate this plane without also considering the people involved and how they contribute to cultural practices. Community and institutional arrangements encompass systems of interpersonal involvement and arrangements for culturally organized activity. These systems influence interpersonal involvement through opportunities for children and adults to participate, so that children become apprentices in certain culturally organized activities.

According to this perspective, the three planes are linked through dynamic and mutually constituting processes, in accordance with much socio-cultural theory (Rogoff 1990; 2003). Culture is inherent in transformation of participation and all people participate in continually changing cultural communities (Rogoff 2003). In taking this position, Rogoff is countering a common tendency in the research literature for culture to be treated as a category or variable, like gender or ethnicity. Instead she uses examples from a wide range of different cultural settings to illustrate cultural processes in everyday activities. Her aim is to open up questions about participation and its transformation rather than about the individual cultural variables that affect development. In pursuing this agenda, she has provided a rich set of detailed descriptions and identified some processes that connect between the individual and social planes, but further specification of these processes is needed.

Activity

As noted above, meaningful activity has a central place in socio-cultural theories. In conceptualizing relations between individual psychological functioning and cultural activity, the individual and cultural activity are seen as part of a single, interacting system such that the individual and the cultural are mutually constitutive elements (Cole 1996; Rogoff 2003; Vygotsky 1978). In this system, human mental processes emerge through practical activity (Cole 1996).

Vygotsky was concerned with the formation of consciousness, or mind, which had been rejected as a legitimate subject of study by the behaviourists. He reasoned that certain activities that distinguished human learning from that of animals were capable of generating consciousness. These were its social character, the capacity to pass information, ideas and artefacts from one generation to another (historicity) and the existence of mental images and schemas prior to practical action, which he dubbed its 'double nature' (Kozulin 1998). The notion of socially meaningful activity became an explanatory principle in his work and that of his followers.

The concept of activity was a controversial topic in Soviet psychology and the interested reader is referred to Kozulin (1996) for a more detailed discussion of this debate. One major point of dispute concerned the significance of practical (material) actions as compared with socially mediated activity. As will become apparent in the next chapter, empirical research has drawn on notions of activity in a somewhat eclectic fashion, without carefully differentiating between the two. Much interest has focused on dialogic exchanges and their role in supporting children's learning.

A feature of activity theory that has proven to be useful when considering interactions is its recognition of goals and motives. As noted above, an early model of activity proposed by Vygotsky (1978) had three components, the subject, a goal (object) or motive and artefacts used by subjects pursuing the goal or object. Leont'ev (1978, as cited in Daniels 2001: 86–7) went on to propose that motives distinguish one activity from another. He was concerned to differentiate between activity and actions and did so by claiming that actions are essentially individual, driven by conscious goals, whereas activities are guided by wider, socially defined motives. He gave a well-known example of hunting for food, an activity that is motivated by the desire for survival. To satisfy this need, humans engage in many actions that are not aimed directly at obtaining food. For example, a hunter oils his gun and a fisherman mends his nets. Likewise, when hunting, members of the hunting party might each have separate actions, such as circling around the animals and moving them towards other hunters. These actions have goals that are subordinate to the overall motive of the activity, which is to obtain food and stay alive. 'To understand why separate actions are meaningful one needs to understand the motives behind the whole activity. Activity is guided by a motive' (Leont'ev 1978, as cited in Daniels 2001: 87). By this he meant that the motive, or purpose of an activity may be collective, whereas goals are individual and tend to emerge during the course of an activity (Engeström 1999).

Leont'ev's distinction between individual and collective goals is useful as a means of connecting individual and collective activity. Engeström (1999) expanded on these ideas and included both the community in which the activity takes place and also rules and division of labour. This expanded activity system provides a means of moving between the analysis of individual actions and the analysis of the broader activity context (Engeström 1999). Cole and Engeström (1993) also use an activity framework to analyse systems of mediation that exist when a novice begins to learn to read from an expert and how these become coordinated into a single system.

An in-depth examination of activity theory is outside the scope of this book and the interested reader is referred to Engeström, Miettinen and Punamiki (1999). The framework is useful though in its acknowledgement of multiple points of view, traditions and interest among those involved in an activity system. Historically, activity systems are shaped and transformed over time and a historical analysis may therefore be useful in reaching a full understanding of such systems.

The theoretical models and frameworks outlined above all draw our attention to links between individuals and their social and cultural settings. There are a number of similarities between them but each has its own perspective, largely stemming from specific research agendas. All attempt to treat the individual and social context as the unit of analysis but as both these components of the unit are highly complex, each approach takes different aspects of the individual and the social context as its focus. Structural analyses are concerned with mapping connections between individual children, their families, schools and other organizations. As the evidence base grows, it becomes clear that some of these factors have stronger impacts on children's achievements and their adjustment. These factors and relationships between them then become the focus of further research. Socio-cultural perspectives offer tools for a more dynamic analysis and those that focus on children's learning suggest that useful ideas to take forward include cultural activities, values, beliefs and goals; customary practices and children's participation in activities. Some of these notions also emerge from comparative studies of classrooms in different cultures and will be explored later in this chapter.

Learning in and out of school

The theories discussed above that take the individual and social context as the unit of analysis often find support in empirical research on learning out of school. This research explores learning that takes place as people engage in everyday activities at home, in the community or in the workplace.

When people think about things they have learned, they tend to think of courses they have taken in school or other organizations. They tend to be less aware of learning that has taken place informally while at work or as part of everyday activities, yet a great deal of learning takes place in this way. Very young children certainly learn a huge amount before they start school, simply by taking part in the activities of family life. As they grow older, young people continue to learn through participation in activities outside school, in the family and community. These range from every day activities such as cooking, shopping, playing and talking to structured sports, music or community activities such as guides and scouts. In these situations, learning often appears to take place spontaneously, as a natural part of performing the activity. For example, cooking involves physical skills and mathematical abilities such as such as weighing and calculating quantities, yet these often go unnoticed.

Complex activities do not have to be formally taught, but may be learned in an informal way through participation alongside experienced practitioners (Lave and Wenger 1991; Scribner 1984). In these apprenticeships, experienced practitioners arrange tasks in such a way that beginners undertake simple parts of the activity and gradually progress to more difficult components. For example, Vai and Gola tailors in Liberia learn their craft from masters who run tailoring businesses, tailor clothes and supervise apprentices. Apprentices first learn to sew by hand, use a treadle sewing machine and press clothes. They start by working on simple garments for children and are given the tasks involved in finishing a garment by hand, such as sewing buttons and hemming. Only later do they learn to sew pieces of the garment together and to cut the cloth. The way that the learning activity is organized, effectively reversing the steps in production of a garment, exposes apprentices to the final production goal, the finished garment, before drawing their attention to the sequence in which the pieces are sewn together, and to the way the fabric is cut.

Lave and Wenger (1991) also drew attention to a transformation that took place, as beginners gradually became part of a community of practice. To begin with, newcomers are on the periphery of this community observing experienced practitioners as they go about their work. In time, however, newcomers become part of the community of practice and their experiences not only increase their knowledge but also change their sense of identity. So a young woman who becomes a midwife acquires both the expert knowledge required to help mothers through pregnancy and delivery and gradually comes to understand what being a midwife means in terms of identity. This form of learning is very common in the world of work and in every everyday activity. It also occurs in schools as part of the hidden curriculum and ethos of schools, through which students learn about expected values and behaviours.

One of the most widely cited examples of learning in an everyday context is a study of Brazilian school children working as sellers in a market (Carraher *et al.* 1985). The children were observed in the market, where they were able to perform accurate calculations of various combinations of amounts for different fruits, such as the price of four coconuts and three pineapples. In a school situation the same children completed the same problems, which were now presented in numerical notation as would be encountered in a classroom.

The children performed the school tasks less accurately, with 74 per cent correct in the market and only 37 per cent correct when problems were presented in a numerical format as would be encountered in school.

Although participation in an activity such as tailoring or selling on the market may be an important condition for learning, it is also true that simply participating in an activity does not necessarily mean we learn all that is required. Apprentice tailors would be fired if they were unable to perform well and children would not earn much as street traders if they were unable to learn the necessary mental arithmetic involved, so it is likely that the samples of adults and children involved in these studies excluded those who had tried and failed.

Nevertheless, the research has been successful in highlighting some differences between formal and informal education (Greenfield and Lave, 1982; Resnick 1987). Greenfield and Lave (1982) argued that in general, informal learning is embedded in everyday activities, as in the examples above, and it occurs as a by-product of those activities. School learning, on the other hand, is set apart from everyday life and becomes an end in itself, rather than having an immediate application. The school curriculum is designed to convey subject knowledge and also skills such as numeracy and literacy that are necessary to acquire that knowledge. Teachers adopt explicit pedagogies for the different subjects they teach, whereas informal education has little explicit pedagogy. This means that even though teaching may be quite structured in informal settings, it is often implicitly rather than explicitly organized. The learner often takes the initiative for finding out about the world around and adults frequently comment that they do not teach yet the child learns.

Another difference between formal and informal education noted by Greenfield and Lave (1982) is that it is unusual for relatives to be a child's teacher in a formal setting, whereas in informal settings, relatives frequently take this role. Also, much learning in informal situations takes place through demonstration and imitation, and children become keen observers, a tendency also noted by Rogoff (1990; 2003). In school there is greater reliance on the linguistic presentation of information, orally or in writing. This is in part a reflection of the subject matter included in the school curriculum, but it may also be an indication of the value placed on language in education. Lastly, Greenfield and Lave (1982) suggest that in informal settings, the main motivation to learn is the desire to become a competent member of adult society, whereas the competition inherent in most education systems encourages greater individual motivation. This may be a somewhat idealized view, yet it draws attention to an important influence on motivation to learn in school.

The embedded nature of much learning out of school leads to contextualized reasoning that incorporates features of the environment, whereas reasoning in school is more often removed from a real world context (Resnick 1987). Children therefore become practised in working with problems that have no obvious connection to the real world. Cole (1998) suggests that this is one of the main differences in cognitive functioning of people who have been to school and those who have not. Individuals who have received at least primary education are better prepared to accept problems in their own right, whereas individuals have not been to school are less willing to do so. A good example is provided by Cole and Scribner (1974), who reported a study by Luria (1971, as quoted in Cole and Scribner 1974), in which he presented syllogistic problems to peasant farmers in Russia. A typical problem had three statements and respondents were asked to say whether the third statement followed from the first two or answered a question. For example:

All bears in Siberia are black
My friend saw a bear in Siberia
What colour was the bear?

A typical answer from a farmer who had not been to school was 'How should I know, I have not been to Siberia. Ask your friend.' This response shows that the farmer had not accepted the problem as one that he was expected to solve solely in its own terms, without reference to his experience of the world. Such problems are commonly encountered by children in school but not in the everyday experience of peasant farmers.

Schools and their associated assessment systems encourage individual cognition, whereas in work and everyday life much responsibility for solving problems is shared. Resnick (1987) cites research by Hutchins on the navigation of a ship entering port, to give an example of the way in which a complex operation such as this involves coordination between several operators. This stands in contrast to much learning in school, where children work alone and are assessed for their individual achievements.

A dichotomous typology such as that above is an oversimplification and there are of course many exceptions to be noted. School learning can be linked with everyday experience and its relevance demonstrated, for example, in relation to project work. There are also some out-of-school contexts in which there is an explicit pedagogy and curriculum. Parents may also behave in a way that is very similar to teachers when they help their children with reading and other school related work at home (Greenhough and Hughes 1998; Thomas 1998). Many work environments are highly specialized and new entrants are expected to have a strong foundation of relevant knowledge and skills. Employers expect the education system to provide this foundational knowledge base.

Perhaps one of the key differences is that in much everyday learning, the learner is involved in completing the whole task, so the need for learning specific skills or information becomes clear. This means that skills and knowledge are acquired on a just-in-time basis, which helps to motivate learning. So, for example, the task of decorating a room with wallpaper involves measuring the room and calculating the amount of wallpaper required. There is a clear motivation for the calculations and an understanding of how the calculations contribute to completing the whole activity. In school, the curriculum is broken down into component parts and students progress from the simpler to the more difficult aspects of the subject. Material is broken down into units that must be learned in sequence and the goal of learning is to acquire skills that will become the means of later activity (Cole 1998). While this is a logical organization, it can make it difficult for students to understand the overall goal of learning, which may seem somewhat abstract and distant.

Assessment systems in education are frequently used to show students their position compared to others, in a very public manner. Assessment in informal situations tends to be criterion referenced, which means that any number of people can pass a test providing they reach the criterion. Good examples of this form of assessment include graded music assessments and the driving test. Performance in these tests is much less public compared to tests in school. Finally, it is undeniable that the learner has restricted choice, autonomy and responsibility in formal education. This means that school learning is often associated with effort and the need for self-regulation, as discussed earlier (Chapter 3).

Concerns about the form of teaching and classroom interaction in US schools led Gallimore and Tharp (1990) to comment that much more effective teaching occurred outside schools for example in child rearing and employee-training programmes. They were particularly concerned about the dominant form of teaching, which largely consisted of recitation. This meant that for most lessons students read assigned texts, completed worksheets and took tests. When students were encouraged to speak, teachers controlled the topic and the way in which children were able to participate. Gallimore and Tharp (1990) recommended, therefore, that principles should be derived from interactions in non-school settings and applied to teaching in school. It may be useful to think about the dominant form of teaching in any classroom and consider whether certain aspects of informal education might suggest ways of improving school learning. Gallimore and Tharp (1990) acknowledge that there are structural and organizational constraints, such as the number of children in a class, which tend to encourage recitation, yet they see that there is scope for teachers to use a wider range of instructional methods with a whole class.

Culture and pedagogy

Examples given above show that a comparative analysis of learning in different cultural settings yields insights into significant features and practices in those settings. Similarly, to analyse school and pedagogic cultures it is useful to make comparisons between systems in different countries or between schools within a country. Without making such comparisons, it can be difficult to analyse classrooms, schools and education systems in our own culture. Most of us think about education in relation to our own experience of schooling, which is usually limited to one or two schools and we tend to assume that these are typical or representative. Even qualified teachers may have experience of only a small number of schools, often in one area of the country.

One way in which education systems in different countries signal the values they espouse is through their national curricula. The aims and goals expressed indicate priorities and values but may be rather broadly conceived so sometimes it is more revealing to examine school curricula. A comparative study of primary schools in five countries (Alexander 2000) found that literacy and numeracy were given prominence in many countries, whereas civic or citizenship education and modern foreign languages had a much more central place in France, Russia, India and the US than in England. Perhaps surprisingly, religious education appeared only in England. Alexander proposes that:

> citizenship and religious education, both signal particular, although contrasting values in respect of how the individual stands in relation to society, while the presence and extent of foreign language teaching conveys an equally important message about how one society stands in relation to others.
>
> (Alexander 2000: 157)

Civic or citizenship education reflects the value placed on the individual's contribution to society and governance, while the extent of foreign language teaching indicates the value placed on understanding and communicating with people in other cultures.

Cultural beliefs and historical developments also permeate schools and classrooms and influence interactions between teachers and pupils within them (Alexander 2000). The structure and form of teaching varies in different systems, a reflection of cultural custom and practice. Moreover, the influence of different pedagogic traditions is evident in the transactions between teachers and pupils. The Central European tradition emphasizes the class as a whole working together while in Russia and France the most prominent activity is structured and public talk. The Anglo-US tradition gives prominence to group and individual work and much time is spent on seatwork, with children working at their desks reading, writing and interacting with peers and the teacher in a relatively unstructured and semi-private manner. Here we see that just as customary practice is a feature of informal learning activities, so it is with formal learning in the education system (Alexander 2000).

Differences in the goals of national education systems are also reflected in pupils' perceptions of the purposes of schooling and in their experiences of secondary school. In a study that compared the English, Danish and French systems of education, Osborn *et al.* (2003) interviewed students in a small number of schools in each country. They found that although students shared some concerns, there were also differences that related to stated priorities in the three national educational systems. The Danish system places an emphasis on collaboration and consensus and students were concerned with good social relationships. This was more important than competitiveness and individual development. The French system also emphasizes social solidarity and promotes equality for all. It aims to bring the majority of children up to a particular standard and according to Osborn *et al.* (2003), differentiation between students is not encouraged. French pupils tended to play down social and academic differences between them. The English system tends to emphasize individualization and differentiation and students in England seemed to be more concerned about issues to do with social identity. These were reflected in a readiness to identify social groups in schools, which frequently related to students' position in the ability hierarchy. For English students, there was a clear link between social identity and learner identity and this was much less evident in the other countries. As this study was carried out in only a small number of schools, care must be taken not to over-generalize the findings.

Summary

Theoretical perspectives linking individuals and their social contexts, outlined above, help to identify and delineate features of culture that have a bearing on children's cognitive growth. Structural models of learners and their contexts map the cultural contexts that bear on children's development, directly or indirectly, whereas socio-cultural models of relations between individuals and their cultural contexts pay more attention to processes that connect individual learning and the social contexts in which it takes place.

Structural analyses highlight the significance of the family and school as sites for children's learning and although they differ in many ways some common theoretical features have been identified. One of these is the significance of parents' and teachers' beliefs concerning children's learning, which have the potential to influence the nature of activities that children are encouraged to engage in. Likewise customary practice sets boundaries on children's activities both in and out of school. Participation in activities provides children with opportunities to learn and to develop their identity. Family preferences and resources may also constrain or open up possibilities for children's participation.

The theoretical integration of the developmental niche into an ecological systems model offers a specific focus on children's learning in the niche. Further combination of this idea of a niche with activity theory opens up a more dynamic approach to learning and one that gives greater recognition to the learner's contribution. There is, however, a curious omission running through all these perspectives and this concerns the nature of learning itself. Socio-cultural theorists work on the premise that learning is a constructive process in which the teacher and the child co-construct meaning together. Researchers working in this tradition give some fascinating insights into strategies that children used to solve problems in everyday contexts and in school. Yet there is little attempt to analyse the demands made by different kinds of learning task and how these relate to the cultural environment and to interactions between adults and children. This issue will be examined in more detail in the next chapter.

5   Interaction and learning

Introduction

As noted in Chapter 4, Vygotsky attributed the development of more advanced types of human learning to our social nature and argued that it is through interaction with other people and the tools and artefacts developed in our culture that we develop advanced ideas and conscious control over our mental processes. His work has raised many questions about the nature of interactions between adults and children and how they relate to cognitive development. These questions inspired a generation of researchers to examine adult–child interactions and develop models of these interactive processes. In general terms this work is concerned with two issues. The first focuses on interactions and aims to understand how these interactions aid learning. It involves detailed observational studies of adults interacting with children as they perform a variety of tasks, with the aim of understanding key features of these interactions. The second is concerned with the wider issue of how adults and children come together and participate in particular kinds of activities. This chapter will consider the first of these, while Chapter 6 is concerned with the second, wider issue.

A dominant view among developmental psychologists, referred to in Chapter 1, is that learning is a constructive process. Both Piaget and Vygotsky thought that learning involved more than simply copying information into the brain and they agreed that individual learners constructed their own understandings of the world, although they proposed different processes were involved. Vygotsky's approach was to consider how a more capable person might provide appropriate guidance and lead a child to more advanced levels of thinking. As noted in Chapter 4 this led him to propose the notion of a 'zone of proximal development', which he defined as a gap between the child's current level and a more advanced level that the child could achieve with help. Vygotsky himself did not undertake a great deal of research on the nature of interactions in the zone of proximal development, so a host of empirical questions remained to be addressed. These include how to identify and measure the boundaries of the zone and questions about the nature of interactions that constitute guidance within it.

These questions have great relevance for education and indeed for the transmission of culture from one generation to another. Tomasello, Kruger and Ratner (1993), for example, propose that the transmission of culture depends on three elements (a) concordance between a learner's capabilities and what the culture has to offer, (b) some person in the culture, a tutor, who can sense what a learner needs and delivers it, and (c) some shared agreement on the part of the tutor and learner about how this arrangement is supposed to work, in this particular culture. The notion of sensing what a learner needs and delivering it again raises questions about how to discover what the learner needs and how best to deliver it. This process may be relatively simple in relation to everyday learning activities but becomes more complex when we consider learning in an institutional setting such as a school or college.

Situation definition and intersubjectivity

When a novice and a more capable other come together to perform an activity, solve a problem or simply have a conversation, they often start from different initial knowledge and understanding of the situation. In order to have a meaningful exchange, the more expert person or teacher has to be able to temporarily adopt the novice learner's position or to see the problem from their perspective (Wertsch 1985). An example from adults' interactions with babies gives a good illustration of this point. Very young babies (up to three months) look around them and are attracted to various perceptual features of their environment such as moving objects, novel objects and human faces but they have very limited voluntary control of attention. If a caregiver wishes to establish joint attention with a baby at this stage of development, a successful strategy is to follow the baby's gaze and interact with them through the object of interest. In this way the adult takes control of establishing joint attention with the child.

Six-month-old infants interact with objects, grasping and manipulating them, and they also interact with people, exchanging babble or expressing emotions. These are dyadic relationships as infants interact with objects or people but they do not coordinate interactions with objects and people. More complex, triadic interactions emerge later, typically between nine and twelve months of age. At first, infants share or check adults' attention, for example looking up at an adult when manipulating an object to check that the adult is watching. Next, infants follow an adult's gaze and finally they direct the adult's attention by pointing, thus establishing joint, triadic engagement between adult, child and object (Tomasello 1999). The emergence of joint attention is an important milestone and one that indicates the child is beginning to understand other persons as intentional agents.

Gradually with age very young children become able to establish joint attention themselves by physically and verbally attracting adults to engage with them. They go on to develop sensitivity to the other's person's perspective, so that as speakers they are able to take account of the perspective of their listeners. This is a major developmental achievement, known as 'intersubjectivity', a term introduced into psychology by Trevarthen (1979; 1980), but now used by many authors.

Wertsch (1984; 1985) used the term 'situation definition' to denote 'the way in which objects or events are represented or defined' (1985: 159). He pointed out that when an adult and a child interact in the zone of proximal development the child may not understand how a problem or task is defined, its components or goal. Thus although the child and the adult are physically in the 'same situation', their representations of the situation may differ in some important respects, so that mentally they may not be in the same situation at all. The challenge for the adult is to

> find a way to communicate with the child such that the latter can participate at least in a minimal way in interpsychological functioning and can eventually come to define the task setting in a new, culturally appropriate way.
>
> (Wertsch 1985: 161)

Here, we see that it is the adult's responsibility to acknowledge the child's representation of the situation and to find a way of incorporating it into their joint activity so that the child can participate and learn. This may be relatively easy to do when building a tower of blocks but far more difficult when teaching school subjects.

Intersubjectivity sets the stage for the child to internalize higher mental functions. Adults have a tendency to hand over responsibility to children as they become more competent and able to manage a task or activity. They adjust their support and guidance in a way that reflects the child's developing competence and thus their interactions reflect the child's intra-mental processes (Wertsch 1985). Building intersubjectivity is an important element in many learning situations. Both the teacher and learner use verbal and non-verbal information to establish key features of an activity. In the process of guided participation, the adult and child both attempt to establish intersubjectivity and learners make great efforts to attend to the features of tasks that adults consider important (Rogoff 1990).

Scaffolding and contingency

Research on the support and guidance provided by more capable others includes many studies of interactions between young children and adults. Much of this work builds on notions of the zone of proximal development, scaffolding and contingency. The metaphor of scaffolding was introduced in seminal research by Wood and his colleagues (Wood *et al.* 1976; Wood *et al.* 1978). In these papers, no explicit link is made with the zone of proximal development. However, Bruner was already familiar with Vygotsky's work as he wrote an introduction to the first English translation of the book

Thought and Language (Vygotsky 1962). This suggests at least an implicit link between Vygotsky's zone of proximal development and the metaphor of scaffolding. Wood *et al.* (1976) observed young children building a tower of intersecting wooden blocks with assistance from an adult. From their analysis of video recordings of these interactions, they proposed that the adult's support was like a scaffold, which was erected to support the child during learning and then taken away once the child could perform the task unaided. They described scaffolding as a form of adult assistance

> that enables a child or novice to solve a problem, carry out a task or achieve a goal which would be beyond his unassisted efforts.
>
> (Wood *et al.* 1976: 90)

They identified several kinds of scaffolding functions, or types of assistance, provided by the adult. Three of these were concerned with managing the task: marking important features, breaking the task into manageable components, or 'reducing degrees of freedom', and keeping the child working towards the task goal. Two of the functions identified were affective, namely recruiting the child's interest and controlling frustration.

These early studies also established principles of levels of control and contingency in adults' interactions with children. Levels of control were identified and formed the basis of later claims about the effectiveness of adults' adjustment of assistance. These levels have been confirmed in later studies with children working at computer-based tasks (Wood and Wood 1996a; 1996b; Wood 1998). They range from very general statements such as 'What might you do next?' to verbal prompts and demonstration.

Level 0: No assistance
Level 1: A general verbal prompt ('What might you do next?')
Level 2: Specific verbal prompt ('You need a big block here')
Level 3: Indicates material ('Try this one')
Level 4: Prepares materials (Selects block and indicates where to put it)
Level 5: Demonstrates

From the findings of their early research, Wood and his colleagues (Wood *et al.* 1976; Wood *et al.* 1978) proposed that adults provided more effective support when they adjusted their interventions in a way that was responsive to, or contingent upon, the child's actions. This led them to propose the contingent shift principle that when the child completed a task successfully the adult should reduce the level of control, and when the child had difficulty the level of control should be increased.

The effectiveness of contingent instruction has been confirmed in a number of studies. When helping children to complete mathematics problems, parents vary in the type of support they offer (Pratt *et al.* 1992). Greater use of the contingent-shift pattern by parents was associated with better performance by children in a subsequent post-test on long-division problems. As this was a cross-sectional study, it was not possible to draw any conclusions about the direction of influence and so no causal links were established. It may be that parents find it easier to maintain contingency with higher attaining children. A subsequent study that controlled for children's initial performance on long-division tasks also found that children made more progress in long division when their parents provided contingent instruction (Pratt and Savoy-Levine 1998).

In a school context, seven- to eight-year-old children who received contingent instruction on balance-beam problems mastered the task with fewer examples than children who received 'nonscaffolded' instruction (Day and Cordon 1993). This study is one of only a small number to include careful assessments of children's intelligence and their competence on a task before instruction started. Students in the scaffolded group needed fewer examples to learn the task and they also performed more consistently in the transfer tests. The performance of students in the non-scaffolded instruction group declined in the transfer tests and was more variable and more strongly related to measured intelligence. More contingent teaching thus appears to promote children's learning and it also reduce differences between the children and increases transfer. It appears, therefore, that children benefit from close calibration of assistance by an adult.

Adults do not find it easy to maintain contingency, even with apparently simple tasks (Wood *et al.* 1978; Wood 1986). Providing such sensitively calibrated support can be very demanding, as it calls for the adult to pay careful attention to the learner and to remember details about their performance. Another reason why it may be difficult to maintain contingency is that students sometimes invent solutions that had not been envisaged by their tutors. A tutor may have one approach to a problem in mind but the student decides to pursue another, reasonable approach. When this happens, tutors must decide whether to offer support for only their solution method or to offer support for the student's chosen way of working. Wood and Wood (1996a) assert that in this situation, the tutor should not restrict support but should instead offer help in relation to the learner's preferred approach and their learning goals. Only in this way will the tutor be able to maintain what they term 'domain contingency', which involves the tutor inferring and supporting the learner's goals. To illustrate this notion, Reichgelt *et al.* (1993) refer to the standard task of a child building a pyramid of blocks. Given such a task, most adults would assemble the four largest blocks to form a square base for the pyramid, then the next largest square and place it on top of the base and so on. At the beginning of the task when all the blocks are spread out on the table, a child, however, might pick up the smallest blocks and start assembling them into a square. A domain-contingent tutor would take this as the starting point and help the child assemble the small square whereas a tutor who was not domain-contingent would direct the child to put down the small blocks and assemble the large square instead. Both tutors could be instructionally contingent, adjusting the level of support to help the child, but only one of them would be considered domain-contingent.

This proposal has important implications as it calls for flexibility on the part of teachers in the way they organize learning tasks for students. Tutors require a good knowledge of a variety of different starting points and sequences through an activity, if they are to adjust and maintain contingency. To achieve such adjustments calls for tutors to appreciate that a task may be accomplished in more than one sequence and to have a sufficiently flexible approach that does not reject unusual or innovative responses. Human tutors are capable of flexibility, whereas computer-based tutoring systems are limited in this respect. Nevertheless, it must be acknowledged that human tutors vary and Putnam (1987) found that some teachers who worked with individual students appeared to follow a standard curriculum script, which was not adjusted for different students.

Assisting performance

Compared with the notion of contingency, which is given a precise definition, the metaphor of scaffolding is more general and open to interpretation. The term has been widely used in developmental psychology and in educational contexts, but critics argue that it is used too loosely and has lost its explanatory value. One concern is that scaffolding has become synonymous with help, as it has been used to denote any type of assistance that helps a learner accomplish a task. It has been argued that scaffolding should only be used if a number of key features are in place (Maybin *et al.* 1992). These include a clearly defined learning outcome that the child is unable to achieve before scaffolding is provided and demonstrates unaided when the scaffolding is removed. There needs to be some evidence that a teacher or parent wishes to help a child acquire a specific skill or reach a specific level of understanding. For scaffolding to be seen as effective there should also be evidence that the child is able to successfully accomplish the task independently, without assistance from the adult. In its original formulation, successful scaffolding was assumed to lead to the child having a better understanding of the process involved in completing a task (Bruner 1983; Wood *et al.* 1976). It is the child's understanding that is being scaffolded, not the tower of blocks.

Another limitation of scaffolding is that the original use of the metaphor was limited to a single isolated task designed for young children, building a pyramid of blocks. Several replications and extensions have also employed relatively simple construction tasks that do not require the formation of complex mental representations. Open-ended tasks and creative activities are less amenable to analysis in terms of scaffolding functions (Blay 2000).

Wood and Wood (1996b) acknowledged that the original concept of scaffolding tended to ignore the nature of the relationship between the adult and child and was limited in its analysis of the communicative mechanisms involved. They accepted Rogoff's analysis of several general features of effective collaboration, as follows:

1 Tutors provide a bridge between the learner's existing knowledge and skills and the demands of the new task.
2 Instructions and assistance are provided in the context of the learner's activity and the tutor helps the learner to keep sight of the overall goal of an activity.
3 Learners play an active part in learning and contribute to the successful solution of problems, even though these are initially beyond their capabilities.
4 Responsibility is transferred from the tutor to the learner.
5 Guided participation occurs in situations where there is no deliberate attempt to teach children, for example during the completion of everyday activities.

In a review of the utility of the metaphor for the field of learning disabilities, Stone (1998) acknowledges the difficulties presented by the wide interpretation of the term but goes on to argue for its retention, as the metaphor captures the essence of helpful interactions between adults and children. He identified four commonly accepted characteristics of scaffolding, as follows.

1 Recruitment by an adult of a child's involvement in a meaningful and culturally desirable activity beyond the child's current understanding or control.
2 Titration of the assistance provided by the adult during the interaction. This is accomplished through ongoing judgment of the child's level of skill and understanding, and adjustment of the support provided.
3 Provision of several types of support might be provided, including gestures and dialogue.
4 Withdrawal of support as the child's confidence grows, thus transferring responsibility from the adult to the child.

Although these two lists of commonly accepted characteristics of effective pedagogic interactions overlap, there are also some differences between them. Both acknowledge that the tutor plays a part in connecting the learner and the activity by encouraging the learner to participate and by providing carefully calibrated assistance. Transfer of responsibility from the tutor to the learner is also a key component. Stone (1998) gives more emphasis to the role of dialogue as a form of support.

Gallimore and Tharp (1990; Tharp 1993) have criticized the notion of scaffolding as it suggested that there were a small number of forms of assistance that could be offered by teachers, whereas in reality teachers assist children in many different ways. They identified seven means of assisting performance that had been studied by psychologists, as follows:

1   Modelling: offering behaviour for imitation. Modelling assists by giving the learner information and a remembered image that can serve as a performance standard.
2   Feedback: the process of providing information on a performance as it compares to a standard. Feedback is essential in assisting performance because it allows the performance to be compared to the standard and thus allows correction.
3   Contingency management: the application of the principles of reinforcement and punishment to behaviour.
4   Instructing: requesting specific action; this assists learners by selecting the correct response and by providing clarity, information and decision-making. It is most useful when the learner can perform some segments of the task but cannot yet analyse the entire performance or make judgements about the elements to choose.
5   Questioning: a request for a verbal response that assists by producing a mental operation the learner cannot or would not produce alone. Question-and-answer interactions can provide useful information about the learner's developing understanding.
6   Cognitive structuring: 'explanations'; cognitive structuring assists the learner by providing explanatory and belief structures that organize and justify new learning and perceptions and allow the creation of new or modified schemata.
7   Task structuring: chunking, segregating, sequencing, or otherwise structuring a task into or from components. This assists learners by modifying the task itself, so the units presented to the learner fit into the zone of proximal development when the entire unstructured task is beyond that zone (Tharp 1993: 271–2).

The inclusion of instructing, questioning and providing explanations in this list draws attention to the use of language as a means of supporting children's learning, and further specification of the communicative mechanisms involved in these interactions will be considered below. Task structuring is also an important element that will be considered in more detail later. Furthermore, teachers may direct the child's attention, offer simple encouragement or hold information in memory.

Others have commented on the tendency of research to focus almost exclusively on the adult's talk and interaction and to give the child's contribution less attention thus implying that adults are the agents for instilling new learning and understanding (Elbers 1996; Rogoff 1990). There has also been a tendency for research on tutoring to ignore or overlook affective components of learning. Researchers imply that adults readily provide assistance that is finely tuned to the child and children are always willing learners, happily following adult guidance. As parents and teachers know all too well, this is not always the case. Finally, there is a need for greater clarity about the interactional processes through which different types of learning takes place (Stone 1998; Wertsch 1985).

Within classrooms it is difficult for teachers to provide scaffolding, due to the number of learners which restricts the amount of time that a teacher spends with any one child. Without a detailed knowledge of each learner, it is difficult for teachers to provide the sensitive support required to maintain contingency (Bliss *et al.* 1996; Gallimore and Tharp 1990). Only in very small groups or individual tutoring is it possible for a teacher to glean sufficiently detailed information about a student to enable effective scaffolding. Gallimore and Tharp (1990) suggest that there is a second reason why assisted performance is rarely found in schools, even though parents appear to be able to achieve it without any special training. They see the teachers' task as more complex than that of parents, requiring a more elaborate set of skills in assisting children's learning. In addition to large classes, teachers are faced with a restricted curriculum and institutional constraints of schooling and this means that teaching has to be a carefully planned and structured activity. Despite these constraints, teachers can learn to use a repertoire of instructional conversations that are more similar to those found in less constrained environments.

Designing and regulating activities

As noted above, many studies of adult–child interactions have employed carefully designed tasks that were easy for the adult to perform and within the child's capability. These have included sorting household objects (Rogoff and Gardner 1984), knot tying (Nilholm and Säljö 1996), weaving (Greenfield 1984), block construction (Gonzalez 1996) and basic arithmetic (Pratt *et al.* 1992; Pratt and Savoy-Levine 1998). In all of these studies, dyads were presented with a task designed by the researchers to be familiar to the adults and within the capability of children in the age group under investigation. This strategy has enabled researchers to describe and compare interactions, however, as the researchers were responsible for designing the tasks for dyads to complete, this method does not allow us to gain insight into the processes through which adults organize and control tasks for children.

Organizing tasks and activities is a process referred to as task structuring (Gallimore and Tharp 1990; Rogoff 1990; 2003; Tharp 1993). According to Rogoff (1990; 2003) children's participation in activities is structured first by the situations in which children are involved and second by the structuring of interactions during activities. Children, caregivers and other companions influence the situations in which children participate and the nature of interactions that occur as the activities unfold. For example, in middle-class European and North American families, caregivers may encourage young children to participate in school-like conversations, literate forms of discourse and book reading, long before they start school.

In a busy home environment, everyday concerns feature prominently and children's learning frequently occurs as a by-product of their involvement in family activities. Parents' main concern is often to get work done and to ensure that their child is safely able to perform the tasks they are allocated. To achieve this, parents arrange tasks in such a way as to gradually increase demands as children become more competent. For example, in many cultures young children are asked to run errands, such as shopping locally for small purchases. At first, a mother might give the right money for one or two items so that the child can go to the shop, point to the items, hand over money and return home. Older children, however, are expected to collect change and to calculate change. Guberman (1999) questioned the parents of 105 Brazilian children about the level of responsibility they gave their children when they sent them to buy goods at local stands on the market. The parents had little formal mathematical education. Most of the children under the age of eight years were given money and expected to wait for change. Children aged 12–14 years were expected to calculate the change themselves. In this manner, children learned arithmetical transactions through participation in the activity of shopping. Parents organized a supportive environment that enabled children to participate in the activity and they gradually increased the demands as children became more competent.

Examples of this form of structuring have been documented in a variety of cultural contexts. Greenfield (1984) observed young women learning to weave in a Mexican village and noted that they were allowed to do the easier parts of weaving central sections of a piece, while experienced adults set up the looms and completed the first few rows, which were the more difficult parts. Likewise, in a study conducted in a Mexican village, tailoring apprentices were given simple sewing tasks, while experienced tailors had responsibility for cutting the cloth (Lave and Wenger 1991). At the time when the research was undertaken, these activities were economically important for the villagers and therefore an important goal of the activity was to avoid expensive mistakes. The teaching strategy adopted ensured that beginners' errors were kept to a minimum by restricting the task components that could be attempted. Only after these were performed to an acceptable level was the learner allowed to proceed to more difficult aspects of weaving or tailoring. Although the main purpose of this way of organizing the activity is to minimize errors, a by-product is that the learner is made aware of the whole process involved in completing the final product. The relevance of the various parts of an activity becomes clear and can provide motivation for acquiring component skills.

There are several different ways in which tasks may be structured and managed to make them accessible to learners. In formal education, it is common for curriculum designers to break tasks down into component parts and develop sequences of activities to teach each component in turn. This method entails a theory about the most appropriate sequence of learning for the majority of learners at a given stage in the curriculum. Sequences may be influenced by theories of instructional design, such as those developed by Gagne and his colleagues (Gagne *et al.* 1992). These theories adopt a logical analysis of tasks to describe the skills and knowledge that a learner needs to complete them. The approach involves working backwards from goals to the requirements of instructional events and specifies a series of events to be undertaken by the teacher to assist the learner. Working backwards from goals in this way is one of the most effective and widely employed techniques for achieving certain types of learning objectives (Gagne and Merrill 1990).

Even apparently simple tasks may involve a number of components. For example, counting a row of five objects includes being able to count to five, counting each object once and only once, using the correct number for each object counted, and knowing that the highest number in the count represents the number of objects in the set (Resnick 1987). A child will have difficulty completing the task if there are weaknesses in any of these subcomponents. Task analysis helps to identify the relevant components and learning activities can then be designed to help the child strengthen those that are weak.

The process of task structuring, or task management, is also an important aspect of tutoring by teachers. The process of task management is similar to task structuring, but the term has been used to refer to the reasoning involved in a tutor's choice of task for a student (McArthur *et al.* 1990). This may involve a complex representation of the structure of knowledge in a particular topic and an ordered sequence of activity that is likely to be effective in teaching. In schools and classrooms, a teacher's choice of tasks for students is an ongoing aspect of their everyday work, and effective teachers design and organize learning activities to make them accessible for learners (Tharp and Gallimore 1988).

Task structuring may be seen as an aspect of assistance in classroom contexts, as teachers select tasks and break them down into sub-tasks using a form of task analysis to ensure that the demands of the activity are not too great for the learner. In the case of solving mathematical problems, for example, this typically involves breaking the whole problem down into a hierarchical set of sub-goals or tasks that constitute the problem (McArthur *et al.* 1990). The process of structuring is not confined to the tutor's choice of task to present to the student, but continues during the tutoring session when the tutor makes ongoing adjustments to calibrate support for the student.

A teacher who realizes that a task is beyond a learner's capability might adjust the task, for example, by presenting an easier problem to solve, or accepting a shorter piece of written work. Alternatively, the teacher might offer hints, prompts or demonstration to support and 'scaffold' the child's completion of the difficult piece of work. Once this has been achieved, the teacher might then give the child an easier problem to solve unaided.

An in-depth understanding of both the subject matter and the learner lies behind effective task structuring and management. For example, in the Reading Recovery programme developed in New Zealand by Marie Clay to develop early literacy (Clay 1985; Clay and Cazden 1990), teachers support children's learning by selecting appropriate texts for them to read. Graded texts for beginning readers may offer a controlled vocabulary, yet they present differences in repetition of words or orthographic regularity. As children's mastery of reading grows, teachers gradually increase the difficulty of the texts. A guiding principle of the programme is that children should be able to read 90 per cent of the words in each text, so teachers must have a detailed knowledge of both the words a child is able to read and the vocabulary used in available texts (Clay 1991).

So far, this section has identified two main ways of structuring tasks. First, an adult performs the difficult parts of a task and gives the child the simpler components. This form of structuring occurs frequently in everyday life and is often motivated by a desire to ensure that the task is completed accurately and safely. The child's learning may be a secondary consideration. A second form of structuring is explicitly designed to promote learning and involves a detailed analysis of the steps required to achieve a learning objective. Thus, the structuring of a task relates to the adult's priorities concerning goals or motives and children's learning. As noted above, an adult who thinks that error-free performance is called for is likely to exert a high level of regulation to ensure that the task is completed accurately. On the other hand, an adult who sees the task as an opportunity to encourage children's learning is more likely to allow the child freedom to make errors in the service of learning. These priorities, or values, connect with the wider culture in which the activity takes place.

Adults' educational level and their interactions with children

In Vygotsky's theory, cultural tools and signs mediate interactions between adults and children. Adults draw children's attention to features of objects they consider important, and they also provide tools for memorizing information and regulating performance. Children who grow up in different cultural contexts are exposed to different cultural signs, tools and practices, which may have consequences for learning and development. Cultural norms and practices influence children's participation in activities, defining social situations where children are allowed to participate and those that are restricted to adults. These cultural norms and childcare arrangements influence the extent of interaction with adults as opposed to peers (Rogoff *et al.* 1993; Paradise 1996). Patterns of interaction between parents and their children also differ from one cultural context to another (Rogoff 1990; 2003). In some cultures, adults rarely have conversations with young children.

Similarly, within a given culture certain aspects of adults' own learning and experience may influence the way they mediate children's learning and experience. One factor that is of interest is parents' educational level, which appears to affect their interactions with children when performing tasks and activities. In cultures without universal education it is possible to investigate whether caregivers' education influences the way they interact with children and the features of tasks and activities to which they attend. Findings from this research indicate that education influences mothers' perceptions of the task goals and whether they involve children in making use of mediating signs.

Wertsch, Minick and Arns (1984) observed interactions between adults and six-year-old children constructing a copy of a three-dimensional barnyard. Six children completed the activity with their mothers who had very little formal education (four years or less) and six completed the activity with teachers who had received 11 years of schooling. An important step in completing this task was to look at the model to see where objects should be positioned and results indicated that the group of children interacting with teachers were more likely to carry out this step. Also, mothers were more likely to assist through direct regulation that involved pointing to or mentioning the pieces, picking up a piece of the puzzle and handing it to the child or putting it in place themselves. Teachers tended to let children do more of the puzzle themselves and encouraged children to look at the model. Wertsch, Minick and Arns (1984) suggested that the mothers and teachers had different interpretations of the task situation. Under the influence of their extensive contact with the institutions of education, teachers saw the activity as an educational opportunity and were keen to encourage the child to learn how to complete the puzzle themselves, even if this involved making mistakes. Mothers who had very limited contact with educational institutions interpreted the situation as one in which they should work with the child to ensure successful completion of the puzzle. Mothers with higher levels of education gave their children more responsibility for completing puzzles (Wertsch *et al.* 1984).

In later research, Wertsch (1985) found that middle-class US mothers and Brazilian teachers almost never physically picked up or placed a piece in the puzzle, whereas this was not unusual for rural Brazilian mothers. Adults who picked up or placed the pieces allowed very little scope for the children to exert strategic responsibility for the task. In general, adults with a higher educational level tend to encourage children to take greater responsibility for task performance (Wertsch 1985).

Similarly, Nilholm and Säljö (1996) found that mothers' interactions with young children related both to their educational background and in their occupation. Mothers who took part in the research were teachers, nurses or factory workers. They were asked to help their six-year-old children use a piece of rope to tie a knot around a wooden stick and were given pictures to illustrate how the knot should be tied. Teachers and nurses encouraged their children to look at the pictures to work out what to do, whereas the factory workers tended to show the children how to tie the knot without drawing the children's attention to the pictures. The teachers also encouraged the children to do more of the knot tying and provided more scaffolding to help the children achieve this. Factory workers tended to give more physical assistance and demonstration than the other groups of mothers.

Neither of these studies included any pre-tests to assess children's competence before the observation sessions, so it is possible that parents were responding to their children's ability to do the puzzle or tie the knot and that this differed in the experimental groups. Nevertheless findings illustrate clearly that even in an experimental situation where participants share the goal of completing the task, individuals have different motives, which influence the way the task is completed. More educated mothers appear to have a notion of pedagogy that is less directive and gives the child greater responsibility for performing this type of activity.

Comparing adults and children as tutors

One way of uncovering the components of effective tutoring is to compare adults and children as tutors. This line of enquiry indicates that adults are more skilled in making sensitive adjustments to the learners' competence and in helping with more sophisticated strategies. Wood *et al.* (1995) compared three-, five- and seven-year-old children working on a computer-based task of building a tower of blocks. After learning to do the activity themselves, the children were then asked to help a same-aged peer. Younger children were less effective at making strategies available and tended to demonstrate or complete the task themselves, they were less contingent and show less intersubjectivity (Wood *et al.* 1995). Seven-year-olds were more contingent than three- and five-year-olds when working with same age peers. This suggests that inter subjectivity and contingency are cognitively demanding.

Older children also appear to be less effective than adults in teaching classification tasks (Ellis and Rogoff 1982) and sophisticated strategies such as planning ahead (Radziszewska and Rogoff 1988; 1991). Ellis and Rogoff (1982) compared the performance of trained nine-year-old children and adults giving assistance in dyads to nine-year-olds completing two sorting tasks. Adult and child teachers gave similar amounts of non-verbal information but the adults gave much more verbal assistance. Learners taught by adults received more information and performed better. Radziszewska and Rogoff (1991) used an errand-planning task in which dyads were shown a town plan with shops and amenities marked and were asked to plan the shortest circuit that could be taken to a list of places. The target children were 30 boys and 30 girls aged nine years who worked with 20 same-age untrained peers, 20 same-age trained peers and 20 parents. Results revealed no differences between trained peer dyads and parent dyads on measures of the planning process. However, the untrained dyads were less skilled, they made more one-step moves and did less exploration. Post-tests indicated that target children in child dyads produced longer routes than those with adults and analysis of interactions between dyads revealed that adults did more strategic thinking aloud and this was associated with better performance by children.

Trained peers used planning strategies but did not explain them. In adult dyads, the children participated more in joint decision-making either working collaboratively with the adult or by actively following. Adults were better at involving the children and verbalizing the strategies they were adopting to complete the task, thus making them more available for appropriation by the children.

One reason for children appearing to be less effective tutors may relate to their knowledge and understanding of tasks and task management. These studies indicate that a tutor needs to be able to judge when to allow the learner to complete the task, or components of it, even if this leads to errors. There is always a temptation for a competent adult or child to take over and do the task instead of standing back and giving the learner a chance. In cognitive terms, the tutor has to suppress a tendency to act. The tutor also needs to be able to take the perspective of the learner and see the problem from their point of view and to be aware of strategies used and to be able to make them available for the learner. These skills are complex, as the tutor has to juggle representations of their own knowledge and strategies as well as those of the student.

Task contexts

Tasks and activities are undertaken in social settings, which help to define and give meaning to an activity and hence influence the manner in which they are completed. Säljö and Wyndhamn (1993) compared children's performance on a task that was presented in a social studies class and a maths class and demonstrated that the context influenced the way in which the children approached the task of finding the correct amount of postage for a letter of given weight. In the mathematics class, most children attempted to calculate the exact cost of the postage, whereas in the social studies class they weighed the letter and then looked for the corresponding postage on a scale.

Several authors suggest that educational systems encourage a hierarchical division of labour in which an individual in a more senior position in the hierarchy takes responsibility for organizing the contributions of others (e.g. Chavajay and Rogoff 2002; Cole 2005). This compares with some traditional cultures where there may be a 'horizontal' organization, with each individual making a contribution to activities and decision-making. Chavajay and Rogoff (2002) explored how mothers in a traditional Maya culture organized a mixed age group of children building a 3D totem pole jigsaw puzzle. Mothers who participated in the study were selected to represent three levels of education and had received 0–2, 6–9 or 12 or more years of schooling. All mothers followed a traditional, shared multi-party structure to some extent however mothers with more schooling gave more direction, pointed out the structure of the activity and proposed a division of labour. This study supports the view that educational systems encourage hierarchical organization. Findings also suggest that children who are unaccustomed to this hierarchical form may not adapt so readily to the organization of activity in school.

Tasks themselves also constitute settings in which interactions take place. Interactions between adults and children are to some extent related to the type of task or activity they engage in. Gonzalez (1996) compared mothers' and fathers' interactions with preschool children completing three different tasks. One was a construction task that required children to construct an object displayed in a picture, the second was reading a picture book together and the third task was playing with household objects. Rates of regulatory interventions by parents were greater for the construction task than for reading a picture book and there was least regulation in the play activity.

During creative or playful activities, adults are more inclined to allow children to take a lead, and in these circumstances there are some interesting changes in the roles adopted by the two participants. For example, when teachers ask children about events in their lives outside school, it is the children who have expert knowledge of people and events, and adults are placed in a position of asking questions to elicit information (Ireson and Blay 1999). The latter ask genuine questions to elicit information from the children, rather than asking known-answer questions that are a common part of classroom dialogue. Similarly during a play activity of building with Lego, during which children decided on the nature of the construction, they sometimes drew inspiration from TV programmes that were unfamiliar to the adult. As a result, adults resorted to questioning in order to establish the type of buildings had in mind. Ireson and Blay (1999) coined the term 'adaptive attunement' to describe the adjustments made by adults during these open-ended activities. This term signals that the adult attempts to adopt the child's position in order to build on it, and it also captures a sense in which the adult may temporarily abandon specific goals intended for the teaching session, accepting that successful learning can be achieved through different sequences of activity. A knowledgeable teacher is able to judge when it is more productive to follow the child's preferred path to learning and when the child must be persuaded to follow the original lesson plan. A flexible teacher is able to make a diversion and still ensure that the original goal is achieved.

Radford, Ireson and Mahon (2006) have also shown that in small group communication tasks there is a close relationship between lesson activities and interactive dialogue between teachers and children. Open-ended tasks such as story writing and speaking book provide opportunities for children to contribute to dialogue. Speaking book is a one-to-one activity during which an adult and child share an exercise book into which pictures have been stuck and use this as a basis for oral discussion. When children are able to draw on their own experience and knowledge and attempt to communicate this to teachers, they not only talk more but they also self-correct errors in their language. In these situations, teachers ask open-ended questions and display interest in the information children provide thereby indicating a genuine desire to engage in dialogue. This form of questioning contrasts with the initiation-reply-evaluation format that is characteristic of much classroom discourse. The standard initiation-reply-evaluation format starts with the teacher asking the class a question and inviting a response from the children, which the teacher then evaluates. This form of questioning provides the children with a very limited response format as they are being invited to provide the correct answer to the question. A more open teacher response may be provided in an initiation-reply-feedback, whereby the feedback may extend a child's response or provide space for discussion of the merits of alternative responses. In contrast with these formats, open-ended tasks in which children are invited to suggest ideas for a storyline and characters for a piece of writing, or to report on their out of school activities are more likely to produce longer contributions to a dialogue.

Evaluating students' level of understanding

Effective task structuring and contingent responding by a tutor both involve detailed knowledge of the student and the task. Few demands are made on adults by tasks such as knot tying, sorting household objects or building a pyramid of blocks, as these are all relatively easy for the adult to perform. Greater demands are made when tutoring older students covering school subjects or degree-level work at university. Detailed observational studies of naturally occurring tutoring of university students suggests that tutors usually adopt subtle methods of evaluating students' understanding. They make sensitive adjustments to activities to account for their students' state of knowledge and motivation. In many instances, these adjustments are made indirectly rather than confronting the student with errors and correcting them immediately (Douglas 1991; Fox 1993; Graesser and Person 1994; Graesser *et al.* 1995; McArthur *et al.* 1990; Merrill *et al.* 1995).

Tutors do not appear to be concerned with overt diagnosis of underlying reasons for student errors, such as knowledge gaps or misconceptions. Instead, they gather information from subtle aspects of the interaction, such as the timing of students' responses; their facial expressions, sighs and laughter, and the extent and speed with which students take up opportunities to complete tutor's sentences (Douglas 1991; Fox 1993; Rogoff 1990). For example, tutors frequently start a sentence and then hesitate before ending, thus giving the student a chance to complete it. If the student does not offer the information, the tutor supplies the ending. This device gives the student an opportunity to demonstrate that they have the necessary knowledge or understanding while providing a safety net in case they do not. Similarly, tutors may employ a series of questions that help to direct the student towards an answer, or they may give opportunities to self-correct (Douglas 1991). This type of help may also form part of an adult's strategy to encourage a child to take responsibility for learning (Rogoff 1990). Tutors also use timing and the way a response is delivered together with the literal content of the response, as a source of diagnostic information (Fox 1991; 1993). So, the sensitive use of hints and prompts may perform two functions: first, providing the tutor with information about the learner's understanding, and, second, encouraging the learner to take responsibility for learning and problem solving.

Discussions between tutors and students are sometimes concerned with cognitive reasoning processes rather than directly with obtaining right answers or completing the next step correctly (McArthur *et al.* 1990). Students in this study were attempting to solve problems in algebra and the discussions focused on the thinking involved in making the next algebraic transformation. When tutors provide assistance in such a way that students are able to correct their own mistakes, this gives further information about their level of understanding.

Students' active participation

As noted above, it is often the adult, whether parent or teacher, who is seen as having responsibility for arranging and structuring activities to enable learning to take place. However learners also play an active part in their own learning. At home, young children initiate a high proportion of interactions with their caregivers (Rogoff 1990; Tizard and Hughes 1984; Wells 1985). Young children are curious about the world and frequently demand information and involvement of caregivers and others around them, 'Children enlist involvement of caregivers in their own activities and attempt to enter into caregivers' activities according to their interests' (Rogoff 1990: 100). In this way children themselves play an active part in extending the boundaries of the zone of proximal development. Both Rogoff (1990) and Elbers (1996) illustrate ways in which children contribute to their own learning. Children often place themselves in a position to observe activities performed by others, or involve themselves in activities and influence the course of activities in which they participate.

Observations of students working with physics and biology tutors indicate that a student's active effort to understand and self-explain is important in successful tutoring (Chi 1996; Chi *et al.* 2001). In one study, Chi *et al.* (2001) observed 11 college students who tutored 12–13-year-old students on the human circulatory system. Tutors worked with their tutees for three sessions, the first session being a pre-test, the second a tutoring session and the third a post-test. In the pre-test, students were asked to define 21 terms and to draw the blood path of the circulation system on an outline of a human body. Students also answered 70 questions, which were designed to test deep and shallow processing of information. Shallow-processing questions called for direct reference to a sentence in the text or text implicit inferences, in other words, inferences that could be drawn from the information provided in the text. Deep-processing questions required knowledge of the double-loop model of the circulatory system or its application to health related issues.

During the tutoring session, the tutor and student worked through a passage from a popular biology text.

When students' prior knowledge, as indicated by the pre-tests, and reading ability were statistically controlled, the tutors' explanations and student responses to scaffolding correlated with shallow learning. Students' reflection correlated with deep learning and students' active response played a more important part than tutors' moves. Students who attempt to make sense of the content of scientific texts gain a deeper understanding, whereas students who do not self-explain tend to gain more superficial knowledge. These findings suggest that the tutor, student and the interactions between them, all influence student learning. Tutors adopted a variety of strategies to encourage students to think about the content and they offered explanations, however they tended to dominate tutorial dialogues, speaking first, taking more turns and speaking for longer than the students. This may be a reflection of their inexperience as tutors.

Handing over responsibility to the learner

A key issue in learning concerns the means by which responsibility for performing a task is transferred from the more expert person to the learner. Vygotsky (1978) proposed that there is a transfer of control from the social (inter-mental) level to the individual (intra-mental level). This view is echoed in thinking about scaffolding and guided participation, whereby an adult has initial responsibility for providing support and there is an assumption that a child will perform a task or solve a problem unaided once they have acquired the competence to do so.

Internalization can be viewed as a constructive process whereby the child appropriates meaning (Vygotsky 1978). Transfer from the interpersonal interaction to the individual child is not a matter of copying information from one level to the other; instead it involves a process of 'appropriation' of meaning, or 'semiotic uptake' (Wertsch and Stone 1985). The child is seen as an active contributor who jointly constructs meaning with assistance from the adult or more expert person.

Further specification of the communicative mechanisms involved now indicates ways in which the transfer of control may be encouraged. Wertsch (1985) argues that adults tend to encourage children's increasing participation, as an aspect of socialization. This is achieved through a number of communicative devices, including reference and abbreviation. He observed parents completing a jigsaw puzzle of a truck with a child and noted that parents used referential language as they attempted to construct a shared situation definition or achieve intersubjectivity. In one case, a young child perceived the wheels of the truck as 'crackers' and appeared to be unable to view them as wheels. This gave the mother great difficulty in establishing effective communication with the child and she used a large number of referential moves before eventually establishing a shared definition of the wheels as circles. First she attempted to establish that they were wheels by telling the child they were not crackers, and by pointing to picture of the truck and suggesting that they find the wheels. When this failed, she resorted to communicative moves that did not require the child to adopt her definition of this object as a truck with wheels. She accompanied these moves with pointing and other gestures which gave the child additional assistance. This mother was forced to adjust her definition of the situation down to the child's level, yet she continued to try and raise the child to her level, using 'semiotic challenge' (Wertsch 1985: 176).

A second device noted by Werstch (1985) is that of abbreviation. Essentially, this involves a gradual transition from specific verbal instructions to more general instructions or hints. These semiotic abbreviations present challenges as they invite the child to identify and carry out subcomponents of a task that are not fully specified by the adult. If the child does not accept the challenge and perform the subcomponents, the adult can take back responsibility and give more specific, less abbreviated instructions.

Tharp and Gallimore (1988; 1991) provide many examples from classrooms to illustrate how teachers fine-tune their talk to children's level of language and to other aspects of their cognitive development. They categorized these into seven forms of assistance, given in an earlier section of this chapter. Even if teachers provide well-tuned assistance in the classroom, the transfer of responsibility for learning can be problematic. Students are not always the eager learners characterized in much of the research carried out with young children.

The method of reciprocal teaching was specifically designed to encourage handover of responsibility to learners (Palincsar and Brown 1984). It was originally developed to teach four strategies for reading comprehension, as noted earlier (p. 66). The reciprocal teaching method builds explicitly on Vygotsky's notion of a zone of proximal development and incorporates elements designed to support a hand over of responsibility for learning from the teacher to the learner (Brown and Palincsar 1989). Working with small groups, the teacher and students first read a passage of non-fiction text and the teacher models the use of the four strategies. Explicit handover of responsibility for the use of the strategies is encouraged by the teacher inviting the students to take turns acting as the learning leader. In this role, each student has responsibility for ensuring that the group asks a question about a paragraph of text, summarizes the paragraph, asked for clarification and make a prediction. The teacher assisted the learning leader through a variety of supports including modelling, prompting and direct explanation.

An interesting aspect of the study was that the researchers provided transcripts of dialogue during the reciprocal teaching sessions. Qualitative and quantitative analyses indicated that the adults provided sensitive assistance to the students and that this became less directive in later sessions, as students provided increasingly clear questions and summaries. The gradual withdrawal of support and accompanying encouragement of students' independent use of strategies suggested that teachers were able to maintain a high level of contingency.

Although this research showed evidence of students' progress in terms of the assessments developed for the programme, there were no statistically significant gains on standardized tests of reading comprehension. A further limitation of the study is that the researchers did not attempt to identify reasons why some students made more progress than others. Differences in students' cognitive and language skills should be assessed to uncover factors that affect progress with reciprocal teaching methods. These might include students' oral language, vocabulary knowledge and verbal intelligence (Cain *et al.* 2004; Perfetti *et al.* 1996), all of which are now known to underpin reading comprehension. Furthermore, multiple studies of reciprocal teaching undertaken since the original research show that there is considerable diversity in the scaffolding that teachers provide (Palincsar *et al.* 1993).

An intervention on a smaller scale indicated that reciprocal teaching methods could be used to improve the communication skills of children with learning difficulties (Lamb *et al.* 1997). A programme of 10 communication games and activities of increasing difficulty was developed to encourage children in an English special school for to plan, organize and express information for others and emphasis was given to answering questions, asking for information and checking understanding. Reciprocal teaching methods were used during which children were given specific support in strategies for self- and other-regulation. Children worked in pairs and were each given a copy of a schematic plan of an island with a number of objects marked. One child, the information-giver, had a route marked on the map and was asked to explain this route to the other child who then marked the route on his or her copy. Findings indicated that in the post-tests, children were talking more, responding to ambiguous instructions more effectively and asking more appropriate questions, mainly when they were in the role of information follower. It may be that part of the success of reciprocal teaching lies in its combination of adult guidance and peer discussion. This combination has been shown to be more effective than adult guidance or peer discussion alone in assisting children's acquisition of road crossing skills (Tolmie *et al.* 2005).

Summary

Vygotsky's work and in particular his notion of the zone of proximal development inspired a generation of educational and developmental research into teaching and learning. This encompasses both parent–child interactions and teacher–student interactions. One major focus of this work has been concerned with the nature of these dyadic interactions and how they may be characterized. Notions of scaffolding and contingency have been productive in generating a considerable amount of research on the performance of simple tasks with clear endpoints. Findings from many of these studies indicate that contingent responding by adults, who increase support when the student encounters difficulties and reduce it when the student makes progress, is beneficial for student learning.

An expanded view of the adult role in tutoring is needed, however, to fully understand how adults help students learn in educational settings. Much of the work undertaken by adults to arrange learning activities occurs before the face-to-face interactions between them and their students. A more developed notion of this aspect of adults' structuring of learning activities should include the tasks and resources selected and the knowledge tutors bring to a tutoring session.

Further expansion of the various ways in which teachers assist students' learning would also enrich understanding of the teaching-and-learning process. These might include modelling, contingency, managing, feeding back, instructing, questioning, and cognitive structuring, as suggested by Gallimore and Tharp (1990). Other semiotic means could usefully be added to this list, including a more finely grained analysis of various types of questioning, and explanations geared to the nature of the learning task. Questioning may be used for a variety of purposes, to check on students' knowledge, elicit information that is unknown to the questioner, provide a hint or prompt or direct the learner's attention to a relevant aspect of a problem or stimulus array.

Finally, students are exposed to a selection of tasks and activities that are available in the contexts in which they find themselves. Families and communities promote certain activities and discourage others. Even activities that are generally encouraged and valued in society are unevenly distributed, as will be illustrated in the next chapter.

6 Exploring connections between individual and culture at home and at school

Introduction

In this chapter the social and cultural factors that form the contexts for interactions between adults and children are focused upon. Every culture provides a variety of settings in which children grow and learn, such as schools, cultural organizations, community activities and home environments. Within each of these settings, children engage in a variety of activities that encourage and support their learning. Reasons for the variations that occur in the participation of children and young people in these activities have to do with a range of cultural factors, including the beliefs and values of parents and teachers, and pedagogical culture. The chapter uses examples drawn from homes and schools to illustrate connections between cultural, pedagogic contexts and children's participation in activities. Connections are to be found at various levels in cultural systems at home and at school, where beliefs, values and customary practices shape the environment in which children grow and learn.

Examples used in the sections that follow include comparative studies of children's activity at home in different cultures and comparative analyses of teaching in different cultures. Linkages are also explored between teachers' pedagogic beliefs and values and their classroom practices, and how school organizational factors may affect the teachers' practices and the learning experience of students in the classroom. Cultural influences are evident in both the pattern of activities that children participate in and the nature of interactions during those activities.

Activity and interaction in home environments

During childhood, parents are instrumental in arranging the home learning environment and are intimately involved in their children's physical, cognitive, social and emotional development. By the time they start school, the vast majority of children are already equipped with an impressive range of relevant skills.

As children move through the education system, parental support for learning includes the provision of home conditions to facilitate learning of skills and knowledge and discussions about a wide range of topics that are relevant to learning in school. Parents also communicate with the child's school, and they help children at home with homework and with educational choices.

In the early years, activities and discussions at home play an important part in children's learning. Parents and children discuss a wide range of topics, thus extending the child's knowledge of the world (Tizard and Hughes 1984). Much children's learning appears to occur spontaneously during everyday activities such as conversations, playing, household chores, and family activities and excursions (Gauvain 1998; 2001; Tizard and Hughes 1984).

Cross-cultural comparisons show that young children growing up in different cultures spend their time in diverse ways. Tudge, Hogan, Lee, *et al.* (1999) compared daily activities of children from four cities, in Greensborough (North Carolina), Suwon (Korea), Obninsk (Russia) and Tartu (Estonia). They examined activity categories of play, lessons, (including both formal and informal instruction), work and conversation. Play was the most common activity in all four cities, but Korean children spent the greatest time playing and Russian children the least. Russian and Estonian children spent more time in lessons and work than Korean and American children and Korean children spent less time in conversation than children in the other three cities. There were also systematic differences between middle-class and working-class children in all four cities. Middle-class children spent more time in lessons and conversation whereas children from working class families spent more time playing.

The researchers also explored connections between parental values and their children's activities (Tudge *et al.* 1999). Parents' values were assessed by asking them to choose from a list of 13 values the three they ranked highest and the three they ranked lowest. From these six, parents then chose the one they valued most and the one they valued least. Of the 13 value statements, five related to self-direction (e.g. 'have self-control'), four to conformity (e.g. 'obey their parents well') and four to social and other aspects of development (e.g. 'gets along well with other children'). Parents' values were quite similar in the four cities, but middle-class parents were more likely than working-class parents to value self-direction in their children. Parents' beliefs about child rearing were also assessed by a questionnaire, which included beliefs about spoiling the child, beliefs about freedom of the child in and around the home and beliefs regarding discipline and control. Parents held beliefs about child rearing that were consistent with the value they placed on self-direction and there was evidence that middle-class children were more likely to engage in activities that would help them to become independent and self-reliant once they entered school. This study demonstrates associations between parental values and beliefs about child rearing and the activities in which young children participate. These values and beliefs vary from one culture to another and also within a given culture.

Parental values and beliefs may also influence parents' pedagogic strategies and their interactions with children. In one of a very small number of longitudinal studies, Greenfield (1998) investigated how cultural change influences parental values and pedagogic interactions in a Mexican village. She reported on a follow-up study of Zinacanteco weavers she observed 10 years earlier in her research of weaving apprenticeship (Greenfield 1984). In her original research, Greenfield described how young girls in the villages were taught to weave, usually by a female relative. Adults were very directive in their teaching, and the girls were prevented from making many errors through a combination of scaffolding and modelling. At the time, Greenfield attributed this to the economic importance of the activity for the Mayan community. Ten years later, she returned to the same community, where the girls had grown up and become mothers and now had daughters of their own who were learning to weave. Her observations revealed that the methods of informal education had changed (Greenfield 1998). The mothers were busy and provided little direct scaffolding and modelling, sometimes delegating the teaching to an older sibling. The young girls were learning by themselves through trial and error or discovery learning. This change in learning process accompanied extensive social change, as the community was more involved in commercial transport businesses and had more links with the city. Although some traditional weaving patterns were produced, many new patterns were being created. Woven artefacts were made of cheaper, commercially produced thread, so mistakes were less expensive and errorless learning was less essential. These changes in weaving apprenticeship were particularly evident in families involved in commercial activity. This research demonstrates that although girls still participated in the activity of weaving, the nature of their interactions with their parents during the activity was altered. Parents' involvement in the wider economic context influenced their values and concerns about error free production and this affected pedagogic interactions with children. Greenfield (1998) points to the importance of considering the mechanisms of learning and apprenticeships as adaptations to particular socio-historical circumstances and therefore subject to variation over time and place.

Further research is needed to confirm the findings of the examples given above and to explore links between values, beliefs, activity and interaction in more detail. Moreover, an important question is whether children's learning is affected in important ways by the activities they engage in and the nature of interactions during these activities. Evidence indicates that educational experiences at home are related to children's attainment in infant school (Tizard *et al.* 1988) and in junior school (Mortimore *et al.* 1988). Children make better progress in reading if they have greater experience of books with their parents reading a variety of books to them and not simply talking about the pictures (Tizard *et al.* 1988). Evidence from a longitudinal study following children from age three to seven years indicates that home learning activities have an impact on their attainment and development (Sylva *et al.* 2004; Melhuish *et al.* 2001). The researchers developed a measure of 'home learning environment' to describe activities in the home that relate to school learning. Parents were asked to report activities such as reading with the child, painting and drawing, library visits, playing with letters, numbers and shapes, teaching songs and nursery rhymes, teaching the alphabet and numbers, taking children on visits and arranging for them to play with other children at home. They found that children who engaged to a greater extent in these activities had higher cognitive development scores, were more co-operative, sociable and confident and engaged in less antisocial behaviour. Parents who were more affluent and educated generally provided a more positive home learning environment for their children. However, there were exceptions and some parents who had limited education and were in low status occupations provided a positive learning environment whereas some parents in high status occupations did not. The home learning environment was only moderately associated with parents' occupational and educational level. It was more strongly associated with children's intellectual and social development, leading the authors to conclude that 'what parents do with their children is more important than who parents are' (Sylva *et al.* 2004: 2). Some children succeed in school despite living in what seem to be difficult material circumstances. It is the kinds of activity that take place at home and the discussions parents have with children that influence children's learning.

Home discussion continues to make an important contribution to school learning as children move through the primary and secondary phases of education. A study of 12–13-year-old students found that home discussions about school activities had a stronger effect on children's achievement than home supervision, such as monitoring the child's homework and out-of-school activities (Sui Chi and Willms 1996). This study controlled statistically for other factors such as family background and socio-economic status, but did not include a measure of students' prior achievement. Other findings from this study include gender effects, with girls engaging in more home discussion than boys. Children with behavioural difficulties engaged in less home discussion and there were also differences between ethnic groups, with Asian and Pacific Island families engaged less than white families.

During adolescence, home discussion conveys parents' hopes and expectations for their child's continuing education and future careers. Parental aspirations have a direct influence on 12–13-year-old student achievement and also an indirect influence through parental involvement in discussions with their children (Singh *et al.* 1995). When the researchers factored out social class in their analysis, parental aspirations had the largest impact on student achievement.

A limitation of these two studies on the effects of home discussion is that they are cross-sectional and do not take account of children's prior achievement. They rely on statistical methods, such as regression analysis, to establish effects and this means that other longitudinal studies, which collect information on the same students over the course of several years will be needed to confirm causal relationships. Longitudinal studies are also required to ascertain whether there are reciprocal relationships, for example parents' aspirations for their children might be affected by information on their progress such as school reports and grades, and progress at school might also be influenced by parental aspirations.

Taken together, the research suggests that the activities children engage in at home and the discussions they have with their parents provide important sites for learning. Parents support their children's intellectual development and they influence motivation to learn through their hopes and aspirations. A review of research by Desforges and Abouchaar (2003) concluded that the involvement of parents at home has strong effects on children's achievement and aspirations. For students in the early years and primary phase of education, parents provide a supportive home environment in which children are encouraged to acquire school-related skills, a sense of self-worth and a positive motivational orientation towards education. During adolescence, parents have less influence on their children's achievement but they retain a significant influence on their aspirations. Children's opportunities to learn at home are mediated through activities in the home and discussion in families. Parents also facilitate older children's participation in a range of activities out of school.

Pedagogic culture

Cultural research and cross-cultural studies, such as those above, draw attention to connections between cultural settings and children's participation in activities. They demonstrate that adults' beliefs and values influence the nature of children's participation. This section turns to educational contexts and how they influence children's participation and learning. Studies of teachers' mediation of the curriculum suggest that their beliefs and values also have an impact on the nature of activities and interactions undertaken.

Research by Blay (2000; Blay and Ireson in preparation) illustrates in a detailed way how teachers' pedagogic beliefs affect the design of learning activities, which in turn influences children's participation and interactions. Blay (2000) observed a cooking activity arranged by four teachers of young children in nursery classes. Cooking was one of the activities normally undertaken in these classes and teachers were asked to design and carry out the activity in the usual way. The researcher observed and recorded the activity and also interviewed the adults to obtain information on their reasons for designing the activity in the way they did and their expectations concerning children's involvement. In one nursery school, two teachers arranged baking activities in their classes, one choosing to bake biscuits and the other cakes. In another nursery school, the activities chosen were cold food preparation, with one class making sandwiches, whereas the other made fruit salad. When asked about these decisions the teachers who selected cold food preparation revealed that they were concerned to maintain their normal pedagogic practice and to take a facilitative role, as opposed to a directive role, in children's learning. For this reason, they offered a selection of breads and fillings for sandwiches, or a selection of fruit for fruit salad so that the children could chose what to make. In this way, teachers' beliefs about appropriate pedagogy transformed an activity that was superficially the same, i.e. cooking, into two different designs, one with a high level of adult regulation and one in which children had greater control. Observations revealed that the adults were directive in the baking activities, taking the children through weighing and mixing ingredients step by step, whereas in the sandwich making there was much less direction and more discussion of the children's choice of different types of breads and fillings and more social conversation. Blay characterized the children as novices in the baking activity as they followed the teacher's instructions and worked at the pace of the group, whereas in the sandwich making, they were designers who selected ingredients and worked at their own pace. Thus, the teachers' pedagogic beliefs influenced the learning activity, children's role in the activity and the nature of interactions in the two different settings.

A second illustration of the link between teachers' pedagogic beliefs and their practices is drawn from the individual teaching of reading. This provides an interesting context in which to study the impact of differing pedagogies on teachers' structuring of learning activities. The reason for this is that there are conflicting views about methods for teaching children to read, which stem from different theories of reading development. In brief, some theories of reading development, sometimes characterized as 'bottom-up' approaches, are based on a logical progression, starting with individual letters and letter sounds before moving to simple, regular words and then combining words and sentences, and finally reading longer texts.

Psycholinguistic theories, on the other hand, encourage a 'top-down' approach to reading development in which reading is seen as a search for meaning. When young learners encounter a word they are unable to read, they are encouraged to think of the meaning of the phrase or sentence and to suggest words that might be reasonable in that context. From an early stage, individual letter sounds and words are learned in the context of reading longer texts. These two theories tend to be associated with different approaches to learning, the bottom-up theory being more behavioural and the top-down approach being more constructivist. In this context, the behavioural approach is taken to mean that the teacher presents information, such as letter sounds, for the learner to memorize and supports learning through feedback and praise. The constructivist approach assumes that learning is a constructive process and that learners strive to make meaning (Stanovich 1994).

In English primary schools, children who do not make satisfactory progress in reading may be offered individual assistance. Tutors who provide this individual assistance offer a variety of forms of support. Some offer very structured, phonic-based programmes, while others offer programmes incorporating a mixture of phonics and book reading. One well-established training programme offered in England is the Reading Recovery programme (Clay 1985; Clay and Cazden 1990). This programme is based on the principle that children utilize several strategies when decoding texts and these strategies should be taught in the context of reading real books. A second well-established programme, known as the Literacy Programme, is based on a linguistic analysis of the English language, and emphasizes the teaching of phonics in an ordered sequence, starting with letter sounds before moving on to blending, then word reading and spelling, then sentences and finally sentences in texts. The teaching techniques are multi-sensory and designed to ensure that the pupil achieves automaticity of response, thereby reducing the load on memory (e.g. Hickey 1977; Hornsby and Shear 1993). Some teachers follow a variety of other courses in literacy development, which combine features and programs.

A small number of teachers were interviewed about their approach to the teaching of reading and were then observed as they worked with individual children (Ireson 2000). When speaking about their approach to the teaching of reading, teachers described activities they incorporated in lessons and they also spoke about the wider curriculum structure of reading. In the Literacy Programme, this was a sequence of teaching points that teachers worked through in strict order, starting with individual letter sounds, then moving on to combinations of letters, then words. Reading Recovery was described in terms of a set of activities that were included in each session. These were reading a familiar text, making and breaking words (using magnetic letters), writing letters and words on a white board, and writing a short story, which was then cut up by the teacher and reassembled and read aloud by the child. A third approach, reported by teachers in a literacy support service, combined elements of Literacy Programme and Reading Recovery into a framework that allowed more scope for adjustment. This started with work on sounds of a small number of consonants, followed by single vowel and consonant-vowel-consonant words that could be made up from the letters already learned. After this, children moved on to sight words, further work on phonics, and book reading.

Observations of teaching sessions were consistent with the teachers' descriptions of their approach. The Literacy Programme teachers spent most of the session doing work on letters and words, and the children's task was to memorize. Reading Recovery sessions included work on letters and words and also on the children's use of strategies, such as self-correcting, reading back or looking at the picture in a book to help work out a word. Children were encouraged to deploy a range of strategies as well as to memorize. These programmes direct children's attention to different aspects of the task of learning to read. The Reading Recovery programme encouraged children's awareness and use of strategies to decode words and understand texts, whereas the Literacy Programme programme emphasized memorization of letter-sound correspondences.

This small-scale study shows how training in contrasting literacy programmes inducts teachers into specific practices that later impact on children's learning experiences. Teachers who had been trained in Reading Recovery or the Literacy Programme incorporated activities that were based on the pedagogic principles of the respective programmes. Ireson (2000) has suggested that these training programmes represent different pedagogic cultures, each of which required extended training to enable teachers to appropriate the cultural tools of the programme and to be inducted into a set of practices, assessments, resources and activities for teaching and learning. Resulting differences in the pedagogic practice adopted by teachers inducted into each programme gave rise to different types of learning experience for the children, all of whom had been identified as making slow progress in learning to read.

This example is given here to draw attention to the way in which pedagogical cultures permeate educational practice in often unnoticed ways. In some respects, the example is unremarkable, as we would expect teachers who have received training in structured literacy programmes to implement them when they work with children making slow progress in reading. Yet it illustrates how teachers who have the same goal of teaching children to read words, make use of different activities to achieve this goal and draw children's attention to different aspects of the learning task.

An influence of teachers' beliefs on their classroom practices is also evident in the teaching of numeracy (Askew *et al.* 1997). Teachers' orientations towards teaching mathematics were characterized as 'connectionist', 'transmission' and 'discovery'. Teachers with a connectionist orientation believed that that most pupils are able to learn mathematics given appropriate teaching. beliefs about what it is to be a numerate pupil included the belief that being numerate involves being both efficient and effective. To illustrate the distinction between efficiency and effectiveness teachers adopting such a perspective might point out that a calculation could be carried out using pencil and paper, or mentally. Both of these methods would be effective, but one might be more efficient than the other for most pupils. Teachers with the connectionist orientation acknowledged that pupils already have mental strategies for calculating and they concentrated on helping pupils to build on these and develop efficient, conceptually based strategies. Misunderstandings were seen as an important part of lessons, as they provide an opportunity to develop understanding. Teachers with a connectionist orientation to teaching also believed that the teaching of mathematics is based on dialogue between teacher and pupils as it is through dialogue that teachers can come to understand pupils' thinking and pupils can gain a better appreciation of mathematical knowledge. These teachers used classroom discussions to introduce links between different representations and meanings. They appear to have a conception of the learner as thinker, in Bruner's categorization, outlined above (Bruner 1996).

Transmission-oriented teachers believed that students should learn a collection of procedures or routines for different kinds of calculation.

In Bruner's terms, they seem to have a view of learners benefiting from didactic exposure. These teachers were less concerned to find out what their pupils already knew, as they did not see the strategies that pupils developed themselves as a basis from which to build more efficient methods. They also tended to believe that pupils varied in ability, so pupils' misunderstandings were seen as requiring remediation in the form of more practice in using the correct method. Teachers adopting this perspective believed that effective teaching consisted of clear explanations and question-and-answer sessions to check that learning had taken place.

Teachers with discovery beliefs were less concerned with teaching procedures and routines and more concerned to give pupils an opportunity to create their own methods. They believed that individual activity was the basis for developing numeracy and that pupils needed to be ready to learn mathematical ideas. Their teaching tended to be based on practical activities that allowed pupils to discover methods for themselves.

The authors acknowledged that the three orientations represent ideal forms and teachers did not always fit neatly into one category. There were commonalities between the classroom practices of teachers with all three orientations. Nevertheless, this study demonstrates clear links between teachers' beliefs and their classroom practice.

On a wider cultural level, research also demonstrates that different activities can be employed to achieve similar learning goals (Alexander 2000; Stigler 1984). Alexander (2000) gives an example of mathematics teaching in Moscow and Michigan where the goal was to translate a real-life arithmetic problem into a numerical calculation. Although the goal was the same, the activity differed in the two schools. In the Moscow school, pupils were expected to recognize which numeric operations were needed and to apply them to the problem, working alone, before a collective process of checking solutions during which pupils were called to the board to discuss their solutions. In the Michigan school, pupils were invited to discuss possible solutions and invent different ways of calculating before sharing their explanations with the rest of the class. All solutions that produced a correct answer were considered to be acceptable. The learning goal, or task, in both cases was the same, to translate a problem into a numerical calculation, but different pedagogic practices transformed the activity so that students in the two schools were exposed to different learning activities. These activities transmit different messages to students about the status of different solution methods. In the Michigan school, students' own solutions were equally acceptable, whereas in the Moscow school the students were expected to know which methods to apply and why some were better than others.

These examples provide clear illustrations of variations in classroom practice across cultures and also demonstrate that there are variations within a given culture. Cultural variations are to be expected and stem from traditions and customary practice in different education systems. Variations within a culture raise questions about factors affecting different practices; the extent to which different practices are tailored to meet learners' needs and the extent to which they affect learning. In the case of literacy teaching, children were offered whichever programme was available in their area. So children in a school offering Reading Recovery had a different experience from children in schools where other programmes were available. Provision did not seem to be determined by the children's specific needs but by the arrangements in place in the different schools (Ireson 2000). This is a common feature of literacy programmes in schools, classrooms and other settings. Programmes are set up and resourced, and teachers adapt them as they see fit to meet the needs of individual children. Although this is understandable from the point of service providers, it suggests that children may not receive provision that is specifically tailored to their individual needs.

Supporting and structuring learning activities

As indicated above, teachers' beliefs and values mediate between cultures and classrooms and thus form links between cultural context and young people's learning experiences. In addition, the organizational context and setting in a school or college supports and structures learning activities. Findings from a study undertaken in an English secondary school suggest some aspects of the setting that may provide this support.

A programme reported by Marriott (1997) was designed to assist students who entered a secondary school with low levels of literacy. Groups of students were taken out of their regular classes and worked on the programme with a teacher. The organizational context and setting of the programme was designed to provide resources to support learning through activities to achieve a series of learning goals. Programme goals for language and literacy learning included addressing pupils' individual needs in relation to reading, particularly reading for meaning; improving decoding skills; and developing spoken as well as written language. These were broken down into sub-goals, and a set of activities developed for each component part. This meant that much expertise was designed into and distributed among the resources supporting the programme (Pea 1993). By distributing expertise into the design of resources in this way, a teacher was able to work effectively with a group of pupils, assessing their individual needs and selecting appropriate activities to extend their capabilities.

In addition to language and literacy goals, the programme set out organizational goals for students, which included developing independent learning, organizational skills, and self-regulation. Although students were in a group setting, they each had their own work and the teacher interacted with each one individually within the group. To enable the teacher to work effectively with individual learners, pupils were encouraged to develop organizational skills such as keeping their work in order, collecting materials they needed and checking their own work, discussing it with a teacher and correcting it before going on to the next task. The programme enabled them to work out what they should be doing next, to see each task in the context of the whole programme and to monitor their progress.

The programme also set out goals for student motivation, recognizing that young people with low achievement in literacy often struggle through primary school and enter the secondary phase lacking confidence in their ability to learn. These difficulties may sometimes lead students to protect their sense of self-worth through inappropriate classroom behaviour or disengaging with school (Covington 1992). For this reason, the programme goals included improving pupils' self-confidence, self-esteem and motivation. Certain activities were designed to enhance motivation, such as listening to tape recorded stories and computer-based activities. Merits for effort and good work were awarded at the end of each lesson and fun activities such as model making were included at the end of each section of work. In addition, pupils were given some choice and control over the order in which they completed tasks.

Another key element of the teaching context was the pedagogic relationship, which had been established at the beginning of the programme, and was constantly reinforced and monitored during the observed teacher–pupil interactions. The framework for this relationship was strongly rooted in the ethos of the department and the school as stated in the school policy on special educational needs and in the views expressed by teachers involved in the programme. It encompassed appropriate areas of negotiation, levels of task engagement, ways of communicating with each other and the availability of teacher support (Marriott 1997).

The design of the programme and the organization of resources were an integral part of the learning activities, and can not be understood fully in isolation from the cultural setting in which they took place. The structuring of this setting started with the recognition that effective teaching of literacy to students in secondary school involves more than imparting knowledge and skills and that learner self-regulation and motivation also require support. Structuring continued through the pedagogic relationship established by the teachers on a daily basis, who worked to gain the learners' trust through a genuine interest in supporting their learning on an ongoing basis (Ireson 2001). The setting afforded particular ways of working that supported affective as well as cognitive aspects of learning. In this environment, students developed a sense of trust that teachers would support their learning.

This example illustrates how the organizational setting supports learning activities. The setting provides material resources and tools for learning, which in this case encouraged students to work independently on activities that extended their learning. Importantly, the setting is also imbued with values about learners and learning that permeate the ethos of the classroom and the pedagogic relationship.

Talking and thinking together

The examples given above illustrate how economic concerns, pedagogical beliefs and educational settings influence the organization and management of learning activities. These activities form an important link between teachers' and parents' pedagogic beliefs and young people's learning experiences, as they provide a vehicle for interactions between adults and young people. Activities have an influence on the nature of interactions between those involved, as will be illustrated below, but they do not do this in a deterministic way. To develop a way of thinking about this indeterminacy, it can be useful to draw on the idea of 'affordance' as developed by Norman (1988) who built on Gibson's earlier work on the ecology of perception (Gibson 1966; 1986). An affordance refers to the properties of an object that constrain how it might be used. These properties may be actual, or as perceived by the user. Norman (1988) wrote about everyday things such as door handles and washing machines and how the design of these objects invites us to use them in particular ways. For example, the design of a door knob does not prevent us from using it in other ways, but it makes it more likely that we will perform a turning action. Object design affects ease of use, with some objects being designed in ways that do not provide enough clues to the specific operations we need to make. Even someone with an engineering degree might have difficulty operating a microwave oven due to the poor design. Lack of visibility makes many computer control devices, such as microwave ovens and washing machines, difficult to use so people tend to learn to use one or two settings and ignore the rest. Likewise, the design of a learning activity invites certain interactions, making them more likely to occur. For example, facing a large number of students in a lecture theatre tends to encourage a formal presentation, whereas a group brainstorming activity encourages a facilitator to invite all members of the group to offer their ideas. Creative lecturers and teachers find ways to encourage student contributions in large groups and a brainstorming activity may elicit few contributions, so the activities do not determine interactions in a precise manner, but they do make some forms of interaction more likely.

The design of learning activities and the setting in which they occur sets up a context, or 'activity setting' (Tharp and Gallimore 1988) in which adults and children engage with and talk about specific subject matter. In educational settings, talk is often a dominant mode of interaction and has become the focus of much research in recent years. In classrooms, it is very common for teachers to ask 'known answer' questions, which invite children to supply the correct answer. The teacher then gives an evaluation of the answer as right or wrong, either in a direct form such as 'yes, that's right' or in a more indirect way. This sequence is referred to as 'initiation–reply–evaluation' or IRE (Edwards and Mercer 1987). The teacher initiates the interaction (I) with a test question, which predicts a pupil response (R) that supplies the known information. Typically teachers then evaluate (E) the pupil's answer in terms of whether it is correct or not. For example, the teacher might ask 'What is the capital of Romania?', inviting a known response (R) 'Bucharest', which is followed by the teacher's evaluation (E) 'Yes, that's right' (Mehan 1985; Mercer 1995). This specific pattern of interaction is very common in classrooms but relatively uncommon in life outside school.

To illustrate this point, in an everyday setting we might go up to someone in the street and ask them if they could tell us the time. Suppose that, when they told us the time, we replied 'that's right'. They would probably look very surprised, as they would be expecting a more usual response to the provision of requested information, such as 'thank you'. In everyday conversations, we usually request information when we are in a state of ignorance, not when we know the answer.

Many learning activities in classrooms place the teacher in a position of authority and thus encourage the IRE form of interaction. It has been found in English primary schools (Alexander 2000; Edwards and Mercer 1987; Mercer 1995; Mroz *et al.* 2000) and early years' settings (Hughes and Westgate 1997). It has also been reported in primary classrooms in the USA, Russia, India and France (Alexander 2000) and is evident in secondary English language lessons in the USA (Gutierrez 1994; Nystrand 1997). Teachers frequently use questions to check on children's current knowledge and the IRE is well suited to this purpose.

The third turn is not always an evaluation of the pupil's response and can be used in other ways, such as giving hints or prompts or other types of feedback. As an acknowledgment of this wider interpretation, the pattern is referred to as IRF or initiation-reply-feedback (Mehan 1985; Mercer 1995). A teacher or parent might also extend a child's response, adding information or specialized vocabulary (Wells 1993), or they may repeat or re-formulate to enlarge the students' response (Cazden 2001; O'Connor and Michaels 1996). A high level evaluation might involve elaboration of important points made by students or exploration of a new line of thought initiated by them (Nystrand 1997).

In the IRE format encountered in classrooms, initiation frequently takes the form of a question. Questions that have received most attention are 'known answer' or closed questions. In contrast, open-ended questions, such as a question about what happened at the weekend, invite the respondent to select information to share with the speaker. Open questioning is generated through the use of particular linguistic forms. These include language that suggests uncertainty or invites a contribution, rather than calling for a specific answer.

Open-ended questions take many different forms such as 'what do you think might happen next?', 'what could we do?', 'how could we work this out?'. Some of these questions invite the child to negotiate rather to provide a correct answer and there is evidence that children produce longer and more complex responses to such questions (Nassaji and Wells 2000). Also, when a teacher asks a question that is a genuine request for information, in the sense that the teacher does not know the answer, the child is more likely to contribute an idea or opinion and the third turn is less likely to take the form of an evaluation (Hughes and Westgate 1997). For example, when a teacher asks a child, 'What did you do at the weekend?' there is a genuine desire for the child to supply information that is unknown to the teacher.

There appears to be a relationship between oral language activities and patterns of classroom dialogue. Radford, Ireson and Mahon (2006) examined forms of initiation in oral language activities and found that teachers were more likely to use open enquiries during a creative writing activity and a speaking book activity than during circle time. Open enquiries are especially likely to occur when the teacher invites children to draw on their own experiences.

As noted above, activities allow scope for interpretation, and while some adults use open-ended, creative activities as an opportunity to engage in discussions, others may not do so (Ireson and Blay 1999). Skilfully managed discussions help to extend young children's language and understanding. 'Sustained shared thinking occurs when a two or more individuals work together in an intellectual way to solve a problem, clarify a concept, evaluate an activity, extend a narrative, etc.' (Sylva *et al.* 2004: 5.). Sustained shared thinking takes place through dialogue that develops and extends thinking and occurs more commonly when children interact one-on-one with an adult or with a single peer partner and during focused group work. In these situations, adults and children are able to contribute to the thinking process and can build on each other's contributions.

In primary schools, exploratory talk, which bears some similarities with sustained shared thinking, is a form of dialogue that may be used by children working together and discussing ideas (Barnes and Todd 1977; Mercer 1995; 2002). Mercer (2002) defines exploratory talk as 'that in which partners engage critically but constructively with each other's ideas' (2002: 150). This form of talk involves following ground rules that help speakers to share knowledge, evaluate evidence and solve problems as partners. It enables groups to work effectively together but as exploratory talk does not always happen naturally when children are asked to work in groups, 'Talk Lessons' were devised to help develop skills in using exploratory talk. The following extracts illustrate differences in children's talk before and after these lessons. The children are working on puzzles from the Raven's Matrices, which require them to complete a series of figures by selecting from several options provided. Each puzzle contains nine items displayed in three rows with one missing item.

Extract 1. Graham, Suzie and Tess doing a test item before the Talk Lessons

TESS: It's that.
TESS: It's that, 2
GRAHAM: It's 2.
TESS: 2 is there.
GRAHAM: It's 2.
TESS: 2 is there.
GRAHAM: What number do you want then?
TESS: It's that because there ain't two of them.
GRAHAM: It's number 2, look one, two.
TESS: I can count, are we all in agree on it? (*Suzie rings number 2 – an incorrect choice – on the answer sheet.*)
SUZIE: No.
GRAHAM: Oh, after she's circled it!

In this extract, Tess offers a good reason for her view (referring correctly to the number of items in a figure) but Graham ignores her and the group agrees on the wrong answer. Tess appears to give up and Suzie is very quiet but is clearly thinking about the solution and indicates her disagreement after circling number 2 on the answer sheet. The group is not working collaboratively.

Extract 2. Graham, Suzie and Tess doing a test item after the Talk Lessons

SUZIE: D9 now, that's a bit complicated it's got to be.
GRAHAM: A line like that, a line like that and it ain't got on a line with that.
TESS: It's got to be that one.
GRAHAM: It's got to be that don't you think? Because look all the rest have got a line like that and like that, I think it's going to be that because ...
TESS: I think it's number 6.
SUZIE: No I think it's number 1.
GRAHAM: Wait no, we've got number 6, wait stop, do you agree that it's number 1? Because look that one there is blank, that one there has got them, that one there has to be number 1, because that is the one like that. Yes. Do you agree? [Tess nods in agreement]
SUZIE: D9 number 1. (*She writes '1', which is the correct answer.*)

(Mercer 2002: 149–50)

In this second extract, Tess disagrees with Graham but Suzie agrees that number 1 is the correct choice. This time, Graham gives a clear explanation of why he thinks number 1 is the correct choice and Tess then agrees. All the children are involved in the discussion and they use language more effectively to express their opinions and persuade others that their explanation is correct.

Exploratory talk can be beneficial when a group of children undertake problem-solving tasks or discuss their understanding of a phenomenon. In these situations it is useful for others in the group to hear explanations and justification for a particular point of view as this reveals thinking processes and reasoning, which can then be debated. Increased use of exploratory talk is associated with better problem solving (Wegerif *et al.* 1999).

Other forms of talk noted above have a positive impact on children's educational progress. Children make better progress in preschools where members of staff encourage sustained shared thinking and employ open-ended questioning that does not constrain children's answers and allows them to make a genuine contribution (Sylva *et al.* 2004). These positive features of interactions in preschool settings are also found in the home (Tizard and Hughes 1984). In these kinds of interactions adults display a genuine interest in children's contribution and treat them as conversational partners. This conveys a message that the child's contribution is valued and at the same time encourages the child's use of language. Similarly 'dialogic teaching' enables children to articulate their reasoning and opens up opportunities for reflection on different points of view (Alexander 2000; 2004). In this sense, it is a vehicle for developing children's thinking and reasoning about problems in the classroom that simultaneously encourages children's awareness of their own cognitive processes and those of others, thus contributing to the development of meta-cognitive processes.

Ability grouping

A final example illustrates how school organization influences the educational experiences of students, which may in turn affect their educational achievement. Ability grouping is an aspect of school organization that has the potential to influence student learning and teachers, parents and policy makers commonly view grouping by ability in a positive light, as it appears to offer a logical way to enable teachers to match work to learners' needs. One means of grouping by ability is through selection for entry to secondary schools and in some parts of the UK children are required to pass the 11-plus examination in order to gain entry to grammar schools. Ability grouping may also be undertaken within schools, where students may be grouped in a variety of ways such as streaming, setting, mixed ability and within class grouping. Streaming is the most rigid form of grouping, as a measure of general ability is used to place students into a class, which is then kept together for most subjects. Setting (regrouping) is a more flexible system, as pupils are grouped on the basis of their attainment in a particular curriculum subject. Schools decide which subjects will be taught in sets, and in which year group setting will be introduced. Students may also be grouped by ability within the class and this form of organization is common in primary schools. Within class groupings are organized by the class teacher who may maintain stable groupings or regroup for different curriculum subjects.

Some key questions are whether ability grouping in schools affects educational outcomes for students and if so, how are these effects mediated? A research programme in non-selective English secondary schools examined the effects of ability grouping on attainment and other outcomes and the factors that might mediate these effects. An additional aim of the research was to understand links between the aims, ethos and management of the school, teachers' attitudes and classroom practices and students' views. It was designed to compare schools employing minimal, moderate and high levels of setting (regrouping) (Ireson and Hallam 2001).

Head teachers, curriculum managers and heads of department supplied information about the school's aims and ability grouping practices. For some, there was a very clear link between these. For example, the head teacher of a school that grouped pupils by ability in every subject said:

> Well, if you look at the aims 'to prepare pupils for their future lives' … that's the first aim of the school … in real life people tend to get put together in ability groupings according to the task … therefore the school reflects that.

In contrast, the head of a mixed-ability school, said:

> The aims of the school start off by saying that we will demonstrate that all members of the school community are of equal value … I think all ability is vital to this … we can't demonstrate that people of equal value if we start to separate them out and say you are better than somebody else or you are worse.
>
> (Ireson and Hallam 2001: 156)

Although these examples illustrate close links between the school's aims and their grouping practices, in other schools such links were not as strong. Some head teachers described a 'mixed philosophy' and they supported a variety of grouping practices in different subject departments. They encouraged each department to make decisions about grouping practices on the basis of what worked best in their subject and for particular groups of students.

Head teachers also spoke of external pressures on the school and how these influenced grouping practices. One of the perceived pressures at the time was the publication of a government White Paper that recommended setting in secondary schools, unless the school could demonstrate that it was getting 'better than expected results through different approach' (DfEE 1997: 38). Also, league tables showing the results of Key Stage tests and national examinations were published in the national press thus raising awareness of the schools' performance in relation to other schools in the vicinity. Additional pressure came from the competitive environment created by the education market, which meant that schools needed to attract a sufficient number of students in order to maintain their funding. Moreover, in order to maintain the school's standing within the local community, some head teachers felt that their school needed to attract students who would perform well.

The structure of the GCSE examination was an additional pressure to group by ability, with about a quarter of head teachers in the sample mentioning tiered examination papers in mathematics and science. Tiered papers restrict the grades that can be obtained by pupils entered for each tier, and it was seen to be problematic to teach a class of students who would be taking different papers. Among the 45 schools taking part in the study, there were differences in the extent to which they were affected by external pressures for ability grouping with schools experiencing greater competition for students if they were in close proximity to one another. The impact of external factors on the extent of ability grouping in schools was also mediated by school ethos and the values of those who worked in the school. Some head teachers actively embraced setting, some actively resisted it, and others used a combination of setting and mixed-ability grouping.

Within schools, heads of department and subject teachers also mediated the implementation of ability grouping. An interesting comparison was made of teachers' reports of their classroom practices with mixed-ability classes and sets, which suggests that teachers' expectations of students relate to the ability composition of the class (Hallam and Ireson 2005). As compared with mixed-ability classes, when pupils were in sets teachers reported that there was greater differentiation of the curriculum. With sets, teachers consistently covered different topics with pupils of different ability whereas in mixed-ability classes pupils of all abilities worked on the same topics at the same time. Teachers also set less homework for students in low-ability groups, whereas in mixed-ability classes the same amount of homework was usually set for all students.

Over 500 teachers completed questionnaires on the approaches they adopted when teaching students in mixed-ability classes and in sets. These teachers had experience of teaching both types of class and completed the same questionnaire items twice, once with reference to their teaching of mixed-ability classes, and once with reference to their teaching of sets. Where pupils were grouped by ability, teachers expected a faster pace of work and they covered topics in greater depth with the more able groups. With lower groups, they covered fewer topics and there were some activities that they would not undertake. In low sets, there was more repetition and rehearsal, structured work, practical activities and question-and-answer sessions. Students in higher sets were allowed more opportunities for discussion, and they were expected to produce more analytical thought (Hallam and Ireson 2005). These findings indicate that the effects of ability grouping are mediated through the activities that teachers provide for students in the classroom. Ability grouping is accompanied by greater differentiation of curriculum content and activities between the groups whereas in the mixed-ability environment, curriculum and activities are more similar for all students. A note of caution is in order here as these findings are based on teachers' self-reports, which may not be an accurate reflection of their actual practice in the classroom. Ideally, these reports should be corroborated with observations in classrooms, but unfortunately this was not possible within the scope of the project.

Observational studies undertaken in US and UK schools with a variety of structured ability grouping patterns tend to support these findings. Several studies and reviews of the literature show that the quality of instruction and the activities undertaken differ in high-, middle-, and low-ability groups (Oakes 1985; Gamoran and Berends 1987). In high-ability groups, pupils are given more independence and choice, there are opportunities for discussion and pupils are allowed to take responsibility for their work. In low-ability groups, instruction tends to be conceptually simplified and proceeds more slowly, there is more structured written work, which can leave work fragmented. From her observations of UK secondary mathematics classrooms, Boaler (1997a; 1997b) reported that teaching in top sets is characterized by a fast pace, a sense of urgency and competition, which reflects teachers' expectations of top-set students. Similarly Hacker and Rowe (1993) found that higher ability groups were set more analytical thinking tasks. There appears to be some agreement between the teacher self-reports and these observational studies, which suggest that teacher reports may be valid reflections of their classroom practice. It seems, therefore, that teachers' expectations of students are based on the ability composition of the class. These expectations affect the cognitive demands made on students and the types of activity they are given, thus affecting their opportunities to participate and learn.

It might be argued that teachers are differentiating work to meet the needs of learners in the ability groups. Effective differentiation should help to ensure that all learners are set work that provides them with sufficient challenge to take their learning forward. There may some truth in this argument yet it is not the whole story, as an analysis of GCSE results reveals that students' achievement is affected by the ability group they are in. When the achievement of students in top, middle and low sets were compared, this revealed that students who had achieved the same levels of attainment in the Key Stage 3 tests taken two years earlier were widely dispersed among the different ability groups. In all schools there was a spread of attainment in a given set and considerable overlap between sets. For example in one school with 12 sets for English, all 12 contained students who achieved level 5 in the Key Stage 3 tests. The question then is whether this dispersal relates to achievement in the GCSE examinations. Figure 6.1 displays the average GCSE results for mathematics for students in top, middle and low sets, according to the Key Stage 3 test results. It shows that students with the same Key Stage 3 levels achieved higher grades if they were in a higher set. This effect was most apparent for students who had achieved average levels in the Key Stage 3 tests. Compared with students in low sets, students who were at level 4 in the Key Stage 3 tests gained, on average, 1.5 grades in mathematics

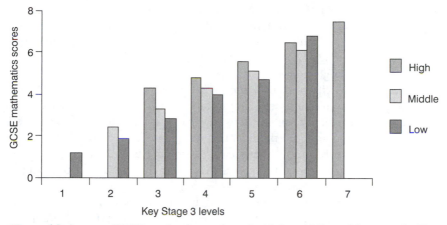

Figure 6.1 Average GCSE grades for students in high, middle and low sets, by Key Stage 3 levels

GCSE if they were in top sets. Students at level 5 gained 0.8 and students at level 6 gained 0.9 of a GCSE grade.

Patterns were similar in English and science. In English, students at levels 5 and 6 gained 0.8 and 0.9 of a GCSE grade respectively if they were in a top set compared to a low set. In science, gains for top-set students were smaller than in the other subjects. Students at levels 4 and 5 gained most, with differences between top and low sets amounting to 0.7 and 0.8 of a GCSE grade respectively (Ireson *et al.* 2005).

These findings demonstrate that values and customary practices in schools have an influence on learners and on their educational achievement. The adoption by schools of different grouping arrangements may be in accordance with explicit values and ethos and may also follow customary practice. Learners are affected by the use of different types of grouping arrangement and these effects are mediated by teachers' values and expectations and their classroom practice, which influence the learning experiences afforded to them. As the effects on achievement and on other educational outcomes are mediated by several factors, it is not surprising to find that the overall effects of ability grouping are relatively small. School organization is a distal factor and as such tends to have smaller effects than proximal factors that affect learners directly, as noted above. Nevertheless the effect for individual students may be great if teachers' classroom practice is such as to affect their learning directly by limiting or extending the opportunity to learn.

Summary

This chapter has used evidence from a variety of cultural and pedagogic settings to demonstrate connections between cultural contexts, learners' participation in activities and their interactions with others in those contexts.

It has deliberately drawn on research in homes and schools as a means of exploring similarities and differences between these two arenas in which children learn. Cross-cultural research is helpful in adding a comparative perspective on homes and schools and highlighting linkages that are less evident within a single culture.

Children's participation in educational activities clearly varies widely according to economic and social circumstances and other factors. Researchers have made progress in identifying activities that assist children to make a good start in school and support them as they progress through the educational system. Parents' role in children's early learning has been recognized for some time, and the support they provide for older children and young people is beginning to be more widely acknowledged.

The chapter has highlighted educational beliefs, values, customary practices and pedagogic cultures as mediators between cultural contexts and children's participation and involvement in activities. These factors are evident in the way that parents and teachers cultivate settings and promote activities that provide opportunities for children to learn. In educational settings, activities are usually designed with specific learning goals in mind, yet teachers often have other goals such as fostering student motivation and self-regulation. These goals affect the way that learning activities are organized and managed.

The organization of schools also affords different opportunities for children to learn. Teachers' beliefs and practices tend to be linked to the perceived characteristics of student groups. As a result, students' experiences of learning are affected by their placement in a particular group. The design of pedagogic interactions, which varies in different cultural settings, also affects students' learning experiences. Teachers may be inducted into a set of practices and unaware of alternative ways of designing these interactions.

Activities provide a link between pedagogic culture, educational interactions and student learning. This link is not deterministic, as individuals' beliefs and values, and the design of activities affords a flexible space in which learning is negotiated. Essentially, mediation at any level introduces indeterminacy, as there is scope for negotiation of the goals and means of an activity.

7 Connecting spheres of learning

Young people grow up within family and cultural settings that offer a variety of opportunities to learn. By participating in activities, they develop a range of skills and capabilities that are promoted in particular cultural settings. Participation sets the stage for learning but interactions between participants play an important part in mediating the learner's orientation to learning and the specific skills and capabilities acquired. Individuals also shape the course of their own learning, building their cognitive capabilities and pursuing particular interests.

The brain and nervous system are designed for learning, and have evolved to allow many different kinds of learning to occur. These include learning to ride a bicycle, use physical tools, play games, learn to speak languages, read and write, do mathematical computations and plan complex events. Other animals demonstrate amazing physical skills but human learning is unique in achieving the capacity to use language and other sign systems such as mathematics, and in the ability to teach others, thus passing on knowledge and skills from one generation to another (Tomasello 1999). Humans are also unique in having the capacity to deliberately plan and regulate their learning.

Some learning occurs almost effortlessly as we go about everyday activities in our lives. The brain appears to be particularly good at noticing patterns and regularities in the world around us, even without conscious efforts to pick them out. It also forms associations between events that occur close together in time, and this is especially true for emotional responses, which readily become associated with places and events. These implicit forms of learning are important for survival in the world. Some of them also form the basis of more conscious and deliberate forms of learning.

The uniquely human ability to use written forms of representation, such as language, mathematics and graphics, enables conceptual tools to be handed down from one generation to another. Humans differ from animals in being able to act with mental models and representations of objects, when those objects are not physically present (Arievitch and Haenen 2005; Tomasello 1999). Cultural tools such as reading and mathematics take years to acquire and for most children take a great deal of effort. Typically, it takes around 10 years to develop these skills to a reasonably high level of proficiency. Complex skills such as reading develop gradually in tandem with oral language acquisition, familiarity with books, and knowledge of correspondence between letters and the sounds they represent.

Practice is clearly an important element in the acquisition of all forms of skill and expertise. It is through practice that skills become automatized and fluent in their execution, which means they can be performed with fewer mental resources, thus freeing up capacity for new learning. Education systems are designed to ensure that students undertake an amount of practice necessary to reach proficiency in culturally valued activities, such as reading and mathematics. Each of these domains has been developed through cultural practices handed down from one generation to the next, with each generation adding to the stock of knowledge and understanding. The acquisition of these domains thus involves learning a large set of component skills and knowledge that must be acquired for proficient performance. It is hardly surprising, therefore, that it takes several years to reach proficiency.

Individuals who go on to reach high levels of expertise generally engage in additional practice of their own volition. Many of them develop techniques for deliberate practice, whereby they focus on and improve specific aspects of a skill, using strategies for self-regulation. This element of self-regulation and application is evident in many biographic accounts of the lives of successful individuals. Some may have had specific aptitudes that facilitated learning, especially in the early stages, but researchers have found it difficult to identify these.

Typical learners, not just those who achieve outstanding success, employ a wide range of strategies to acquire knowledge and skills, develop understanding, plan and solve problems and accomplish tasks set in the classroom. Cognitive and meta-cognitive strategies for learning and remembering are closely linked to a learner's growing stock of knowledge. These strategies tend to emerge in tandem with increasing knowledge and may appear spontaneously. More successful learners deploy a variety of self-regulatory strategies before, during and after completing tasks (Pintrich 2000; Zimmerman 1998). They tend to be aware of their own preferences and arrange environments that are conducive to learning. They set goals during the preparatory phase of a task, use appropriate strategies, monitor progress and evaluate both their performance and their use of self-regulatory strategies.

Family nurturing of learning in the early years can give children a head start on the trajectory towards successful achievement. Early learning environments can have profound effects on children's achievements and parents who value and enjoy academic, musical or sporting accomplishments tend to devote time and effort in activities that encourage and support these. Children are then initially introduced to these activities as a natural part of everyday life at home. Dedicated attention to children's learning rests on beliefs about the nature of childhood, the role of parents and whether teaching is desirable or necessary, especially in the early years. Parents who invest heavily in their children's learning may offer sustained support well into adulthood. This investment is an indication of the value placed on their children's achievement in a specific domain.

The family environments of individuals who go on to exceptional achievements tend to be extreme in providing support for their children (Bloom 1985; Howe 1990). Parents place considerable value on success and achieving the best one can in life. They often structure the child's life around an activity they themselves enjoy and assume the role of teacher when the child is very young, supervising homework and practice and spending time with the child, giving support and encouragement. This strong sense of the value and importance of achievement stems in part from the individual parents' own valuing of an activity and in part from the cultural value placed on specific accomplishments in a domain such as arts, science, mathematics or sports.

It seems, therefore, that the value of an activity may arise from a number of factors. It may be that parents enjoy an activity themselves and want their children to share their enjoyment, in which case the child then has an early introduction to the activity and also observes parents enjoyment of it, their intrinsic reasons for taking part. Children and young people who develop their own interest and enjoyment, can be said to find intrinsic value in the activity. Other reasons for valuing an activity may be more extrinsic. Accomplishments in sports, music, arts and achievement in school may be seen as means to enable children to have a good, interesting job and a comfortable life style. Parents who work long hours in poorly paid occupations frequently see education as a means for their children to have a better way of life. Education is also valued in its own right as a means of developing the mind.

Cross-cultural perspectives draw attention to variations in opportunities for children in different cultures around the world. In all societies, young children are given considerable encouragement to engage in culturally valued activities, which vary in ways that relate to wider ecological, economic and other factors and customary practice. This diversity is reflected on a smaller scale within a given culture, where the differences in children's opportunities to learn are less extensive yet may be significant.

Customary practices are shaped by historical developments and accompanied by cultural beliefs. This is clearly seen in both informal learning activities and in education systems with different cultural traditions. For example, the prominence of structured, public talk in classrooms in Central Europe contrasts with the Anglo–US tradition of group and individual work undertaken in a semi-private manner. The Central European tradition emphasizes the class as a whole working together whereas the Anglo–US tradition emphasizes individualization and differentiation (Alexander 2000). Contrasting customary practices are also found within, as well as between, particular cultures. For example, teachers who are inducted into different schools of thought with regard to the teaching of reading use contrasting methods and activities each of which may be employed to address a variety of learners' difficulties in reading.

Participation in an activity is a necessary but not sufficient condition for learning as the pedagogic interaction also plays a part in influencing what is learned and how effectively this is achieved. Adults who provide effective support for children's learning calibrate and adjust their input in light of the child's performance of tasks and problems. They adjust their verbal, material and physical input to achieve a good level of adaptive attunement (Ireson and Blay 1999; Ireson 2000), which may be achieved through contingent teaching and scaffolding (Wood and Wood 1996a; 1996b), guided participation (Rogoff 1990) or assisted performance (Tharp and Gallimore 1988). Tutors also provide support through careful selection and organization of learning tasks, which they adjust in light of a learner's performance and developing competence. Adaptive attunement is most readily achieved when an adult works with a single child. Nevertheless, it is possible to achieve a good level of attunement when working with groups in the classroom, most notably when tasks are carefully structured and teaching expertise is designed in to and distributed among the resources used by children working individually or in small groups.

Classroom talk may also be used to encourage children's participation in meaningful exchanges that build on and develop their ideas and lines of thinking. Particular forms of interaction encourage these types of exchange, especially those that reduce the teacher's traditional, domination of classroom talk through transmission of information. Exchanges that encourage dialogic, as opposed to monologic, styles of interaction provide students with space to explore and express their own ideas and think about them in relation to those of their classmates and their teacher. At the same time, dialogue that builds on the learner's input indicates that the teacher acknowledges the learner's valid contribution to a discussion.

Connecting the cognitive, interpersonal and cultural spheres of learning

In recent years considerable advances have been made in understanding the mental processes involved in remembering information, solving problems and reasoning. Much relevant research is based on experimental studies, which provide a strong evidence base. However, the majority of these studies involve learning over very short periods of time rather than the longer time-scales that are characteristic in most real-life learning. Such studies help to describe how cognitive processes work but they do not tell us enough about how they are acquired. They provide useful insights for educators and ways of thinking about children' learning, but do not necessarily constitute a basis for direct application in the home or classroom.

Contemporary theory on the acquisition of skills and expertise offers a unifying framework that may be applied to a wide range of learning from language comprehension and production, mathematical operations, sporting activities and social stereotypes (Speelman and Kirsner 2005). Learning in each of these domains involves the acquisition of a large number of component processes, through involvement in activities that call for their use. Taking part in any activity involves neuronal processing in the brain and affects linkages in the changing web of competing connections. Connections are strengthened when a goal is achieved and thus goal directed activity forms an important link between the neural and cultural spheres of learning.

Opportunities for children to participate in activities that have goals relating to school learning vary considerably from one cultural context to another. Cultural goals, values and customary practices affect the opportunities offered to children and are mediated through parents, teachers and others who influence the activities children engage in. For example, parents who read to their young children, take them to libraries, teach them songs and nursery rhymes, the alphabet and numbers, help them to acquire skills and knowledge that are relevant in school (Sylva *et al.* 2004). Parents continue to support children's learning after they start school. Customary practices within a culture may encourage or discourage such activities or make them accessible only to certain groups of children. In some cultural settings, these 'school-like activities' may be seen as irrelevant and therefore rarely provided. The primary concern of a family may be with economic survival, in which case school learning is not a priority as children as expected to work as soon as they are able to do so.

Mediation and indeterminacy

Mediation of learning by signs, tools and other people in a culture introduces forms of indeterminacy, in the sense that there is potential for change, creativity and transformation. Mediation by other people, in the zone of proximal development, provides a space for cultural development and change (Cole 1985). It involves a negotiation of shared meaning as individual students receive, store and use information in a form that is similar to, but not identical with, that of their teachers and parents. This is due to the way that connections are formed in the brain somewhat idiosyncratically, reflecting an individual's experience. New learning is appropriated and transformed by the learner during the process of internalization and as no two individuals share exactly the same experiences, there will always be differences in their stock of knowledge and their mental representations of concepts and events.

Several aspects of the teaching and learning encounter introduce additional elements of indeterminacy. First, participants' attention to specific features of a task or activity means that they may see it quite differently. Even apparently simple learning activities present an array of information and individuals attend selectively, orienting themselves towards different features of information presented. Participants have their own interests and priorities concerning their involvement in a task and the learning outcomes, which influence their orientation towards task features and the nature of their engagement with the task and with one another. A good teacher will draw the learner's attention to those features that are relevant for the task at hand.

A second source of indeterminacy stems from the variety of conceptions of learning and teaching held by teachers, parents and students. In the early years, children have a relatively restricted view of learning as doing and they gradually expand on this as they grow older and move through the education system. By adulthood, conceptions encompass learning to do, to know, to understand, memorize, to see the world in a different way and change as a person. Older learners thus appear to retain basic concepts of learning as doing and knowing, alongside an array of additional conceptions. The coexistence of these adult notions means that one or other of them may be to the fore during an interaction with a learner and thus affect the quality of a learner's experience of learning.

Moreover, during an interaction between teacher and learner, one or more of these notions of learning may be to the fore, for each individual. So there may be discrepancies between the dominant notions of a teacher and student or parent and child. For example, a teacher who is concerned to develop understanding might have difficulty with a student who sees learning as acquiring facts and procedures and producing correct answers. A similar issue arises if the teacher is concerned with factual learning and the student is more concerned with understanding content and seeing the relevance of this in a broader perspective. In both situations there is a difference of view that may cause difficulties unless it is recognized and addressed. There may be a need for negotiating common ground in relation to the nature of the learning that is being undertaken. This is in addition to the negotiation that is undertaken between participants' understandings of the content itself. In both cases, recognition of the different perspectives is a first step in the process of negotiation.

Different conceptions of learning and beliefs about learners thus infuse interactions between teachers, parents and young people. In this way, the cognitive architecture connects with the wider socio-cultural architecture through participants' belief systems as well as their cognitive knowledge systems. These belief systems may be implicitly learned and thus not readily brought to mind or verbalized with the result that their influence on participants' behaviour is largely through unconscious processes.

Third, adults' concerns about and regulation of task completion give learners more or less freedom in learning. There is a tendency for adults who are concerned with efficient, error-free performance of a task, to exert a high level of regulation. When mistakes are costly in economic or other terms, adults tend to be more restrictive, whereas when mistakes are not costly, adults do not regulate children's activities to the same extent. Just as adults teaching girls to weave tend to regulate the activity closely when it is economically important (Greenfield 1984; 1998), so teachers who are judged on the basis of their children's performance in national tests and examinations are likely to exert greater regulation of their students' learning. Their orientation towards reaching externally set targets may override their concern with children's mastery and understanding of the subject. These concerns can have an impact on the learners' use of self-regulatory strategies as adults tend to give children more control as a means of encouraging them to regulate their own learning and become more independent learners.

Finally, learners are not passive recipients of input from adults but play an active part in the nature of the interaction and the learning that takes place. Those who strive for a deep understanding of a subject are more actively engaged, asking questions and seeking explanations. The origins of this deep orientation to learning are not fully understood and most likely stem from a number of individual and relational factors such as prior learning, interest, intellectual capability and the extent to which deep learning is valued by significant others. More remains to be discovered about the interplay between individual and cultural factors that encourage children to persist with particular forms of learning.

These various sources of indeterminacy introduce scope for creative invention and change. Learners are not simply passive recipients of information but are able to negotiate shared meaning, thus allowing the process of learning to be one of active transformation and appropriation of knowledge. The process of negotiation involves agreeing on the salient features and goals of an activity, task or problem. It may also involve negotiation of the meaning of learning itself.

Bringing together socio-cultural and cognitive frameworks

Studies of interaction between adults and children have been very productive in providing insight into the processes through which parents and teachers support and guide children's learning. We now know a good deal about interactions between parents and young children completing certain types of task that have clear and agreed solutions. These tasks involve physical actions, such as building a tower of blocks, tying a knot and organizing household objects. They are carefully selected to be within the participants' capabilities and can be completed in a fairly short time.

Older children are able to perform actions with 'material representations' rather than the physical objects themselves (Arievitch and Haenen 2005). Material representations might be diagrams and models, such as a plan or map of a town showing the location of shops in an errand planning task (Radiszewska and Rogoff 1988; 1991), written numerical notation for long division problems (Pratt *et al.* 1992). Material representations are at one remove from physical actions on objects. They supply a connection with the problem to be solved and enable a solution to be found without physical manipulation of the objects themselves. When solving problems of this type, social interaction assists in the formation of linkages between different types of representation.

At the heart of a cultural view of learning is the ability of humans to recognize another's point of view and achieve intersubjectivity. This ability appears to rest on communication through language, which by its very nature encourages individuals to see different perspectives. Linguistic representation allows us to look at the world from different viewpoints and to understand that there is more than one possible interpretation of a given situation. It also enables us to preserve new ideas and ways of understanding that may be passed on to the next generation. Recognition of another's point of view rests on shared conceptions so that teachers and others are able to temporarily adopt, or approximate, the learner's standpoint and use that as a starting point for their calibration of support.

Effective calibration of support is an important issue in education, where the concept of matching tasks to students' capabilities is well known and widely accepted. The notion of a zone of proximal development (Vygotsky 1978) raises questions about whether task demands should be set at the level of the child's current capability or at the level of potential development, or somewhere in between. It may be most productive to work at a level that is just beyond current competence, always drawing the child forward and pushing against the outer boundary of the zone. To do this, the teacher and learner must orient towards the goal of a task and towards significant features of the task or problem, if necessary reminding the learner of the goal as the activity unfolds. If the learner's definition of the task does not correspond to the teacher's, the teacher may need to adopt the learner's definition as a first step in order to establish some common ground. Once this has been achieved the teacher then works to draw the learner towards a more advanced position. To make a task meaningful, orientations may involve linking between actions at the physical, material, verbal and mental levels. Arguably, interactions with adults and other knowledgeable others can help learners make connections between these levels (Arievitch and Haenen 2005; Shayer and Adey 2002).

Conclusions

The cognitive and socio-cultural perspectives presented in this book provide frameworks for understanding connections between cultural, social and individual spheres of learning. They will hopefully be useful to teachers and others concerned with children's learning and cognitive growth. They specifically draw attention to the nature of children's participation in learning activities and how this may affect not only the skills and knowledge they acquire but also their beliefs and orientations towards learning itself.

A central argument running through this book is that there are strong connections between the various spheres of learning. What happens in the brain affects and is affected by cultural activity. The plasticity of the human brain makes it capable of learning over long periods of time, building up knowledge and skills that are available for later use. Cultural settings provide children with a wide variety of opportunities to learn, as adults' beliefs, values, ethnotheories and customary practices lead them to promote specific activities. By engaging in these activities the brain forms connections that affect learners' performance in component skills. There is thus a constant interplay between the cultural and biological formation of mind, which is mediated by people, tools and artefacts and is dynamically changing, somewhat like the sea's interaction with the shore. Waves moving against the sand deposit material and take material away in an ever-shifting process, so the shoreline and the sea itself are re-constituted in a process of constant interaction and change.

Schools provide a specific set of opportunities to learn, designed to ensure that the majority of young people acquire culturally valued knowledge and skills. The vast majority of typically developing children have the capability to acquire these, provided that they devote sufficient time to learning in productive ways and are not de-motivated by home, school, classroom or other factors. Some children take longer than others as they start school with fewer components in place, but provided that teaching achieves a good level of adaptive attunement it will enable them to progress.

Differences in customary practices at home and between parents' beliefs about learning mean that children have very different opportunities to learn and acquire component skills that form the basis for school learning. Educators should not be too quick to categorize children as having more or less ability when they start school but should concentrate instead on identifying existing component skills and helping children to build on them. We should expect to find diversity in these skills and also in children's beliefs about and orientations towards learning. These beliefs and orientations also have a significant influence on children's progress. Awareness of this diversity among learners of all ages will hopefully enable educators to see children's learning in a different way.

Although much progress has been made, there remain many challenges for the future. One of these challenges is to raise awareness of the different forms of learning and to encourage discussion of the educational environments that promote them. Such discussions might include uncovering values and beliefs that shape the design of learning activities and the pedagogic interactions that take place as activities unfold. The design of learning activities involves not only careful structuring to achieve curriculum objectives but also what might be termed 'affective structuring' to support valued dispositions, beliefs and aspirations.

There are also many gaps in our understanding of the links between learning and the various settings in which it takes place. For example, there is more to be discovered about the factors that encourage learners to develop conceptions of learning that go beyond the accumulation of factual information; when awareness of learning is beneficial; and how pedagogic interactions relate to activities, tasks and individual factors. The part played by learners themselves in this process is under-represented in much of the research to date.

In the past, when employment was widely available in unskilled or semi-skilled occupations, it was sufficient for the UK to educate a minority of the population for employment in the civil service and in other professional and managerial occupations. In the twenty-first-century global economy there is much less manual work available in his country and education is an increasingly important passport to a wide range of occupations. This means that the education system must be designed to equip all learners, not just those who appear to be the most able, with the knowledge and skills required for future employment. Moreover, as there is less likelihood of remaining in one job or career for life, many adults can expect to enter different occupations and learn new skills during their working lives and even into retirement. In this context, personal qualities of adaptability and the disposition and capacity to continue learning throughout life are important for individuals to acquire. Such personal qualities as the disposition to learn are learned through participation in settings imbued with practices that value learners and their learning. Arguably an education system that develops pedagogic settings and practices to assist all young people to acquire these dispositions and capabilities will simultaneously serve them and the country as a whole.

References

Abernethy, B. (1991) 'Visual search strategies and decision-making in sport', *International Journal of Sport Psychology*, 22(3/4): 189–210.

Adey, P. and Shayer, M. (1993) 'An exploration of long-term far-transfer effects following an extended intervention programme in the high school science curriculum', *Cognition and Instruction*, 11(1): 1–29.

Adey, P., Robertson, A. and Venville, G. (2002) 'Effects of a cognitive acceleration programme on year 1 pupils', *British Journal of Educational Psychology*, 72(1): 1–25.

Alexander, R.J. (2000) *Culture and Pedagogy: International Comparisons in Primary Education*, Oxford: Blackwell.

Alexander, R.J. (2004) *Towards Dialogic Teaching*, Cambridge: Dialogos UK Ltd.

Alexander, P.A., Schallert, D.L. and Hare, V.C. (1991) 'Coming to terms: How researchers in learning and literacy talk about knowledge', *Review of Educational Research*, 61(3): 315–43.

Anderson, J.R. (1983) *The Architecture of Cognition*, Cambridge, MA: Harvard University Press.

Anderson, J.R (2000) *Cognitive Psychology and its Implications*, New York: Worth Publishers.

Arievitch, I.M. and Haenen, J.P.P. (2005) 'Connecting sociocultural theory and educational practice', *Educational Psychologist*, 40(3): 155–65.

Askew, M., Brown, M., Rhodes, V., Johnson, D. and Wiliam, D. (1997) *Effective Teachers of Numeracy*, Final Report, London: School of Education, King's College.

Bandura, A. (1977) *Social Learning Theory*, Englewood Cliffs, NJ: Prentice Hall.

Bandura, A. (1986) *Social Foundations of Thought and Action*, Englewood Cliffs, NJ: Prentice Hall.

Bandura, A. (1997) *Self-efficacy: The Exercise of Control*, New York: WH Freeman.

Barnes, D. and Todd, F. (1977) *Communication and Learning in Small Groups*, London: Routledge & Kegan Paul.

Bennett, N., Desforges, C., Cockburn, A. and Wilkinson, B. (1984) *The Quality of Pupil Learning Experiences*, London: Lawrence Erlbaum.

Bereiter, C. and Scardamalia, M. (1989) 'Intentional learning as a goal of instruction', in R. Glaser (ed.) *Knowing, Learning and Instruction*, London: Lawrence Erlbaum.

Bereiter, C. and Scardamalia, M. (1993) *Surpassing Ourselves: An Inquiry into the Nature nd Implications of Expertise*, Chicago, IL: Open Court.

Berliner, D.C. (1986) 'In pursuit of the expert pedagogue', *Educational Researcher*, 15(7): 5–13.

Berry, D.C. and Broadbent, D.E. (1984) 'On the relationship between task performance and associated verbalisable knowledge', *Quarterly Journal of Experimental Psychology*, 36A(2): 209–31.

Biggs, J.B. (1987) *Student Approaches to Learning and Studying*, Melbourne: Australian Council for Educational Research.

Biggs, J.B. (1996) 'Enhancing teaching through constructive alignment', *Higher Education*, 32(3): 347–64.

Biggs, J.B. and Collis, K.F. (1982) *Evaluating the Quality of Learning: The SOLO Taxonomy*, New York: Academic Press.

Biggs, J.B. and Moore, P.J. (1993) *The Process of Learning*, London: Prentice Hall.

Biggs, J.B., Kember, D. and Leung, D.Y.P. (2001) 'The revised two-factor study process questionnaire', *British Journal of Educational Psychology*, 71(1): 133–49.

Blakemore, S.-J. and Frith, U. (2005) *The Learning Brain: Lessons for Education*, Oxford: Blackwell.

Blay, J. (2000) 'Social interaction in the nursery: evaluating a model of guided participation', unpublished PhD thesis, London: Institute of Education, University of London.

Blay, J. and Ireson, J. (in preparation) 'Pedagogical beliefs, activity choice and structure, and adult–child participation in nursery classrooms'.

Bliss , J., Askew, M. and Macrae, S. (1996) 'Effective teaching and learning: scaffolding revisited', *Oxford Review of Education*, 22(1): 17–35.

Bloom, B.S. (1985) 'Generalisations about talent development', in B.S. Bloom (ed.) *Developing Talent in Young People*, New York: Ballantine Books.

Boaler, J. (1997a) 'When even the winners are losers: evaluate the experiences of 'top set' students', *Journal of Curriculum Studies*, 29(2): 165–82.

Boaler, J. (1997b) *Experiencing School Mathematics: Teaching Styles, Sex and Setting*, Buckingham: Open University Press.

Borkowski, J.G. and Muthukrishna, N. (1995) 'Learning environments and skill generalisation: how contexts facilitate regulatory processes and efficacy beliefs', in F.E. Weinert and W. Schneider (eds) *Memory Performance and Competencies: Issues in Growth and Development*, Mahwah, NJ: Erlbaum.

Boulton-Lewis, G., Smith, D.J.H., McCrindle, A.R., Burnett, P.C. and Campbell, K.J. (2001) 'Secondary teachers' conceptions of teaching and learning', *Learning and Instruction*, 11(1): 35–51.

Broadbent, D.E., Fitzgerald, P. and Broadbent, M.H.P. (1986) 'Implicit and explicit knowledge in the control of complex systems', *British Journal of Psychology*, 77(1): 33–50.

Bronfenbrenner, U. (1989) 'Ecological systems theory', in R. Vasta (ed.) *Annals of Child Development*, Greenwich, CT: JAI Press.

Bronfenbrenner, U. (1993) 'The ecology of cognitive development: research models and fugitive findings', in R. Wozniak and K.W. Fischer (eds) *Development in Context*, Hillsdale, NJ: Erlbaum

Brophy, J. and Good, T.L. (1986) 'Teacher behavior and student achievement', in C.M. Wittrock (ed.) *Handbook of Research on Teaching*, 3rd edn, New York: Macmillan.

Brown, A. and Palincsar, A.S. (1989) 'Guided, cooperative learning and individual knowledge acquisition', in L. Resnick (ed.) *Knowing, Learning and Instruction*, London: Lawrence Erlbaum.

Brown, A.L., Armbruster, B.B. and Baker, L. (1986) 'The role of metacognition in reading and studying', in J. Orasano (ed.) *Reading Comprehension: From Research to Practice*, Hillsdale, NJ: Lawrence Erlbaum Associates.

Brown, A.L., Bransford, J.B., Ferrara, R.A. and Campione J. (1983) 'Learning, remembering and understanding', in J. Flavell and E.M. Markman (eds) *Handbook of Child Psychology*, 4th edn, *Cognitive Development*, New York: Wiley.

Brown, S. and McIntyre, D. (1992) *Making Sense of Teaching,* London: Routledge.

Bruner, J.S. (1983) *Child's Talk: Learning to Use Language*, Oxford: Oxford University Press.

Bruner, J.S. (1996) *The Culture of Education*, Cambridge, MA: Harvard University Press.

Bryan, W.L. and Harter, N. (1899) 'Studies on the telegraphic language: the acquisition of a hierarchy of habits', *Psychological Review*, 6(4): 345–75.

Bryant, P.E. (1982) 'The role of conflict and agreement between intellectual strategies in children's ideas about measurement', *British Journal of Psychology*, 73(2): 243–52.

Butler, D.L. (1998) 'The Strategic Content Learning approach to promoting self-regulated learning: a report of three studies', *Journal of Educational Psychology*, 90(4): 682–97.

Cain, K. and Dweck, C.S. (1989) 'Children's theories of intelligence: a developmental model', in R. Sternberg (ed.) *Advances in the Study of Intelligence*, Hillsdale, NJ: Lawrence Erlbaum.

Cain, K., Oakhill, J. and Bryant, P. (2004) 'Children's reading comprehension ability: concurrent prediction by working memory, verbal ability and component skills', *Journal of Educational Psychology*, 96(1): 31–42.

Carey, S. and Spelke, E.S. (1998) 'Domain-specific knowledge and conceptual change', in L.A. Hirschfield and S.A. Gelman (eds) *Mapping the Mind: Domain Specificity in Cognition and Culture*, Cambridge: Cambridge University Press.

Carraher, T.N., Carraher, D.W. and Schliemann, A.D. (1985) 'Mathematics in the streets and in schools', *British Journal of Developmental Psychology*, 3(1): 21–9.

Cazden, C. (2001) *Classroom Discourse: The Language of Teaching and Learning*, Portsmouth, NH: Heinemann.

Chase, W.G. and Simon, H.A. (1973) 'Perception in chess', *Cognitive Psychology*, 4(1): 55–81.

Chavajay, P. and Rogoff, B. (2002) 'Schooling and traditional collaborative social organization of problem solving by Mayan mothers and children', *Developmental Psychology*, 38(1): 55–66.

Chi, M.T.H. (1978) 'Knowledge structure and memory development', in R. Siegler (ed.) *Children's Thinking: What Develops?*, Hillsdale, NJ: Erlbaum.

Chi, M.T.H. (1996) 'Constructing self-explanations and scaffolded explanations in tutoring', *Applied Cognitive Psychology*, 10(7): 33–49.

Chi, M.T.H., Feltovitch, P.J. and Glaser, R. (1981) 'Categorisation and representation of physics problems by experts and novices', *Cognitive Science*, 5(2): 121–52.

Chi, M.T.H., Glaser, R. and Rees, E. (1982) 'Expertise in problem solving', in R. Sternberg (ed.) *Advances in the Psychology of Human Intelligence*, Hillsdale, NJ: Erlbaum.

Chi, M.T.H., Siler, S. A., Jeong, H., Yamauchi, T. and Hausmann, R.G. (2001) 'Learning from human tutoring', *Cognitive Science*, 25(4): 471–533.

Chinn, C.A. and Brewer, W.F. (1993) 'The role of anomalous data in knowledge acquisitions: a theoretical framework and implications for science instruction', *Review of Educational Research*, 63(1): 1–49.

Clay, M. (1985) *The Early Detection of Reading Difficulties*, Portsmouth, NH: Heinemann.

Clay, M. (1991) *Becoming Literate: The Construction of Inner Control*, Portsmouth, NH: Heinemann

Clay, M. and Cazden, C. (1990) 'A Vygotskian interpretation of Reading Recovery', in L.C. Moll (ed.) *Vygotsky and Education: Instructional Implication and Applications of Sociohistoric Psychology*, Cambridge: Cambridge University Press.

Cole, M. (1985) 'The zone of proximal development: where culture and cognition create each other', in J.V. Wertsch (ed.) *Culture, Communication and Cognition: Vygotskian Perspectives*, London: Cambridge University Press.

Cole, M. (1996) *Cultural Psychology: A Once and Future Discipline*, Cambridge, MA: Harvard University Press.

Cole, M. (1998) 'Cognitive development and formal schooling: the evidence from cross-cultural research', in D. Faulkner, K. Littleton and M. Woodhead (eds) *Learning Relationships in the Classroom*, London: Routledge.

Cole, M. (2005) 'Cross-cultural and historical perspectives on the developmental consequences of education', *Human Development*, 48(4):195–216.

Cole, M. and Engeström, Y. (1993) 'A cultural-historical approach to distributed cognition', in G. Salomon (ed.) *Distributed Cognitions*, Cambridge: Cambridge University Press.

Cole, M. and Scribner, S. (1974) *Culture and Thought*, London: John Wiley & Sons.

Collins, A., Brown, J.S. and Newman, S. (1989) 'Cognitive apprenticeship: teaching the crafts of reading, writing and mathematics', in L.B. Resnick (ed.) *Knowing, Learning and Instruction*, London: Lawrence Erlbaum.

Covington, M. (1992) *Making the Grade: A Self-Worth Perspective on Motivation and School Reform*, New York: Cambridge University Press.

Crossman, E.R. (1959) 'The theory of the acquisition of speed-skill', *Ergonomics*, 2(2): 153–66.

Daniels, H. (2001) *Vygotsky and Pedagogy*, London: Routledge.

Dasen, P.R. (2003) 'Theoretical frameworks in cross-cultural psychology', in T.S. Saraswathi (ed.) *Cross-Cultural Perspectives in Human Development*, New Delhi: Sage Publications.

Day, J.D. and Cordon, L.A. (1993) 'Static and dynamic measures of ability: an experimental comparison', *Journal of Educational Psychology*, 85(1): 75–82.

de Groot, A.D. (1965) *Thought and Choice in Chess*, The Hague: Mouton.

de Groot, A.D. (1966) 'Perception and memory versus thought: some old ideas and recent findings', in B. Kleinmuntz (ed.) *Problem-Solving: Research, Method and Theory*, New York: Wiley.

Deci, E.L. and Ryan, R.M. (1987) 'The support of autonomy and the control of behaviour', *Journal of Personality and Social Behaviour*, 53(6): 1024–37.

Desforges, C. (1995) 'How does experience affect theoretical knowledge for teaching?', *Learning and Instruction*, 5(4): 385–400.

Desforges, C. and Abouchaar, A. (2003) *The Impact of Parental Involvement, Parental Support and Family Education on Pupil Achievement and Adjustment; A Review of Literature*, DfES Research Report number 433, London: DfES.

Desforges, C. and Cockburn, A. (1987) *Understanding the Mathematics Teacher*, Lewes: Falmer Press.

DfEE (Department for Education and Employment) (1997) *Excellence in Schools*, CM 3681, London: HMSO.

Douglas, S.A. (1991) 'Tutoring as interaction', in P. Goodyear (ed.) *Teaching Knowledge and Intelligent Tutoring*, Norwood, NJ: Ablex Publishing Corp.

Doyle, W. (1986) Classroom organisation and management, in M. Wittrock (ed.) *Handbook of Research on Teaching*, New York: Macmillan.

Driver, R. (1994) *Making Sense of Secondary Science: Research into Children's Ideas*, London: Routledge.

Driver, R., Guesne, E. and Tiberghien, A. (1985) *Children's Ideas in Science*, Milton Keynes: Open University Press.

Duncan, T.G. and McKeachie, W.J. (2005) 'The making of the Motivated Strategies for Learning Questionnaire', *Educational Psychologist*, 40(2): 117–28.

Dunkin, M.J. and Biddle, B.J. (1974) *The Study of Teaching*, New York: Holt, Rinehart and Winston.

Dweck, C.S. (1999) *Self-Theories: Their Role in Motivation, Personality and Development*, Philadelphia, PA: Taylor and Francis.

Dweck, C.S. (2001) 'The development of ability conceptions', in A. Wigfield and J. Eccles (eds) *Development of Achievement Motivation*, London: Academic Press.

Eccles, J.S. and Wigfield, A. (2001) 'Development of academic achievement motivation', *International Encyclopaedia of the Social and Behavioural Sciences*, Oxford: Elsevier.

Eccles, J.S, Adler, T., Futterman, R., Goff, S., Kaczala, C., Meece,J. and Midgley, C. (1983) 'Expectancies, values, and academic behaviors', in J.T. Spence (ed.) *Achievement and Achievement Motivation*, San Francisco, CA: WH Freeman.

Eccles, J.S., Wigfield, A. and Schiefele, N. (1998) 'Motivation to succeed', in N. Eisenberg (ed.) *Handbook of Child Psychology*, 5th edn, New York: Wiley.

Edwards, D. and Mercer, N. (1987) *Common Knowledge: The Development of Understanding in the Classroom*, London: Methuen.

Eisenberger, R. (1998) 'Achievement: the importance of industriousness', *Behavioural and Brain Sciences*, 21(3): 412–13.

Elbers, E. (1996) 'Cooperation and social context in adult-child interaction', *Learning and Instruction*, 6(4): 281–6.

Ellis, S. and Rogoff, B. (1982) 'The strategies and efficacy of child versus adult teachers', *Child Development*, 53(3): 730–5

Engeström, Y. (1999) 'Activity theory and individual and social transformation', in Y. Engeström, R. Miettinen and R.-L. Punamiki (eds) *Perspectives on Activity Theory*, Cambridge: Cambridge University Press.

Engeström, Y., Miettinen, R. and Punamiki, R.-L. (eds) (1999) *Perspectives on Activity Theory*, Cambridge: Cambridge University Press.

Entwistle, N. and Marton, F. (1993) 'Knowledge objects: understandings constituted through intensive academic study', *British Journal of Educational Psychology*, 64(11): 161–78.

Entwistle, N. and Ramsden, P. (1983) *Understanding Student Learning*, London: Croom Helm.

Entwistle, N. and Waterston, S. (1988) 'Approaches to studying and levels of processing in university students', *British Journal of Educational Psychology*, 58(3): 258–65.

Ericsson, K.A. (1996) 'The acquisition of expert performance: an introduction to some of the issues', in K.A. Ericsson (ed.) *The Road to Excellence: The Acquisition of Expert Performance in the Arts and Sciences, Sports, and Games*, Mahwah, NJ: Erlbaum.

Ericsson, K.A. (2002) 'Attaining excellence through deliberate practice: insights from the study of expert performance', in C. Desforges and R. Fox (eds) *Teaching and Learning. The Essential Readings*, Oxford: Blackwell.

Ericsson, K.A. and Kintsch, W. (1995) 'Long-term working memory', *Psychological Review*, 102(2): 211–45.

Ericsson, K.A. and Lehmann, A.C. (1996) 'Expert and exceptional performance: evidence on maximal adaptations on past constraints', *Annual Review of Psychology*, 47: 273–305.

Ericsson, K.A., Krampe, R.T. and Tesch-Romer, C. (1993) 'The role of deliberate practice in the acquisition of expert performance', *Psychological Review*, 100(3): 363–406.

Evans, S. (2001) 'What is learning? A study of the conceptions of year 9 students', unpublished Masters dissertation, London: Institute of Education, University of London.

Eysenck, M.W. and Keane, M.T. (2005) *Cognitive Psychology: A Student's Handbook*, Hove: Psychology Press.

Fitts, P.M. and Posner, M.I. (1967) *Human Performance*, Belmont, CA: Brooks/ Cole.

Flavell, J.H. and Wellman, H.M. (1977) 'Metamemory', in R.V. Kail and J.W. Hagen (eds) *Perspectives on the Development of Memory and Cognition*, Hillsdale, NJ: Lawrence Erlbaum Associates.

Fox, B. (1991) 'Cognitive and interactional aspects of correction in tutoring', in P. Goodyear (ed.) *Teaching Knowledge and Intelligent Tutoring*, Norwood, NJ: Ablex Publishing Corporation.

Fox, B (1993) *The Human Tutorial Dialogue Project*, London: Lawrence Erlbaum.

Frederiksen, J.R. and Collins, A. (1989) 'A systems approach to educational testing', *Educational Researcher*, 18(9): 27–32.

Gagne, R.M. (1970) *The Conditions of Learning*, New York: Holt, Rinehart and Winston.

Gagne, R.M. and Merrill, M.D. (1990) 'Integrative goals for instructional design', *Educational Technology Research and Development*, 38(1): 23–30.

Gagne, R.M., Briggs, L.I. and Wager, W.W. (1992) *Principles of Instructional Design*, London: Harcourt Brace Jovanovich.

Gallimore, R. and Tharp, R. (1990) 'Teaching mind in society: teaching, schooling and literate discourse', in L.C. Moll (ed.) *Vygotsky and Education: Instructional Implications and Applications of Sociohistorical Psychology*, Cambridge: Cambridge University Press.

Gamoran, A. and Berends, M. (1987) 'The effects of stratification in secondary schools: synthesis of survey and ethnographic approaches', *Review of Educational Research*, 57(4): 415–35.

Garner, R. (1986) *Metacognition and Reading Comprehension*, Norwood, NJ: Ablex Publishing.

Gauvain, M. (1998) 'Thinking in niches: sociocultural influences on cognitive development', in D. Faulkner, K. Littleton and M. Woodhead (eds) *Learning Relationships in the Classroom*), London: Routledge.

Gauvain, M. (2001) *The Social Context of Cognitive Development*, New York: Guilford.

Gibson, J.J. (1966) *The Senses Considered as Perceptual Systems*, Boston, MA: Houghton Mifflin.

Gibson, J.J. (1986) *The Ecological Approach to Visual Perception*, Hillsdale, NJ: Lawrence Erlbaum.

Glaser, R. (1984) 'Education and thinking: the role of knowledge', *American Psychologist*, 39(2): 93–104.

Glaser, R. and Chi, M.T.H. (1988) 'Overview', in M.T.H. Chi, R. Glaser and M. Farr (eds) *The Nature of Expertise*, Hillsdale, NJ: Erlbaum.

Gobet, F. and Waters, A.J. (2003) 'The role of constraints in expert memory', *Journal of Experimental Psychology: Learning, Memory and Cognition*, 29(6): 1082–94.

Gonzalez, M.-M. (1996) 'Tasks and activities: a parent–child interaction analysis', *Learning and Instruction*, 6(4): 287–306.

Goodnow, J. (1996) 'Acceptable ignorance, negotiable disagreement: Alternative views of learning', in D.R. Olson and N. Torrance (eds) *The Handbook of Education and Human Development: New Models of Learning, Teaching and Schooling*, Cambridge: Blackwell.

Graesser, A.C. and Person, N.K. (1994) 'Question asking during tutoring', *American Educational Research Journal*, 31(1): 104–37.

Graesser, A.C., Person, N.K. and Magliano, J.P. (1995) 'Collaborative dialogue patterns in naturalistic one-to-one tutoring', *Applied Cognitive Psychology*, 9(6): 495–522.

Greenfield, P.M. (1984) 'A theory of the teacher in the learning activities of everyday life', in B. Rogoff and J. Lave (eds) *Everyday Cognition*, London: Harvard University Press.

Greenfield, P.M. (1998) 'Cultural change and human development', in E. Turiel (ed.) *New Directions in Child Development*, San Francisco, CA: Jossey-Bass.

Greenfield, P.M. and Lave, J. (1982) 'Cognitive aspects of informal education', in D.A. Wagner and H.W. Stevenson (eds) *Cultural Perspectives on Child Development*, San Francisco, CA: W. Freeman.

Greenhough, P. and Hughes, M. (1998) 'Parents' and teachers' interventions in children's reading', *British Educational Research Journal*, 24: 4, 383–98.

Greenhough, W.T., Black, J.E. and Wallace C.S. (1987) 'Experience and brain development', *Child Development*, 58(3): 539–59.

Guberman, S.R. (1999) 'Supportive environments for cognitive development: illustrations from children's mathematical activities outside of school', in A. Goncu (ed.) *Children's Engagement in the World*, Cambridge: Cambridge University Press.

Gutierrez, K.D. (1994) 'How talk, context and script shape contexts for learning: a cross-case comparison of journal sharing', *Linguistics and Education*, 5(3–4): 335–65.

Hacker, R.G. and Rowe, M.J. (1993) 'A study of the effects of an organisation change from streamed to mixed-ability classes upon science instruction', *Journal of Research in Science Teaching*, 30(3): 223–31.

Hallam, S. and Ireson, J. (1999) 'Pedagogy in the secondary school', in P. Mortimore, (ed.) *Pedagogy and its Impact on Learning*, London: Sage Publications.

Hallam, S. and Ireson, J. (2005) 'Secondary school teachers' pedagogic practices when teaching mixed and structured ability classes', *Research Papers in Education*, 20(1): 3–24.

Hastings, N. and Schwieso, J. (1995) 'Tasks and tables', *Educational Research*, 37(3): 279–91.

Hickey, K. (1977) *Dyslexia: A Language Training Course for Teachers and Learners*, Staines: Dyslexia Institute.

Hornsby, B. and Shear, F. (1993) *Alpha to Omega. The A-Z of Teaching Reading, Writing and Spelling*, Oxford: Heinemann Educational.

Howe, M.J.A. (1990) *The Origins of Exceptional Abilities*, Oxford: Blackwell.

Howe, M.J.A. (1991) 'Learning to learn: a fine idea, but does it work?', *Educational Section Review*, 15(2): 43–57.

Howe, M.J.A., Davidson, J.W. and Sloboda, J.A. (1998) 'Innate talents: reality or myth?', *Behavioural and Brain Sciences*, 21(3): 399–442.

Hughes, M. and Westgate, D. (1997) 'Assistants as talk-partners in early years classrooms: some issues of support and development', *Educational Review*, 49(1): 5–12.

Ireson, J. (2000) 'Activity and interaction in pedagogical contexts: towards a model of tutoring', in H. Cowie, G. van der Alsvoort and N. Mercer (eds) *Advances in Learning and Instruction: Social Interaction in Learning and Instruction*, Amsterdam: Elsevier Science.

Ireson, J. (2001) 'Tutoring activity in school: pedagogic principles and participation', in R. Nata (ed.) *Progress in Education*, vol. II, Huntingdon, NY: Nova Science Publishers.

Ireson, J. and Blay, J. (1999) 'Constructing activity: participation by adults and children', *Learning and Instruction*, 9(1): 19–36.

Ireson, J. and Hallam, S. (2001) *Ability Grouping in Education*, London: Paul Chapman.

Ireson, J., Hallam, S. and Hurley, C.J. (2005) 'What are the effects of ability grouping on GCSE attainment?' *British Educational Research Journal*, 31(4): 313–28.

Kail, R. (1990) *The Development of Memory in Children*, New York: W.H. Freeman.

Kant, I. (1781 [1968]) *Critique of Pure Reason*, trans. N.K. Smith, London: Macmillan.

Klahr, D. and MacWhinney, B. (1998) 'Information processing', in D. Kuhn and R.S. Siegler (eds) *Handbook of Child Psychology*, vol. 2, *Cognition, Perception and Language*, 5th edn, New York: Wiley.

Kozulin, A. (1996) 'The concept of activity in Soviet psychology', in H. Daniels (ed.) *An Introduction to Vygotsky*, London: Routledge.

Kozulin, A. (1998) *Psychological Tools: A Sociocultural Approach to Education*, Cambridge, MA: Harvard University Press.

Kuhn, D. (1995) 'Microgenetic study of change: what has it told us?', *Psychological Science*, 6(3): 133–9.

Kulik, J.A. and Kulik, C.L.C. (1992) 'Meta-analytic findings on grouping programs', *Gifted Child Quarterly*, 36(2): 73–7.

Lamb, S.J., Bibby, P.A., and Wood, D.J. (1997) 'Promoting the communication skills of children with moderate learning difficulties', *Child Language Teaching and Therapy*, 13(3): 261–78.

Lave, J. and Wenger, E. (1991) *Situated Learning: Legitimate Peripheral Participation*, Cambridge: Cambridge University Press.

Lesgold, A., Glaser, R., Rubinson, H., Klopfer, D., Feltovitch, P. and Wang, Y. (1988) 'Expertise in a complex skill: diagnosing x-ray pictures', in M.T.H. Chi, R. Glaser and M. Farr (eds) *The Nature of Expertise*, Hillsdale, NJ: Erlbaum.

McArthur, D., Stasz, C. and Zmuidzinas, M. (1990) 'Tutoring techniques in algebra', *Cognition and Instruction*, 7(3): 197–244.

Marriott, J. (1997) 'An investigation of small group literacy teaching in year 7', unpublished Masters dissertation, London: Institute of Education, University of London.

Marton, F. and Booth, S. (1997) *Learning and Awareness*, Mahwah, NJ: Lawrence Erlbaum.

Marton, F. and Säljö, R. (1976) 'On qualitative differences in learning II: outcome as a function of the learner's conception of the task', *British Journal of Educational Psychology*, 46(2): 115–27.

Marton, F. and Säljö, R. (1984) 'Approaches to learning', in F. Marton, D. Hounsell and N.J. Entwistle (eds) *The Experience of Learning*, Edinburgh: Scottish Academic Press.

Marton, F., Dall'Alba, G. and Beaty, E. (1993) 'Conceptions of learning', *International Journal of Educational Research*, 19(3), 277–300.

Marton, F., Watkins, D. and Tang, C. (1997) 'Discontinuities and continuities in the experience of learning: an interview study of high school students in Hong Kong', *Learning and Instruction*, 7(1): 21–8.

Maybin, J., Mercer, N. and Stierer, B. (1992) '"Scaffolding" learning in the classroom', in K. Norman (ed.) *Thinking Voices: The work of the National Oracy Project*, London: Hodder and Stoughton for The National Curriculum Council.

Meece, J. (1994) 'The role of motivation in self-regulated learning', in D.H. Shunk, and B.J. Zimmerman (eds) *Self-regulation of Learning and Performance: Issues and Educational Applications*, Hillsdale, NJ: Erlbaum.

Mehan, H. (1985) 'The Structure of classroom discourse', in T.A. van Dijk (ed.) *Handbook of Discourse Analysis*, vol. 3, *Discourse and Dialogue*, London: Academic Press.

Melhuish, E., Sylva, K., Sammons, P., Siraj-Blatchford, I. and Taggart, B. (2001) *Social Behavioural and Cognitive Development at 3–4 Years in Relation to Family Background*, Technical Paper 7, London: Department for Education and Employment/Institute of Education.

Mercer, N. (1995) *The Guided Construction of Knowledge*, Clevedon: Multilingual Matters.

Mercer, N. (2002) 'Developing dialogues', in G. Wells and G. Claxton (eds) *Learning for Life in the 21st Century*, Oxford: Blackwell Publishers.

Merrill, D.C., Reiser, B.J., Merrill, S.K. and Landes, S. (1995) 'Tutoring: guided learning by doing', *Cognition and Instruction*, 7(3): 315–72.

Mortimore, P., Sammons, P., Stoll, L., Lewis, D. and Ecob, R. (1988) *The Junior School Project*, London: ILEA Research and Statistics Branch.

Mroz, M., Smith, F. and Hardman, F. (2000) 'The discourse of the Literacy Hour', *Cambridge Journal of Education*, 30(3): 379–90.

Nassaji, H. and Wells, G. (2000) 'What's the use of triadic dialogue?: An investigation of teacher–student interaction', *Applied Linguistics*, 21(3): 376–406.

Nicholls, J.G. (1989) *Democratic Education and the Competitive Ethos*, Cambridge, MA: Harvard Press.

Nicholls, J.G. (1992) 'Students as educational theorists', in D. Schunk (ed.) *Students' Perceptions in the Classroom*, Hillsdale, NJ: Lawrence Erlbaum.

Nicholls, J.G. and Miller, A. (1983) 'The differentiation of the concepts of difficulty and ability', *Child Development*, 54(4): 951–9.

Nilholm, C. and Säljö, R. (1996) 'Co-action, situation definitions and sociocultural experience: an empirical study of problem solving in mother–child interaction', *Learning and Instruction*, 6(4): 325–44.

Nisbet, J. and Shucksmith, J. (1986) *Learning Strategies*, London: Routledge.

Norman, D.A. (1978) 'Notes towards a theory of complex learning' in A.M. Lesgold (ed.) *Cognitive Psychology and Instruction*, New York: Plenum Press.

Norman, D.A. (1988) *The Psychology of Everyday Things*, New York: Basic Books.

Nussbaum, J. (1985) 'The Earth as a cosmic body', in R. Driver, E. Guesne and A. Tiberghien (eds) *Children's Ideas in Science*, Milton Keynes: Open University Press.

Nystrand, M. (1997) *Opening Dialogue: Understanding the Dynamics of Language and Learning in the English Classroom*, New York: Teachers College Press.

O'Connor, M.C. and Michaels, S. (1996) 'Shifting participant frameworks: orchestrating thinking practices in group discussion', in D. Hicks (ed.) *Discourse, Learning and Schooling*, New York: Cambridge University Press.

Oakes, J. (1985) *Keeping Track: How Schools Structure Inequality*, New Haven, CT: Yale University Press.

Osborn, M., McNess, E., Planel, C. and Triggs, P. (2003) 'Culture, context and policy: comparing learners in three European countries', in R. Sutherland, G. Claxton and A. Pollard (eds) *Learning and Teaching, Where World Views Meet*, Stoke on Trent: Trentham Books.

Owings, R.A., Petersen, G.A., Bransford, J.D., Morris, C.D. and Stein, B.S. (1981) 'Spontaneous monitoring and regulation of learning: a comparison of successful and less successful 5th graders', *Journal of Educational Psychology*, 72(2): 250–6.

Palincsar, A.S. and Brown, A.L. (1984) 'Reciprocal teaching of comprehension-fostering and comprehension-monitoring activities', *Cognition and Instruction*, 1(2): 117–75.

Palincsar, A.S., Brown, A.L. and Campione, J.C. (1993) 'First-grade dialogues for knowledge acquisition and use', in E. Forman, N. Minick and C.A. Stone (eds) *Contexts for Learning: Sociocultural Dynamics in Children's Development*, Oxford: Oxford University Press.

Paradise, R. (1996) 'Passivity or tacit collaboration: Mazahua interaction in cultural context', *Learning and Instruction*, 26(4): 379–90.

Paris, S.G. and Paris, A.H. (2001) 'classroom applications of research on self-regulated learning', *Educational Psychologist*, 36(2): 89–101.

Pask, G. (1976) 'Conversational techniques in the study and practice of education', *British Journal of Educational Psychology*, 46(1): 12–25.

Pavlov, I.P. (1927) *Conditioned Reflexes*, trans. G.V. Anrep, London: Oxford University Press.

Pea, R.D. (1993) 'Practices of distributed intelligence and designs for education', in G. Salomon (ed.) *Distributed Cognitions*, Cambridge: Cambridge University Press.

Perfetti, C.A., Marron, M.A. and Foltz, P.W. (1996) 'Sources of comprehension failure: theoretical perspectives and case studies', in C. Cornoldi and J. Oakhill (eds) *Reading Comprehension Difficulties: Processes and intervention*, Mahwah: NJ: Lawrence Erlbaum.

Perkins, D., Jay, E. and Tishman, S. (1993) 'New conceptions of thinking', *Educational Psychologist*, 28(1): 67–85.

Piaget, J. (1936/1963) *The Origins of Intelligence in Children*, New York: Norton.

Piaget, J. (1964) 'Development and learning', *Journal of Research in Science Teaching*, 2(3): 176–86.

Pintrich, P.R. (1989) 'The dynamic interplay of student motivation and cognition in the college classroom', in M.L. Maehr and C. Ames (eds) *Advances in Motivation and Achievement: A Research Annual*, London: Jai Press.

Pintrich, P.R. (1999) 'The role of motivation in promoting and sustaining the self-regulated learning', *International Journal of Educational Research*, 31(6): 459–70.

Pintrich, P.R. (2000) 'The role of goal orientation in self-regulated learning', in P.R. Boekaerts, P.R. Pintrich and M. Zeidner (eds) *Handbook of Self-Regulation*, London: Academic Press.

Pintrich, P.R. and de Groot, E.V. (1990) 'Motivational and self-regulated learning components of classroom academic performance', *Journal of Educational Psychology*, 82(1): 33–40.

Pintrich, P.R. and Garcia, T. (1991) 'Student goal orientation and self-regulation in the college classroom', in M.L. Maehr and P.R. Pintrich (eds) *Advances in Motivation and Achievement: Goals and Self-Regulatory Processes*, vol. 7, Greenwich, CT: JAI Press.

Pintrich, P.R., Smith, D.A., Garcia, T. and McKeachie, W. J. (1991) *A Manual for the Use of the Motivated Strategies for Learning Questionnaire* (MSLQ), Technical Report No. 91–B-004, Ann Arbor, CT: University of Michigan, School of Education.

Pramling, I. (1988) 'Developing children's thinking about their own learning', *British Journal of Educational Psychology*, 58(3): 266–78.

Pramling, I. (1996) 'Understanding and empowering the child as a learner', in D. Olson and N. Torrance (eds) *The Handbook of Education and Human Development*, Oxford: Blackwell.

Pratt, M.W. and Savoy-Levine, K.M. (1998) 'Contingent tutoring of long-division skills in fourth and fifth graders: Experimental tests of some hypotheses about scaffolding', *Journal of Applied Developmental Psychology*, 19(2): 287–304.

Pratt, M.W., Greene, D., MacVicar, J. and Bountrogianni, M. (1992) 'The mathematical parent: parental scaffolding, parenting style and learning outcomes in long-division mathematics homework', *Journal of Applied Developmental Psychology*, 13(1): 17–34.

Prawat, R.S. (1989) 'Promoting access to knowledge, strategy and disposition in students: a research synthesis', *Review of Educational Research*, 59(1): 1–41.

Putnam, R.T. (1987) 'Structuring and adjusting content for students: a study of live and simulated tutoring for addition', *American Educational Research Journal*, 24(1): 13–48.

Puustinen, M. and Pulkinen, L. (2001) 'Models of self-regulated learning', *Scandinavian Journal of Educational Research*, 45(3): 269–84.

Radford, J., Ireson, J. and Mahon, M. (2006) 'Triadic dialogue in oral communication tasks: what are the implications for language learning?', *Language and Education*, 20(3): 191–210.

Radziszewska, B. and Rogoff, B. (1988) 'Influence of adult and peer collaboration on children's planning skills', *Developmental Psychology*, 24(6): 840–8.

Radziszewska, B. and Rogoff, B. (1991) 'Children's guided participation in planning errands with skilled adult or peer partners', *Developmental Psychology*, 27(3): 381–9.

Reber, A.S. (1993) *Implicit Learning and Tacit Knowledge*, Oxford: Oxford University Press.

Reichgelt, H., Shadbolt, N., Paskiewicz, T., Wood, D. and Wood, H. (1993) 'EXPLAIN: On implementing more effective tutoring systems', in A. Sloman (ed.) *Prospects for Artificial Intelligence*, Brighton: University of Sussex, Society for the Study of Artificial Intelligence and Simulation of Behaviour.

Resnick, L. (1987) 'Learning in school and out', *Educational Researcher*, 16(9): 13–20.

Resnick, L., Wang, M.C. and Kaplan, J. (1973) 'Task analysis in curriculum design: a hierarchically sequenced introductory mathematics curriculum', *Journal of Applied Behaviour Analysis*, 6(4): 679–710.

Richardson, K. (1988) *Understanding Psychology*, Milton Keynes: Open University Press.

Rogoff, B. (1990) *Apprenticeship in Thinking: Cognitive Development in Social Context*, Oxford: Oxford University Press.

Rogoff, B. (2003) *The Cultural Nature of Human Development*, Oxford: Oxford University Press.

Rogoff, B. and Gardner W. (1984) 'Adult guidance of cognitive development', in B. Rogoff and J. Lave (eds) *Everyday Cognition*, London: Harvard University Press.

Rogoff, B., Mistry, J., Göncü, A. and Mosier, C. (1993) *Guided Participation in Cultural Activity by Toddlers and Caregivers'*, Monographs of the Society for Research in Child Development 58, Chicago, IL: University of Chicago Press.

Ryan, R.M. and Deci, E.L. (2000) 'Intrinsic and extrinsic motivation: classic definitions and new directions', *Contemporary Educational Psychology*, 25(1): 54–67.

Sabers, D., Cushing, K.S. and Berliner, D. (1991) 'Differences among teachers in a task characterised by simultaneity, multi dimensionality, and immediacy', *American Educational Research Journal*, 28(1): 63–88.

Säljö, R., and Wyndhamn, J. (1993) 'Solving problems in the formal setting: an empirical study of the school as a context for thought', in S. Chaiklin and J. Lave (eds) *Understanding Practice: Perspectives on Activity and Context*, Cambridge: Cambridge University Press.

Samuelowicz, K. and Bain, J.D. (1992) 'Conceptions of teaching held by academic teachers', *Higher Education*, 24(1): 93–111.

Scribner, S. (1984) 'Studying working intelligence', in B. Rogoff and J. Lave (eds) *Everyday Cognition: Its Development in Social Context*, Cambridge, MA: Harvard University Press.

Shayer, M. and Adey, P. (2002) 'Cognitive acceleration comes of age', in M. Shayer and P. Adey (eds) *Learning Intelligence: Cognitive Acceleration Across the Curriculum from 5 to 15 Years*, Buckingham: Open University Press.

Siegler, R.S. (2000) 'The rebirth of children's learning', *Child Development*, 71(1) 26–35.

Siegler, R.S. and Alibali, M. (2005) *Children's Thinking*, 5th edn, Upper Saddle River, NJ: Prentice Hall.

Simon, H.A. and Chase, W.G. (1973) 'Skill in chess', *American Scientist*, 61(4): 394–403.

Singh, K., Bickley, P.G., Keith, T.Z., Keith, P.B., Trivette, P. and Anderson, E. (1995) 'The effects of four components of parental involvement on 8th grade student achievement: structural analysis of NELS-88 data', *School Psychology Review*, 24(2): 299–317.

Skinner, B. (1953) *Science and Human Behaviour*, New York: Macmillan.

Skinner, B. (1954) 'The science of learning and the art of teaching', *Harvard Educational Review*, 24(1): 86–97.

Sloboda, J. (1986) 'What is skill?' in A. Gellatly (ed.) *The Skilful Mind*, Milton Keynes: Open University Press.

Speelman, C. and Kirsner, K. (2005) *Beyond the Learning Curve*, Oxford: Oxford University Press.

Stanovich, K. (1994) 'Constructivism in reading education', *The Journal of Special Education*, 28(3): 259–74.

Sternberg, R.J. (1985) *Beyond IQ: A Diarchic Theory of Human Intelligence*, Cambridge: Cambridge University Press.

Sternberg, R.J. and Ben Zeev, T. (2001) *Complex Cognition*, Oxford: Oxford University Press.

Stigler, J.W. (1984) 'Mental abacus: the effect of abacus training on Chinese children's mental calculations', *Cognitive Psychology*, 16(2): 145–76.

Stigler, J.W. and Hiebert, J. (1999) *The Teaching Gap: Best Ideas from the World's Teachers for Improving Education in the Classroom*, New York: Free Press.

Stigler, J.W., Chalip, L. and Miller, K.E. (1986) 'Consequences of skill. The case of abacus training in Taiwan', *American Journal of Education*, 94(4): 447–79.

Stone, C.A. (1998) 'The metaphor of scaffolding and its utility for the field of learning disabilities', *Journal of Learning Disabilities*, 31(4): 344–64.

Sui Chi, E.H. and Willms, J.D. (1996) 'Effects of parental involvement on eighth grade achievement', *Sociology of Education*, 69(2): 126–41.

Super, C.M. and Harkness, S. (1986) 'The developmental niche: A conceptualisation at the interface of child and culture', *International Journal of Behavioral Development*, 9(4): 545–70.

Sylva, K., Melhuish, E., Sammons, P., Siraj-Blatchford, I. and Taggart, B. (2004) *The Effective Provision of Preschool Education (EPPE) Project – the Final report: Effective Pre-school Education*, Technical Paper 12. London: DfES/Institute of Education.

Tait, H., Entwistle, N. and McCune, V. (1998) 'ASSIST: a reconceptualisation of the approaches to studying inventory', in C Rust (ed.) *Improving Student Learning: Improving Students as Learners*, Oxford: The Oxford Centre for Staff and Learning Development.

Tharp, R. (1993) 'Institutional and social context of educational reform: practice and reform', in E.A. Forman, N. Minnick and C.A. Stone (eds) *Contexts for Learning: Sociocultural Dynamics in Children's Development*, New York: Oxford University Press.

Tharp, R.G. and Gallimore, R. (1988) *Rousing Minds to Life: Teaching, Learning and Schooling in Social Context*, New York: Cambridge University Press.

Tharp, R.G. and Gallimore, R. (1991) 'A theory of teaching as assisted performance', in P. Light S. Sheldon and M. Woodhead (eds) *Learning to Think*, London: Routledge.

Thomas, A. (1998) *Educating Children at Home*, London: Cassell/Continuum.

Tizard, B. and Hughes, M. (1984) *Young Children Learning: Talking and Thinking at Home and at School*, Cambridge, MA: Harvard University Press.

Tizard, B., Blatchford, P., Burke, J., Farquhar, C. and Plewis, I. (1988) *Young Children at School in the Inner City*, Lawrence Erlbaum.

Tolmie, A., Thomson, J.A., Foot, H.C., Whelan, K., Morrison, S. and McLaren, B. (2005) 'The effects of adult guidance and peer discussion on the development of children's representations: evidence from the training of pedestrian skills', *British Journal of Psychology*, 96(2): 181–204.

Tomasello, M. (1999) *The Cultural Origins of Human Development*, London: Harvard University Press.

Tomasello, M., Kruger, A.C. and Ratner, H.H. (1993) 'Cultural learning', *Behavioral and Brain Sciences*, 16(3): 495–552.

Trevarthen, C. (1979) 'Communication and cooperation in early infancy: A description of primary intersubjectivity', in M. Bullowa (ed) *Before Speech: The Beginning of Interpersonal Communication*, New York: Cambridge University Press.

Trevarthen, C. (1980) 'The foundations of intersubjectivity: development of interpersonal and cooperative understanding in infants', in D. Olsen (ed.) *The*

Social Foundations of Language and Thought: Essays in Honor of J.S. Bruner, New York: W.W. Norton.

Tudge, J., Hogan, D., Lee, S., Tammeveski, P. Meltas, M., Kulakova, N., Snezhkova, I. and Putnam, S. (1999) 'Cultural heterogeneity: parental values and beliefs and their preschoolers activities in the United States, South Korea, Russia, and Estonia', in A. Goncu (ed.) *Children's Engagement in the World: Sociocultural Perspectives*, New York: Cambridge University Press.

van Rossum, E.J. and Schenk, S.M. (1984) 'The relation between learning conception, study strategy and learning outcome', *British Journal of Educational Psychology*, 54(1): 73–83.

Vermunt, J.D. (1998) 'The regulation of constructive learning process', *British Journal of Educational Psychology*, 68(2): 149–71.

Vermunt, J.D. and Vermetten, Y.J. (2004) 'Patterns in student learning: relationships between learning strategies, conceptions of learning, and learning orientations', *Educational Psychology Review*, 16(4): 359–84.

Vygotsky, L.S. (1962) *Thought and Language*, Cambridge, MA: M.I.T Press.

Vygotsky, L.S. (1978) *Mind in Society*, Cambridge, MA: Harvard University Press.

Vygotsky, L.S. (1981) 'The genesis of higher mental functions', in J.V. Wertsch (ed.) *The Concept of Activity in Soviet Psychology*, Armonk, NY: Sharpe.

Wang, M.C., Haertel, G.D. and Walberg, H.J. (1993) 'Towards a knowledge base for school learning', *Review of Educational Research*, 63(3): 249–94.

Watson, J.B. and Rayner, R. (1920) 'Conditioned emotional reactions', *Journal of Experimental Psychology*, 3(1): 1–14.

Wegerif, R., Mercer, N. and Dawes, L. (1999) 'From social interaction to individual reasoning: an empirical investigation of a possible cultural model of cognitive development', *Learning and Instruction*, 9(5): 493–516.

Weinberg, S.S. (1991) 'Historical problem solving: a study of the cognitive processes used in the evaluation of documentary and pictorial evidence', *Journal of Educational Psychology*, 83(1): 73–87.

Weinstein, C.E. and Mayer, R.E. (1986) 'The teaching of learning strategies', in M. Wittrock (ed.) *Handbook of Research on Teaching*, New York, NY: Macmillan.

Weinstein, C.E. and Palmer, D.R. (2002) *Learning and Study Strategies Inventory (LASSI): User's Manual*, 2nd edn, Clearwater, FL: H & H Publishing.

Weinstein, C.E., Shulte, A.C. and Palmer, D.P. (1987) *Learning and Study Strategies Inventory*, Clearwater, FL: H & H Publishing.

Wellman, H. and Gelman, S.A. (1998) 'Knowledge acquisition in foundational domains', in W. Damon (series ed.) and D. Kuhn, and R.S. Siegler (eds) *Handbook of Child Psychology*, vol. 2, *Cognition, Perception, and Language*, 5th edn, New York: Wiley.

Wells, G. (1985) '*Language, Learning and Education*', Windsor: NFER-Nelson.

Wells, G. (1993) 'Re-evaluating the IRF Sequence: a proposal for the articulation of theories of activity and discourse for the analysis of teaching and learning in the classroom', *Linguistics and Education*, 5(1): 1–37.

Wertsch, J.V. (1984) 'The zone of proximal development: some conceptual issues', in B. Rogoff and J.V. Wertsch (eds) *Children's Learning in the Zone of Proximal Development*, San Francisco, CA: Jossey Bass.

Wertsch, J.V. (1985) *Vygotsky and the Social Formation of Mind*, London: Harvard University Press.

Wertsch, J.V. and Stone, A. (1985) 'The concept of internalization in Vygotsky's account of the genesis of higher mental functions', in J. V. Wertsch (ed.) *Culture,*

Communication and Cognition: Vygotskian Perspectives, Cambridge: Cambridge University Press.

Wertsch, J., Minick, N. and Arns, F.J. (1984) 'The creation of context in joint problem solving', in B. Rogoff and J. Lave (eds) *Everyday Cognition: Its Development in Social Context*, London: Harvard University Press.

Whiting, B.B. and Whiting, J.W.M. (1975) *Children of Six Cultures: A Psycho-Cultural Analysis*, Cambridge, MA: Harvard University Press.

Whitty, G., Edwards, A., Power, S. and Wigfall, V. (1998) *Destined for Success? Educational Biographies of Academically Able Pupils*, End of award report to the Economic and Social Research Council. Swindon: ESRC.

Winne, P.H. (1995) 'Inherent details in self-regulated learning', *Educational Psychologist*, 30(4): 173–87.

Winne, P.H. and Perry, N.E. (2000) 'Measuring self regulated learning', in M. Boekaerts, P.R. Pintrich and M. Zeidner (eds) *Handbook of Self-Regulation*, London: Academic Press.

Wood, D.J. (1986) 'Aspects of teaching and learning', in M. Richards and P. Light (eds) *Children of Social Worlds*, Cambridge: Polity Press.

Wood, D.J. (1998) *How Children Think and Learn: The Social Contexts of Cognitive Development*, Oxford: Blackwell.

Wood, D. and Wood, H. (1996a) 'Vygotsky, tutoring and learning', *Oxford Review of Education*, 22(1): 5–17.

Wood, D. and Wood, H. (1996b) Commentary: contingency in tutoring and learning. *Learning and Instruction*, 6(4): 391–7.

Wood, D., Bruner, J.S. and Ross, G. (1976) 'The role of tutoring in problem solving', *Journal of Child Psychology and Psychiatry*, 17(2): 89–100.

Wood, D., Wood, H. and Middleton, D. (1978) 'An experimental evaluation of four face-to-face teaching strategies', *International Journal of Behavioral Development*, 1(2): 131–47.

Wood, D., Wood, H., Ainsworth, S. and O'Malley, C. (1995) 'On becoming a tutor: towards an ontogenetic model', *Cognition and Instruction*, 13(4): 565–81.

Woods, P. (1990) *The Happiest Days? How Pupils Cope With School*, London: Falmer Press.

Yuill, N. and Oakhill, J. (1991) *Children's Problems in Text Comprehension*, Cambridge: Cambridge University Press.

Zeidner, M., Boekaerts, M. and Pintrich, P.R. (2000) 'Self-regulation: directions and challenges for future research', in P.R. Boekaerts, P.R. Pintrich and M. Zeidner (eds) *Handbook of Self-Regulation*, London: Academic Press.

Zimmerman, B.J. (1998) 'Academic studying and the development of personal skill: a self-regulatory perspective', *Educational Psychologist*, 33(2/3): 73–86.

Zimmerman, B.J. and Martínez-Pons, M. (1986) 'Development of a structured interview for assessing student use of self-regulated learning strategies', *American Educational Research Journal*, 23(4): 614–28.

Zimmerman, B.J. and Martínez-Pons, M. (1990) 'Student differences in self-regulated learning: relating grade, sex and giftedness to self-efficacy and strategy use', *Journal of Educational Psychology*, 82(1): 51–9.

Index

ability grouping 74, 131–5, 154
ACT theory 38
accommodation 13
achievement 1, 13, 21, 30, 31, 47–9, 52–3
activity: activity goals 82; activity theory 85–6, 92, 151; classroom activity 34–6; cognitive activity/mental activity 28, 77, 81–2; cultural activity 83, 85, 144, 158; everyday activity 87; learning activity 19, 59–60, 73, 87, 121, 127; mathematical activity 80; meaningful activity 81, 85; neuronal activity 141; practical activity 85
affordance 127
Aristotle 7–8
assimilation 13
Associationism 7

Bandura, A. 12, 59, 147
behaviourist 6–8, 10–12, 14, 22–3, 28, 64–5, 68, 77, 85, 119, 121, 151, 154–5
belief/s: adults' beliefs 120, 145; beliefs about child rearing 117; beliefs about learners 142; cultural beliefs 3, 91, 139; educational beliefs 136; learners' beliefs 3, 63; motivational beliefs 51, 59, 63, 68–9; parents/parental beliefs 117, 145; pedagogic beliefs 116, 120–1, 127; share/d beliefs 73; teachers' beliefs 82, 92, 121, 123–5, 136
Bronfenbrenner, U. 3, 70–1, 73, 148

chunks 5, 16, 35, 101
classroom dialogue: practice; talk 3, 84, 109, 129

classroom interaction 44, 90
classroom: organisation 151
cognitive conflict 12, 28–9, 61, 94, 113, 119, 148–9, 150, 153, 155, 158, 160–1
cognitive skill 2, 16, 30–1, 38, 43, 50, 56, 61
cognitive strategies x, 2–3, 19, 23, 51–2, 56–8, 64–7, 69, 138
community x, 3, 19, 48, 70–1, 76, 81, 84, 86–7, 116–18, 132–3
component process theory 40–1, 141
conceptions: of children as learners; of learning 2, 4, 6, 8, 23–6, 28, 61–3, 65, 68–9, 142, 145, 155, 160
contingency 3, 96–9, 101–2, 107, 114–15, 161
contingent instruction/contingent tutoring 97–8/157
cross-cultural 73, 117, 120, 136–9, 150
cultural context: cultural development 77–8, 80, 141; cultural environment 19–20, 48, 80, 93; cultural practice/s 1, 82–4, 138; cultural setting/s 2–3, 23, 84, 86, 90, 120, 126, 136–7, 141, 145; cultural tools 78, 80, 83, 105, 123, 137; cultural value 48, 73, 82, 139
customary practice 3, 73, 82–3, 86, 91–2, 116, 124, 135–6, 139, 141, 145

Dasen, P.R. 72–3, 82, 150
declarative knowledge 38, 40
deliberate practice 43–4, 47–8, 51, 138, 152
developmental niche 3, 71–4, 81–2, 92, 159
differentiation 49, 92, 133–4, 139, 156

discussion: 27, 44, 51, 68–9, 109–11, 114, 117, 123, 129, 145, 156, 160
domain knowledge 33, 50

ecological systems 70, 74, 92, 148
elaboration 17, 52, 65, 128
expectancy-value theory 59–60
expert 30–7, 40, 42–8, 79, 86–7, 95, 109, 112, 148–52
expertise 30–7, 41–4, 46–8, 50–1, 56, 81, 125, 138, 140, 147, 149, 153, 155
exploratory talk 129, 131

Gauvain, M. 81–2, 153
goal setting 51–2, 54, 63–4, 67–8
goals: cultural goal 82, 141; goal directed activity 141; learning goals 48, 59, 61, 98, 124–5, 136; literacy goals 125; performance goals 61; programme goals 125–6; task goals 41, 61, 63, 106

higher mental functions 20, 75, 77, 96, 160–1
home 1, 31, 71, 73, 84, 86, 89, 103, 111, 116, 120, 131, 138, 140, 145, 160
home discussion 119
home learning environment 116, 119

imitate/ion 11–12, 28, 88, 101
implicit learning 21, 158
indeterminacy 4, 127, 136, 141–3
individualization 92, 139
informal education 88, 90, 118, 153
information processing 16, 18, 22–3, 58, 154
interaction: adult–child interaction 94, 102, 114, 151, 153; pedagogic interactions 2, 100, 118, 136, 140, 145; social interaction 68, 77–8, 144–8, 154, 160; triadic interactions 95;
intersubjectivity 95–6, 107, 112, 144, 160
IRE 127–8

Kant, I. 7, 154

learning activity 7, 19, 59–60, 73, 87, 121, 127
learning curves 31–2

learning experiences: goals 123, 125, 127, 135–6, 147
learning strategies 51–2, 59, 62–4, 68–9, 156, 160–2
levels of control 97
literacy programmes 123, 125

mastery: goals 61–2
maturation 13, 75, 77–8
meaningful learning 52, 62
mediation 20, 70, 75, 80–1, 120, 135, 141
mental models 137
microsystem 71–3
modelling 22, 101, 113, 115, 118
motivation: achievement motivation 59, 151; extrinsic motivation 60, 158; motivation to learn 59, 88, 120; motivational beliefs 51, 59, 63, 68–9
novice viii, 33–7, 86, 95, 97, 149

observational learning 11–12, 28
organisation 151, 153
organizational context: goals, setting 125
parent 97, 107, 111, 128, 142
parents: *see also* parental belief under 'beliefs'
parental aspiration 119–20; parental ethnotheories 82; parental support 45, 47, 117, 151; parental values 117, 118, 160
participation: children's participation/ in activities 86, 92, 102, 105, 116, 120, 136, 140, 144;
guided participation 83–4, 96, 100, 112, 140, 148, 158
Pavlov, I. 8, 9, 156
pedagogic belief: culture; relationship; setting 116, 120–1, 127
performance: goals 43, 61
Piaget, J. 6–7, 12–14, 20, 22–3, 28, 75, 83, 94, 157
Plato 7
practice: 10-year rule 30, 32, 50
procedural knowledge 12, 38

questions: known-answer questions 109, 127; open-ended questions 109, 128

reading: reading comprehension 40, 66, 113–14, 149, 152, 157; reading development 121; teaching

of reading 66, 121–2, 139; word
    reading 122
Reading Recovery 104, 122–3, 125,
    150
reciprocal teaching 66, 113–14, 156
rehearsal 52, 62, 65, 133
representation 21, 32–4, 36, 38, 56, 96,
    104, 123, 137, 144, 149
Rogoff, B. 11, 20, 83–5, 88, 96, 100–2,
    105, 107–8, 110–11, 140, 143, 149,
    151, 153, 158, 161
rote learning 24, 52

scaffolding 3, 96–7, 99–100, 102, 106,
    112, 114, 118, 140, 148, 155, 157,
    159
self-evaluation 51,54, 57, 65, 67
self-regulated learning 3, 19, 51–3,
    58–9, 62, 65, 68–9, 155–7, 161–2
self-regulation 3, 19, 23, 51–3, 55–64,
    66–9, 79, 81, 90, 125–6, 136, 138,
    155–7, 161–2
semiotic challenge 131
sets 10, 20, 49, 79, 92, 96, 127, 131,
    133–5, 137
setting 1, 23, 38, 52, 54, 63, 66–7, 88,
    95, 108, 125–8, 131–2, 136, 148,
    158
siblings 19, 70
Siegler, R.S. 37, 57–8, 149, 154,
    158–9, 161
situation definition 95–6, 112, 156
social learning 19, 22, 147
socio-cultural 2, 5, 19, 22–3, 28, 70,
    75, 81–3, 85–6, 92, 142–44

SOLO taxonomy 14–16, 148
spontaneous learning 6, 77
strategies 16–19, 23, 26–9, 32–3, 37,
    51–69, 80, 92, 107–8, 112–14,
    118, 122, 138, 143, 147, 149, 151,
    156–7, 160–2
sustained shared thinking 129, 131

tacit knowledge 21–22, 158
task management 104, 108
task structuring 101–2, 104, 110
time management 54, 57, 64
tutoring: children as tutors; effective
    tutoring; tutors 101–2, 104, 107,
    110–12, 115, 149–57, 161
tutors 65, 98–100, 107–8, 110–12,
    115, 121, 140

value 30, 48, 59–60, 64, 69, 88, 91, 99,
    138–9, 146
values x, 3, 48, 59, 64, 72–3, 82, 86–7,
    91, 105, 116–18, 120, 126, 133,
    135–6, 145, 151, 160
Vygotsky, L. 3, 6–7, 19–20, 23, 66, 75,
    77–9, 80–1, 83, 85, 94, 96–7, 105,
    112–14, 144, 150, 152, 154,
    160–1

Wertsch, J. 79, 96, 106, 112–13, 150,
    160–1
Wood, D. 96–9, 107, 154, 158, 161–2

zone of proximal development 78–9,
    83, 94, 96–7, 101, 111, 113–14,
    141, 144, 150, 161